It's All in the Frijoles

100 Famous Latinos Share
Real-Life Stories,
Time-Tested Dichos,
Favorite Folktales, and
Inspiring Words of Wisdom

Yolanda Nava

A Fireside Book
Published by Simon & Schuster
New York   London   Toronto
Sydney   Singapore

FIRESIDE
Rockefeller Center
1230 Avenue of the Americas
New York, NY 10020

FIRESIDE and colophon are registered trademarks
of Simon & Schuster, Inc.

Designed by Ruth Lee

Manufactured in the United States of America

10   9   8   7   6   5   4   3   2   1

Library of Congress Cataloging-in-Publication Data

It's all in the Frijoles : 100 famous Latinos share real-life stories,
time-tested dichos, favorite folktales, and inspiring words of
wisdom / [edited by] Yolanda Nava.
        p. cm.
      Includes bibliographical references and index.
      1. Virtues—Quotations, maxims, etc. 2. Latin Americans—
Quotations. 3. Hispanic Americans—Conduct of life. I. Nava,
Yolanda.

BJ1521.I77 2000
170'.89'68073—dc21

                                                                    00-024858

ISBN 0-684-84900-3

Acknowledgments

This book would not be possible without the guidance, support, and love of many people. First of all, I am most grateful to my mother, Consuelo Chavira Sepulveda, for underscoring all of her life's teaching on that sun-lit afternoon in her home as she was dying, and giving me yet one more precious gifts. *Frijoles,* how perfect! How simple! Her wisdom, her love, her courage, dignity, and grace have been an inspiration to me.

To my children, Joaquin and Danielle, who have reminded me of how much there is to learn from, and teach, our young. You are the precious jewels of my life! Joaquín, called long distance from New York, asking questions and encouraging me to keep on schedule. Danielle assisted with filing, faxing, trips to the library and bookstore, mailings, and computer work, not to mention trips to the market to keep us supplied with food. How can I thank you?

I owe immense debt and gratitude to all the contributors to *Frijoles.* Each and every one of you has given so much to the world by sharing your many talents with us. Your willingness to recall your stories helps us realize that those priceless words of advice and those curious lessons about life we received from our parents and *abuelitos* are still worth remembering and sharing. Some of you I knew and loved before this project, others have become new, cherished friends. I hope we can do more good things together. You make me proud of *nuestra raza, nuestra cultura. ¡Adelante!*

My deepest appreciation to Dolores and John Sanchez and Tony Castro at Eastern Group Publications for providing me the opportunity to write a weekly column. The seminal column "Mother's Deathbed Wisdom" has spawned a book! To Frank del Olmo at the *Los Angeles Times,* who reprinted that column, which literary agent Betsy Amster read. To Betsy for challenging me to write a book and helping me to get it published. And to Heidi Wall whose Flash Forward Mastery class provided the framework and tools required to initiate and complete this book.

Then, there were the friends without whom such a project cannot move forward. I am blessed to have all of you in my life: Jim Banks, beloved attorney and friend who negotiated contracts, organized my office, supplied the recording and playback devices (complete with footpedal!), and responded to all my pleas for help when my computer malfunctioned; Janet Rouse for her keen insights and comments; Marta Baca at Georgina & Associates for providing translation assistance on an as-needed basis; and UCLA Professor Juan Gomez-Quiñonez who introduced me to Antonio Caso's work and other historically relevant material.

To Carolyn Carradine, Cecelia Cole, Kathy Williamson, Pat Quinn, and Regina Cordova for sharing humor, *cariños,* encouragement, nourishment, good times, advice, patience, and friendship, and to Marta Monahan, mentor and dear friend whose own work, now in book form as *Strength of Character and Grace,* has been so inspirational. I wish you and my mother could have met.

And a very special thanks to my editors Becky Cabaza and Marcela Landres for their enthusiasm in shepherding this book to completion. They made the work a delight.

Beyond those of you I know personally, I respectfully acknowledge *mi gente trabajadora, respetuosa y humilde, que tiene tanta fe y que viven con responsabilidad, lealtad, integridad, valentía, prudencia, fortaleza, caridad, moderación, castidad, y que siempre busca la justicia.* You are the inspiration for all of us to maintain our beautiful traditions.

This book is lovingly dedicated to my mother,

Consuelo Chavira Sepulveda,
and to my children

Joaquín and Danielle,
con todo cariño.

May you carry on the wisdom of our elders.

Contents

It's

All

in the

Frijoles

Introction

To raise children with strong moral values in today's topsy-turvy world, parents—not just Latino parents—need all the help they can get. "Blood is inherited," Mamá used to say, "but virtue is acquired." I really didn't fully understand this as a child but, the older I get, the more Mamá's words ring true. My own moral education at my mother's hands was unambiguous and direct. Her lessons for life were delivered firmly but lovingly.

My mother was a woman of tremendous character and spiritual strength. She was graceful and dignified, opinionated yet softspoken. Her wisdom was uttered in both beautiful Spanish *dichos,* proverbs, and in English, which she worked very hard to perfect. She read widely in her free time, and especially enjoyed the biographies of great men and women. A woman of modest means and limited formal education, she demonstrated that character has nothing to do with titles or wealth.

Born in Chihuahua, Mexico in 1909, Consuelo Chavira Sepulveda grew up in San Buenaventura in the home of her maternal grandfather. Her father was a carpenter and draftsman, a progressive thinker who left the revolution-torn country in 1914 to make a new life for his family in Arizona. There, he built twenty schools in the southern part of the state before moving his growing family to Los Angeles. Mamá survived *La Revolución* and, on this side of the border, the Great Depression. She worked most of her life as a fine seamstress, became a naturalized United States citizen, and went back to attain her high-school diploma in the evenings at Hollywood High School while in her forties after her seventeen-year marriage to my father ended in divorce. This was a time when she realized my precocious questions outran her eighth-grade education. She was prudent with her money and, as a reward, was able to pay off the mortgage on her home by the time she retired.

Mamá radiated what all Latinos recognize as *educación*, "good breeding." That quality of behaving in the world with good manners, dignity, and *respeto,* respect for others, ultimately begins within. Her parents had raised her well and, in turn, she saw it as her responsibility to pass these same teachings on to me, her only child. This she did with a good measure of discipline and love, all of it colored by her Mexican roots.

But it took her death to make me realize just how deeply she had influenced me, and how very important her lessons in living had been in shaping who I am. How appropriate it was that her last lesson should have been so simple on the surface, yet so profound; a final, offhand pronouncement whose real significance would initially elude me, while, at the same time, keeping me close to her even after she was gone.

What do you do when the one who gave you life, who soothed your fevers and dried your tears, who wept at your wedding, and helped welcome your children into the world, is diagnosed with a terminal illness? What do you do when the doctors give the petite woman you love and call Mamá only six weeks to live? I did what I instinctively knew to be the only thing I could do. Out of love and respect for her, I took her back to the home I grew up in and began a long, painful goodbye.

We spent many hours alone, the two of us, even though different family members and friends came and left, each paying their respects. I read her poetry, inspirational passages from the Bible, and the words of her spiritual guide, Mary Baker Eddy. From the moment I opened my eyes in the morning until they closed for what I hoped would be a good night's rest, I felt a compelling need to soak up as much of her as she could give. And I asked her questions which had been with me from childhood. Questions, about her life before I knew her, about her difficult marriage and divorce, about things done and not done. What did she think would happen when she died? About God? And the question that seemed most important: What was the source of her fortitude?

"What makes you so strong?" I asked her one afternoon as she lay in the big bed, the skin of her face pale even against the white of the sheets and of her nightgown. The end was drawing near. Her frailty was obvious now, reminding me daily how our roles had shifted. It was my hand that held the water glass, tucked in the sheets, and, most important, conjured up words of comfort until her dark eyes closed and her thin chest rose and fell in the orderly rhythm of sleep.

"What makes you so strong?" I asked again.

"Beans," she said. "Beans have made me strong."

Beans! *¡Frijoles!* Was I to take her words literally? I laughed at her brief response, but I was also somewhat disappointed that she didn't leave me with a stronger message.

It wasn't until several months after her death, as I stood at the kitchen sink preparing *frijoles de la olla,* beans from a clay pot, that these words came back to me: Mamá took great care in washing and sorting her beans. After running water over the *frijoles* several times, she would spread the beans on a tray or large dish, then pick out and discard any imperfectly shaped, shriveled, or discolored beans. Each bean for her pot had to be a perfectly flawless pinto.

As I set aside all those less than perfect pintos, just as I had been taught to do as a child, I heard my mother telling me, her finger wagging, "*¡Ten cuidado, mija!* Pay attention! One bad bean can spoil the pot."

Frijoles de la olla is a simple dish: beans simmered with salt pork, onion, garlic, and bay leaf, seasoned with salt. But Mamá always prepared it with great care. As I prepared the beans in my own kitchen, with her beloved clay *olla* on the stove, I finally realized that her last lesson was not about the nutritional power of beans. It was about *character.*

"Character is everything," she always told me, speaking of the moral, ethical, and religious qualities that mold and sculpt who we are. Character traits such as honesty, responsibility, respect, and courage were among the virtues she admired in others and insisted upon in her own daughter, virtues she herself encompassed. From the moment of my birth, she had seen her duty as nothing less than to shape my character, and the virtues she taught me very quickly set me apart from many of my peers. She was saying that the virtuous life is the product of constantly weeding out flaws and weaknesses, and choosing right over wrong, just like preparing a good pot of beans.

Mamá believed perfection was not out of our reach if only we would aim for it, taking a small step each day toward expressing our inherent goodness. "Remember, *mijita,* God is in the details. God is in the pots and pans. In every small thing we do or say."

As I approach my middle years, with my two children growing into adulthood, I find that it is still my mother's steadfast values, reshaped in part by my own life experience, that I have passed on to my children. It is my mother's voice that I hear, her words that have framed solutions and provided healing during troubled times.

Throughout my working life, first as a teacher and youth counselor, then as a television news reporter/anchor, followed by several years as a communications and family-literacy consultant with the Los Angeles Unified School District, I have seen how the stresses of adjusting to life in this county affect many of the Latino families with whom I have come into contact. Most of these parents want nothing more than to give their children the same kind of moral, ethical, and religious direction they had growing up—something to anchor them as they seek a better life. Yet, with each generation, the cultural and moral traditions of their own Hispanic heritage have become more foreign, the stories of elders forgotten. Sometimes, even the language is lost. The emphasis upon the building blocks of character—*las virtudes,* the virtues—is often ignored in the struggle to achieve economic security, producing a decline in the civil character of society. What societal factors are responsible for all of this? How is it that we increasingly fail to acknowledge and reinforce the wise teachings that nourish character? For me, the solution is in the symbolism of the *frijoles*. What I now want to do for other Latino parents is pass on the beautiful gifts my Mamá gave me to help them do the same for their own children.

In 1996, I wrote about my mother's deathbed wisdom in one of my weekly columns for the Eastern Group Publications. The column later became the basis for this book, as I realized that the virtues Mamá emphasized must be preserved as a precious part of our cultural heritage. I knew I needed to share this wisdom with others to nourish the best in all of us.

Like beans, which have been a staple of life for generations, giving nourishment throughout Europe and the Americas, I see *las virtudes,* the virtues, as part of the collective unconsciousness that has fueled great cultures, Indo-Hispanic and many others, for thousands of years. The riches and truths of this universal collective past are still with us today to give us strength and direction, if only we acknowledge, accept, and incorporate its wisdom into the conscious living of our present lives.

In the lore of our indigenous roots from the Olmecs, Incas, Mayans, Aztecs, and the *mestizo* peoples of the West and Southwest, I found the roots of our deep kinship with the earth, the ideals of stewardship and caretaking, an appreciation for education, and of a responsibility to something larger and more majestic than any single soul. From Spain came an exquisite language, a rich intellectual tradition, and the Christian religion, particularly Catholicism, which, out of necessity, adapted to and embraced the mysticism of the indigenous peoples of the Americas. Examples from the modern world, songs and poetry, childhood memories, and the words of contemporary leaders have all contributed to the teaching of virtues. This book contains all this and much more.

Perhaps my most comforting discovery in writing this book is that parents who share these concerns have been striving to teach their children to lead virtuous lives for as long as there have been parents and children!

It's All in the Frijoles is part anthology and part first-person recollections from my own experiences, as well as those of such Hispanic luminaries as writers Isabel Allende and Pablo Neruda; actors Hector Elizondo, Edward James Olmos, and Ricardo Montalban; football superstar Joe Kapp; politicians Gloria Molina and Cruz Bustamante; and news anchors María Salinas and Soledad O'Brien.

Each of the fourteen chapters weaves together literature and recollections to explore the various aspects of a single virtue: responsibility, respect, hard work, loyalty, honesty, faith, courage, humility, temperance, prudence, justice, fortitude, charity, and chastity.

While you are reading *It's All in the* Frijoles I hope you will discover the similarities among different Spanish-speaking countries and appreciate the nuances of uniqueness across geographical boundaries. Somewhere along the way, you may meet a childhood poem or tale your *abuelita* used to share with you, or "hear" familiar music as you read the words of a song your Mamá sang to you as a child. I believe this book will stimulate other memories as well. You can tell your own stories to your children as you make your way through the book.

It's All in the Frijoles contains examples of those qualities that can sculpt us into more perfect beings, in the same way that Mamá's recipe for the perfect pot of beans is also a lesson for life. It is a book with simple yet profound concepts that you and your children can explore and read together. I hope that you open its pages to look for inspiration when you're demoralized or anxious, or when you're seeking some *dicho* (saying) you heard as a child but cannot remember. These words—these stories, poems, myths, sayings, and recollections—spring from thousands of years of tradition. They have survived for the simple reason that they have proven across time and adverse conditions to exemplify the moral, ethical, and religious concepts our ancestors cherished enough to defend, write down, and pass on for future generations. Even what is new carries within it echoes of the old. They remind us of the good within, comfort us as they teach, and help us bring past and present together. I know, as I rediscover these pieces of my past and the virtues they evoke, I can hear my mother's voice more clearly than ever.

Yolanda Nava
December 1999
South Pasadena, California

I

Responsibility
Responsabilidad

Political crises are moral crises.
> —OCTAVIO PAZ, "Postscript," 1970.
> Mexican poet, writer,
> 1990 Nobel Prize Laureate in
> Literature.

Tell me thy company, and I'll tell thee what thou art.
> —MIGUEL DE CERVANTES,
> *Don Quixote*, 1615

T*he virtue* responsabilidad y obligación—*responsibility and obliga-tion—acts as the keystone that holds the expansive arch of our culture together. Obligation encompasses one's duty to others, beginning with the responsibility of each parent to provide children with the necessi-ties of life—food, clothing, shelter, and, of course, love, as well as tak-ing care of one's elderly family members. From these primary duties, responsibility spreads out in ever-larger concentric rings to embrace the wider community, of which family is a part. In one direction it leads to the ideas of respect and loyalty, in another to courage, humil-ity, and hard work.*

Mamá taught this important virtue in the same way in which she learned it in her youth. Hispanic culture teaches that one's behavior is guided by its effect or impact on others, rather than by its sole effect on the individual. By thinking this way, we see our every action is considered a reflection on our parents, our good family name, our community, and our raza. *As family members, we are bound by our obligations, our duty to one another. Often the agreement is an un-written one, reinforced by the deep intimacy within Latino families where grandparents, aunts, uncles,* compadres, *and a host of other* fa-miliares *form a network of responsible, caring adults that guide the young members of the household. Whether by words or actions, we learn very early on that we will be cared for, taught what behavior is expected of us, taught what roles we are to play in our family, and* shown that we must care for those who are older, younger, or weaker than ourselves.

Responsibility, obligation, and duty are synonyms that seem almost anachronistic in these self-indulgent times in which commitments are often ignored but are, in reality, vital to human relationships. How can one person rely on another if we are not bound by our word, or if we have no sense of obligation to one another beyond what might be upheld in a court of law?

Just as Mamá's duty to me was the driving force in her life, she let me know it was my responsibility to work hard at my studies, to be well behaved, and to obey her. Boundaries were clearly defined. So were right and wrong. She wisely allowed me to learn the consequences of my actions in both obvious and subtle ways, after setting out the guidelines of appropriate and expected behavior. You knew that if you violated the rules, or stepped out of bounds after initial warnings, you would be punished. Whack! No questions asked.

As I was an only child, Mamá encouraged my love of animals and allowed me pets of all varieties. She let me know I was completely responsible for them. The feed store was blocks and blocks away, and we had no car. I can still remember carrying fifteen-pound sacks of dog food and chicken and bird feed through the hot streets and up the long hill to our house above Sunset Boulevard, much as, I now realize, my mother carried home, by bus and on foot, shopping bags of food from Grand Central market in the center of downtown Los Angeles. She did this because the Central market had the freshest produce and best meat at reasonable prices, and because she could stop there after work.

One summer, I learned the hard way that not fulfilling your responsibilities can have serious consequences. Among my pets were seven parakeets of various striking colors, who lived in a cage on a shaded, enclosed porch. Mamá had told me that they needed fresh water and seed every day. That summer I discovered many new friends on the block, and we spent most of the long, hot days playing games and cavorting about the neighborhood with other children.

Several days running, I was so eager to go out in the morning *that I forgot about the birds. On the third day, I returned home to find them all lying on the bottom of the cage, dead. I was miserable and guilty, and felt like a very bad person as my mother explained that they, like humans, need water more than anything else to live. It was a failure of fulfilling a responsibility that I would never make again.*

Why is responsibility so important? Fulfilling obligations to family and others is essential to achieve harmonious relations. Assuming responsibility is a requisite of leadership.

Katherine Ortega
Former United States Treasurer

My father was the one who taught us responsibility. If you were given a job you were responsible for doing it and, if you said you were going to do something, you'd better do it or have a very good reason for not doing it. To this day, I get very upset with people who say they are going to do something, then don't do it. He also taught us to be on time. If you said you were going to be there at eight, you had to be there at eight, not eight-thirty. I think he was somewhat typical of that generation.

My father was a very proud person. Crippled as a young man, he developed himself and was very physically and mentally strong. He taught us that you were responsible for yourself and your family, that you should not depend on other people to take care of you. Nor did he believe in handouts, and refused to accept food or other support during the Great Depression.

I remember him working two or three jobs, whatever it took, and saying that his children may have had patched clothes, but they were clean.

His sense of responsibility and obligation also extended to the community where we lived. He was a member of the school board, helped at the church, and built a church in Bent, New Mexico.

My father emphasized the importance of being prepared. He wanted all of us to be independent—including the girls—to be self sufficient, not to depend on anyone for our well-being. He even said his agenda was for us to learn how to make a living, because "if you get married and if he doesn't treat you right, I want you to pick up and walk out. If you're not treated right, you don't have to stay."

We all had our responsibilities around the house, and we were expected to come straight home after school to complete them. We all had to work. The boys had to wash the windows and clean the yards, and the girls had to make the beds, help with the house, prepare meals, and do the dishes. We could not stand around. As we got older, he gave us responsibilities in his upholstery and furniture business. That's how my sister and I learned accounting. To this day, I can't be idle. I'm constantly doing something, and I always find something to do.

He encouraged us to share his interest in politics. Back in those days, he received the afternoon paper. He would read it from cover to cover, sometimes staying up until eleven o'clock at night, reading, and tell us "You have to be informed." In order to change things, he said, "You have to be involved." He even got involved at school. He would talk to our teachers, and find out from the principal how things were going. He wanted to be informed, so that he would be able to participate.

Being responsible to the community was important to my father. He told us that if things were going to be done right you had to keep an eye on them and be involved. My oldest sister and a couple of my brothers became involved by serving on state commissions.

Manuel T. Pacheco, Ph.D.

President, University of Missouri System

I grew up in New Mexico as the oldest of eleven brothers and sisters in a farming family. In a large family, there were certain values that, of necessity, were inculcated in us right from the outset. We were responsible for each other and, because the resources we had were limited, they had to be shared. Our values were also shaped by my parents' and grandparents' strong religious beliefs. Religion was the driving force for our family.

As a child, I had responsibilities on the farm before I went to school. I had to feed the calves and do other chores. I remember very specifically that I neglected my responsibilities for a very short period. One of the calves that I was supposed to have fed died because I hadn't taken care of it. So there were very, very real consequences, which didn't only have an effect on me. I remember I got a really bad spanking because my parents had depended on me, and I hadn't lived up to the responsibility. Not only was it bad for the animal, but it also meant that money that my family needed wasn't going to be available because we weren't going to be able to sell that calf, so that was a hard lesson.

How I was raised has influenced my role as president. I organize responsibilities in such a way that everybody is able to maximize their abilities. I don't have to be in charge, for which I am criticized sometimes. However, I believe it important to give somebody else the authority and the responsibility to carry out the job. This approach happens to coincide with the new style of management, but that isn't the reason I take this approach. I believe that better decisions are made when many people are involved, instead of pretending the only answer comes from the titular head.

I've always had the belief that the success of society depends on individual actions, and that those individual actions have to be coor-

It's All in the Frijoles

dinated with others' in order to achieve group success. If a person has a strong talent, it's part of my personal philosophy that the person has the responsibility to use it. It's the conglomeration of those individual talents that move issues forward. All this comes from a basic belief in the goodness of people. I think I learned these things from my upbringing, because we knew we were dependent upon each other.

Isabel Allende, an exiled Chilean writer now living in the United States, is well known for her magical, funny, uplifting novels, the best known of which is House of the Spirits. *She remembers growing up in a Chile divided, where everything outside was danger and chaos, but where, inside her house, she was surrounded by her mother's powerful love. When we talked, she recalled how aware she was of her obligations to her own family and all its members.*

Isabel Allende
Author

I grew up in a place where you couldn't expect anything from the state. The first message I received as a child was, "If you are lost, never approach a policeman." You didn't expect anything from the government or from the state. There was no proper welfare, no medical insurance, no life insurance. Nothing worked. Things have changed and are today quite different in Chile but, at the time when I was growing up, whatever happened—old age, disability, pregnancy, unwanted pregnancy, you lost your job, whatever—you went back to your family. And your family had to provide. In the same way, you had to give when you were in a better position. So, if any member of your family would come to you and say, "I'm homeless," you would have to take them in. There was no way you could refuse. You had the responsibility, but you also got back the support when you needed it. This sort of unconditional support from the family was the first rule that I learned.

You also keep in touch. Once a week, it was compulsory to have lunch at my grandfather's house, the family mansion. If you failed once because you had something to do it was okay, but, if it happened two or three times in a row, some of the family elders would come by to talk to you.

I remember once I put highlights on my hair. I knew my grandfather was going to hate it, hate it absolutely, so I didn't go to lunch for two weeks. The third week, I realized I had to choose between the highlights or my family. I got rid of the highlights!

Say the word obligación *to any Spanish-speaking person and the thoughts that come to mind will be* cumplir *and* cuidar, *"to fulfill" and "to take care of." You will see these themes repeated over and over again, from the nursery song "Pin Pon," which encourages children to learn obedience in the simplest ways, to the Aztec speech of the Elders, which stretches that sense of responsibility to touch the earth itself.*

"Pin Pon" is a children's song from Mexico, which parents sing with their little ones, helping them to make the appropriate motions as they sing together. As in many cultures, such songs involve the children physically at the same time they teach simple lessons, starting from the first glimmers of an infant's understanding, to passing on a picture of the world they will grow into.

"Pin Pon" reinforces the toddler's understanding of his very first responsibilities—to wash, to be polite and friendly, and—the fondest wish of parents the world over—to go right to bed when the sun goes down.

It's All in the Frijoles

Pin Pon

Pin Pon es un muñeco,
muy guapo y de cartón.
Se lava sus manitas con
 agua y jabón.

Se desenreda el pelo con
peine de marfil,
y aunque se da estirones
no llora ni hace así.

Pin Pon toma la mano con
fuerte apretón que dice
 quiere ser tu amigo
Pin Pon, Pin Pon.

Y cuando las estrellas em-
 piezan
a salir, Pin Pon se va a la
cama y se acuesta a dormir.

Pin Pon

Pin Pon is a pretty doll,
 made of cardboard.
He washes his little hands
 with soap and water.

He untangles his hair with
an ivory comb, and even if
 it pulls too hard he
 doesn't cry or go like this.
(Make an unhappy face.)

Pin Pon takes your hand
with a strong grip to say
he wants to be your friend.

And when the stars begin
to come out Pin Pon goes to
his bed and goes to sleep.

"¡No seas malcriado!" "Don't misbehave!" Or, "¡Malcriada!" "You bad girl!" Every Latino child hears these phrases from time to time. The story "The Boy Who Wouldn't Listen to His Parents" brings to mind my mother's reaction to my testing the limits of appropriate behavior. Like the disobedient boy, I was often too curious for my own good, or wanted to impose my will on the situation even when it was not appropriate. This story reminds us that we must learn to be obedient and act responsibly at all times, not just when someone is watching us.

The appearance of the beans in this tale is no accident, either. Just as they are a staple of life in Latin America, frijoles are a feature of many stories and myths, both as a comforting symbol of the familiar and a reminder that, though the tale may be fantastic and the characters larger than life, the lesson applies to all of us. In this case, the boy learns that it's a good idea to keep your eyes on the beans—the small things in life—and to fulfill your obligations.

The Boy Who Wouldn't Listen to His Parents

Many, many years ago there was a small boy who never listened to his parents. No matter what they tried to teach him, he refused to listen.

One sunny morning, the boy ran away from home. He hoped to find someone who wouldn't tell him what to do. Far, far from the village he ran, past the houses and down the path into the forest. Wandering deeper and deeper, he at last came upon a small house in a clearing. On the porch sat a round old man. The boy went up to the man and stood there, staring.

"What do you want, boy?" asked the man.

"I want something to eat," replied the boy.

The man, who had heard tales of the boy in the village, said, "You need to stop being so bad. No one will love you or take care of you unless you change your ways."

The boy only laughed.

At that, the old man smiled. "Come in. I will feed you, and you can stay with me for a while."

The little boy followed the old man into the house.

The next morning, the old man had to go to work. "Listen, *mijo*. While I am gone, you must stay inside. The only thing I ask is that you put the beans on to cook in the afternoon. But be careful. Do not put more than thirteen beans in the pot. Do you understand what I am telling you?"

The boy nodded, and the old man left. Later in the day, the boy filled the clay pot with water and put it on the fire. Carefully he counted out thirteen beans and tossed them in.

"That doesn't seem like very much," he said to himself. "There won't be enough to eat unless I add more." So, back and forth he went, throwing in several dozen more beans. When the water began to boil, the beans swelled up, first filling the pot, then overflowing into the fire. The boy was shocked. Quickly he found another pot and divided the beans. Soon both pots were overflowing. They tipped over and broke under the cascade of beans.

When the man returned home he found beans everywhere, and shards of pots.

"Why didn't you do as I told you?" he angrily said to the boy. The boy studied his feet and said nothing. The old man got a broom and began to clean up the mess.

The next morning, the old man once again left for work. "Listen, boy. Tomorrow I want you to cook the beans exactly the way I told you. And, by the way, don't open that little red door in the kitchen. Understand?"

Again the boy nodded to show he understood. The man took his leave.

Later that day, the boy carefully took out the pot, filled it with water, placed it on the fire, and counted exactly thirteen beans into it. After doing this, he went to sit at the table. The chair faced the little red door. He wondered what was behind that door. Surely, it couldn't cause any harm just to take a peek. Finally, he got up and opened the door.

There was a small earthen room just beyond the red door, with three large *ollas* (pots) each covered with a plate. There was also a large bureau. When he opened the top drawer he found three capes—green, yellow, and red.

What was in the *ollas*? Curious, he lifted the plate on the first *olla*, and dark clouds poured out of the *olla* and out the open window, filling the sky. Frightened and cold, the boy grabbed the red cape and pulled it around his shoulders. Suddenly, a clap of thunder shook the skies. The boy was turned into thunder and rose into the skies, where he became part of a great storm.

The old man heard the thunder as the skies grew dark, and knew

Responsibility/*Responsabilidad*

something had happened. Rushing home, he discovered the *olla* was open, still pouring out dark clouds. He quickly covered it, then noticed the bureau drawer was open and the red cape missing. Immediately he put on the green cape and rose into the skies, calming the storm. When he returned, the unconscious boy, still cloaked in the red cape, was in his arms.

The little boy regained consciousness some time later, lying on the bed. The room was warm and he was dry. The old man stood by his side. After some time, he spoke:

"You are lucky I heard the storm and came to look for you. You could have been lost forever among the clouds. I did not tell you to stay away from the red door for no reason. Your defiance has almost cost you your life."

The boy was silent, pondering this, as the man continued to speak.

"I am Qich Mam, he who controls the rains and the skies. I forgive what you have done: I wish you no harm. When I gave you directions, it was for your own good. So it is with your parents. Promise me you will no longer disobey them."

The boy smiled. "I promise."

Qich Mam patted the boy tenderly. "I believe you."

The little boy returned home to his parents, who were very glad to see him. From that day, he made himself useful to his parents and to those around him. He became very well known, and well loved. And he often thought, with gratitude, of the round old man who held the secrets of the skies in his hands.

"Usted es el arquitecto de su propio destino." You are the architect of your own destiny, my mother would say. She then would elaborate on how we build our lives each day, according to our thoughts and actions.

Her way of thinking, and the everyday tools she used to teach it—the dichos, the stories, the fables—belong to a great tradition, parts of which can be traced back to many pre-Columbian indigenous cultures that ruled Central and South America until the arrival of the

It's All in the Frijoles

Conquistadors. When Cortez arrived near what is now Mexico City, he met Moctezuma, ruler of a civilization that predated Christ, a civilization that had mastered irrigated agriculture and astronomy, and that had constructed towering monuments and pyramids in the jungle where the Aztecs worshiped their gods.

The ancient tlamatinime, the Aztec wisemen, believed that it was their duty to "to place a mirror before the people, that they might become wise and prudent; to endow with wisdom the countenances of others, so that a face [personality] might be assumed and developed . . . to humanize the will of the people." This desire to "make wise the countenance of others" began at birth. Boys and girls were raised in a strict manner. Parents taught their children specific lessons by repeating stories and rhymes over and over again. One of the simplest lessons, and one in which we can hear a cross-cultural echo of the Ten Commandments, is "The Wisdom of the Aztec Elders."

The Wisdom of the Aztec Elders

Obey and honor your parents.
Enter houses after your elders.
Respect the gods and do their bidding.
Do not steal or cheat.
Always give food to the hungry.
Learn good manners.
Tell the truth.

Early historical documents tell us that life during the time of the Aztecs was very hard, and lived according to rigid rules. This was intended to strengthen the heart. By adhering to the prescribed practices and performing penances, the human will was given shape and directed toward self-control and discipline. As one ancient text explains:

The mature man
Is a heart solid as a rock,

Is a wise face.
He is able and understanding.
Possessor of a face, possessor of a heart.

All of this, as well as a greater responsibility to the natural world and everything and everyone it, is found in an Aztec Huehuetlalli, *a speech of the elders.*

Huehuetlalli
Aztec Poem

Act! Cut wood, work the land,
Plant the cactus, plant the maguey.
You will have drink, food, clothing.
With this you will stand straight.
With this you shall live.
For this you shall be spoken of, praised.
In this manner you will show yourself.
To your parents and relatives.

Someday you shall tie yourself to a skirt and blouse.
What will she drink? What will she eat?
Is she going to live off the air?
You are the support, the remedy;
You are the eagle, the tiger.

————————

Dichos are proverbs, a delightful part of the oral tradition of the Latin peoples, which can guide our lives. All of us who grew up with a grandparent or parent who spoke Spanish grew up hearing dichos, *those short, plain, old-fashioned-sounding sayings, which carried us back to the old country, wherever it was. In a few words, these sayings carried a deep message. It sometimes takes a while, but ultimately we* all get the message and wonder why we didn't listen to our parents and abuelos *more attentively years ago.*

You will find dichos *here and at the end of each chapter, and sometimes at the beginning, which bring to mind different aspects of each virtue. Dichos feel good on the tongue—they are, after all, a verbal shorthand which my elders used countless times to remind me to behave wisely. Say them aloud and talk about them together. You'll find they make just as much sense today—and sound as good!—as when your great-grandmother first heard them. (For a very thorough listing, see José Antonio Burciaga's* In Few Words, *published by Mercury House.)*

Dichos
Proverbs

Del dicho al hecho hay mucho trecho.
From saying it to doing it is a long way.

Dime con quién andas y te diré quién eres.
Tell me with whom you travel, and I will tell you who you are.

El árbol se conoce por su fruta.
The tree is known by its fruit.

El buen padre en la casa comienza.
The good parent begins at home.

El consejo de la mujer es poco y él que no lo agarra es loco.
The advice of a woman is very scarce, and the person who does not heed it is crazy.

El que entre los lobos anda, a aullar se enseña.
He who walks among the wolves learns to howl.
(Beware of the company you keep.)

Costumbres de mal maestro, sacan hijo siniestro.
A bad master's habits make a sinister son.

Buena es la libertad pero no el libertinaje.
Liberty is good, but not the libertine.

2

Respect
Respeto

Obey and honor your parents,
respect and obey the gods,
be honest, tell the truth,
and don't eat too quickly
at the table.

—AZTEC TEACHING

Amor de padre o madre, que lo demás es aire.
Love of father and mother, the rest is pure air.

—SPANISH SAYING

El respeto ajeno es la paz.
The respect for the rights of others is peace.

—BENITO JUÁREZ, President
of Mexico

E l respeto ajeno es la paz." *These often-quoted words, originally ut-tered by Benito Juárez, President of Mexico, capture the essence of the virtue respect. "The respect of others is peace." They are simple words that convey a powerful meaning. Coupled with the Biblical Com-mandment "Honor thy father and thy mother," and the fundamental teachings of the ancient pre-Columbian people of Meso-America, they form part of the foundation for desired behavior passed on by genera-tions of Hispano parents.*

When the Spaniards arrived in the valley of Mexico in the year 1519, the Aztecs were already a highly cultured and powerful nation. Their city of Tenochtitlán was one of the most beautiful in the world. It had temples, schools, hospitals, palaces, parks, and zoos. There were strict rules for youth. Children were taught to obey and honor their parents, to respect and obey the gods, to be honest, to tell the truth, and not to eat too quickly.

Respect for our elders, for our cultural traditions, and for the earth which sustains us, are themes that are stressed under the virtue respect. Appropriate behaviors are learned, which means they must first be modeled by parents and other significant adults. If there is in-consistency in a parent's behavior, it is unproductive to tell a child to "Do as I say, not as I do." Parents, themselves, must first behave with respect.

Because we are taught to respect our elders, young Latino chil-

dren are open to learning from their elders' wisdom. We respect los ancianos, our elders, because they are older, more experienced, wiser. And, when we grow wiser ourselves, we are fully able to appreciate their teachings. "Always treat grandma with respect, mijita," Mamá would say. "You must not talk in a loud voice or whine, but must speak softly and politely. Always address adults as Mr. or Mrs. So and So, never by their first name." She taught me to greet my elders, shake hands, give a kiss or hug, and quietly listen to the adult conversation around me without interrupting. Anyone who has experienced polite, well-spoken Spanish-speaking children is often charmed by their demeanor. I know I am.

It is the modeling of appropriate behavior by our elders and the use of proverbios and dichos that serve as our teachers. Uttered in a firm but thoughtful tone of voice, Mamá's proverbios were lessons in morals, rules of etiquette, and personal conduct. She used every possible opportunity to teach me some aspect of behaving correctly, that is, in a manner that encouraged harmony between family members and others.

What some may see as a highly ritualized form of social interaction is actually a training ground for self-respect, along with respect for others whom we do not know or who are different from us. Respect also means to be open to people who have differing opinions, and being able to talk about these opinions and feel excited about these differences. Taking care in our use of the resources God has provided us is also part of this important virtue.

Respect is the highest form of love. It includes a reverence for life and for all living things.

As it was a highly prized virtue in our home, there was little tolerance for breaches of respect. Mamá demanded it, and often reminded me that her father would control his children's behavior with a look. "He rarely had to spank the boys," she would tell me, drawing upon a family standard set long before I came on the scene. Mamá also believed in and quoted the Biblical adage, "Spare the rod, spoil the child." In our home, there was no room for negotiation. Rudeness, rebellion, and lack of respect were not tolerated. I knew the standard of *behavior that was expected. And I knew it was important to respect Mamá's teachings because Mamá, other elders, and the Bible told me so.*

Filmmaker Moctezuma Esparza's memories of his early training as a youngster are reminiscent of the ways in which the best Latino parents instill this important virtue in their children.

Moctezuma Esparza
Film Producer

I learned from my dad that if you weren't familiar with someone you used the formal address, *usted*. To this day when I talk to my aunts and uncles I address them using *usted*. This form was used as an indication of respect, including respect for elders. That was also very much a part of my everyday life.

Throughout my entire life I called my father *usted* and, as a consequence, felt a respect and appreciation for all elders for their life experience, wisdom, and knowledge. I remember a funny little saying, *"El diablo no es diablo por ser diablo sino por viejo."* (The devil is not the devil because he's the devil, but because he's so old.) It reminds me that life experience is the greatest value, because you've seen so much and you've experienced so much. Early on, my father let me know that I could either learn from his experience or I could learn from my own mistakes; both were valuable. He said it was up to me how I was going to approach things, but it certainly would be less painful if I learned through his experience.

Along with respecting elders, a quality my father had that he passed to me was to treat everyone the same, that is, with respect, no matter what their station in life was, no matter whether they were

It's All in the Frijoles

a president, a rich person, a farmworker, a dishwasher, or anyone else.

He very much pushed me as a child—I was fairly shy—to talk to people. He'd say, "Go be friendly, go say hello," to this person. The idea was that one should always be introducing oneself, welcoming people, and extending hospitality to anyone in one's home, or wherever one was. And I was to do so without regard to a person's apparent station in life, status, or achievement, since people's worth was not in their earthly station, but in their character.

It certainly has served me well, in that I didn't grow up intimidated by anybody as no one was unapproachable, as long as you treated them with respect. If I treat everyone with respect, then everyone is available to me.

My dad communicated these ideas to me by telling me stories, either stories about the family or stories of other people. There were also all the pithy sayings I grew up with.

There was this story about a saint who came across someone who was afflicted by a parasitic worm. This person was asking for a healing. This particular saint cut off some of his flesh to envelop the worm, so the worm would not be killed in curing the person.

I still remember that story to this day because the point my father was communicating to me was that all life is sacred, nature, plants, every living thing. It wasn't just a sense of communicating religion or Bible stories, but it was very much a way of looking at the world. He shared with me an understanding that everything is alive. Instead of going about indiscriminately killing anything that was in front of us—even insects—he attempted to find a way to shoo a spider out, or open the door for something to fly out. I still have that habit now. I see a beetle or spider, and I throw them outside. I got that from my father. I must admit, though, I kill fleas.

He also taught me to appreciate and respect our Latin heritage. He was always telling me how the Incas had already achieved brain surgery and dentistry, or that the Mayans had discovered zero, and had an infinitely complex understanding of cosmology and the nature of time. I remember him telling me that when the Aztecs came to the valley of Mexico, the famous pyramids of the sun and moon were already very ancient, and that there was a deep, profound civilization and spirituality that existed, and that still exists.

To treat people well, to be well behaved, that was what was more important, rather than to be full of information or to be lacking in upbringing. I remember him saying *"No seas malcriado. ¿Que no tienes educación?"* Those words translate to "Don't be a person who has been badly raised, ill-bred, poorly mannered, or a person who is without education."

My father made the distinction between book learning and education as a person. I remember that if someone were discourteous, or if I was discourteous to someone, he would ask me if I had not been educated: *"¿Que no tienes educación?"* So I came to understand the word education not as something we learned in school, not as the gathering of information, but as a way to be and to treat other people with respect.

The film Stand and Deliver *was based on the inspiring teacher Jaime Escalante, who motivated students at Garfield/Roosevelt High School in the* barrio *of East Los Angeles to perform at previously unheard-of levels of excellence.*

Jaime Escalante
Teacher

If you believe in yourself, that means you're thinking positively, and you'll make it; you're gonna do it! However, if you have a negative image about yourself, you'll really kill yourself. One of the greatest things in life is that no one has the authority to tell you what you want to be. You're the one who'll decide what you want to be. Respect yourself and respect the integrity of others as well. The greatest thing

It's All in the Frijoles

you have is your self image, a positive opinion of yourself. You must never let anyone take it from you.

Three hundred years ago, Jesuit scholar Baltazar Gracián was one of Spain's greatest writers. He was a contemporary of Saint Teresa de Avila and Saint John of the Cross. He was a keen observer of many in positions of power, thus his work draws on a careful study of statesmen and potentates who managed to combine ethical behavior with worldly effectiveness. His maxims offer us valuable insight into the art of living and the practice of achieving.

Baltazar Gracián (Spain)
(1601–1658)

The Art of Worldly Wisdom

B*e known for your courtesy:* it alone can make you worthy of praise. Courtesy is the best part of culture, a kind of enchantment, and it wins the goodwill of all, just as rudeness wins only scorn and universal annoyance. When rudeness comes from pride, it is detestable; when from bad breeding, it is contemptible. Better too much courtesy than too little, or the same sort for everyone, for that would lead to injustice. Treat your enemies with courtesy, and you'll see how valuable it really is. It costs little, but pays a nice dividend: Those who honor are honored. Politeness and a sense of honor have this advantage: We bestow them on others without losing a thing.

Spanish-speaking people are trained to be respectful of elders and people in authority. However, respect is a two-way street. One cannot demand respect without giving it.

Marta Monahan

Author, **Strength of Character and Grace**

As a girl, I attended a small Catholic boarding school with only 125 girls. I loved Mother Superior. Everyone always hated me because I was the pet, but I earned it. Not because I ingratiated myself with her, but because I earned it. I knew the value of respect and discipline, and I was an easy child. I was not rebellious. Mother Superior was an outstanding woman. People came from all kinds of places to ask for her advice. One day I was in the little park and a famous prostitute came—let's call her La Dolores. Everybody knew who she was, because she was such a beautiful woman. She was about thirty years old, and very famous. I saw her come in and I thought, "Oh, my God. Why is this woman coming to see Mother Superior?" And Mother Superior came and she saw me looking at her and didn't say anything. And the woman stayed about an hour or two. She came out and Mother Superior came out to say goodbye to her. And Mother Superior came to me and said, "Do you have a question?"

"I know who she is," I said. "She is called La Dolores. And she is from the happy life."

"Remember" she told me, "whenever anybody comes to your house, no matter their position, their wealth, or their name, and they come with the respect due you, they deserve to be treated with the finest, highest dignity that ever stepped on your threshold. Any more questions?"

I said, "No."

"Understood?"

"Yes." And I thought about that. It is the same rhythm: You give respect first, and you receive it. If you do not receive it, you have a right to demand it, but not unless you give it. However, if you give it only to those you think deserve it, you will have a very uneven character and way of being. I know people who only greet those they want

It's All in the Frijoles

to impress, or those that they are impressed by, with graciousness, but don't treat everyone with the same grace.

Jesus Treviño
Director, Chicago Hope

As a child, I used to visit my grandmother every summer in Mexico. At the end of each visit, before I returned to Los Angeles, I would always be blessed. I would have to get down on my knees and she would apply the oil on my face and on my hands and bless me. As I got older, I thought this was a little old hat. I thought it was quaint. The summer before I entered Occidental College, we were going to do this ritual. I was down on my knees; I was feeling my oats, and she was giving me this blessing. I think she detected a smirk on my face. She hauled off and whacked me right across the face—the biggest slap I'd ever had in my life. She said *"Pórtate bien, hay que respetarme."* (Behave yourself, you must respect me.) I felt terrible because I thought, "You little creep, how dare you? Here's this grandmother that's been with you since you were a child and you are making fun of her. How could you do that?"

Then there are all the values of respect that my mother instilled in me and that the culture instills into you from the beginning—to respect your elders and to behave yourself. Sometimes the cultural messages work against us. I think we have a very complex culture and, while I embrace a lot of it, I think some elements of our culture need to be reexamined. *Machismo* is certainly one of them. So is the attitude of just being compliant, which in our culture is associated with being a good person—*te portas bien*—you don't make noise, you don't make waves.

You go to Hollywood and don't make waves, and you're dead! The squeaky wheels get the grease in Hollywood, but our culture teaches us not to be squeaky wheels. So, you have to know how to modify our cultural values, and learn the difference between applying that kind of respect in your household and being so respectful of people around you at work, including your boss, that you never ask for the raise you deserve, or you allow yourself to be taken for granted. That's been a hard thing for me to learn.

María Conchita Alonso
Actress, Singer, Television Host

Respect is everything for me. I can become like a tiger if I am not treated with respect. Sometimes I hear people say that I'm a little difficult to work with. I am not difficult at all, only I demand respect, and to be treated as an equal human being. I don't think that someone who has millions of dollars should be treated better than someone who doesn't have a cent. I think people should be respected for what they are inside, for their soul, for the good actions that they do in life, not for how powerful they are or for how much money they have.

Of course, when someone works very hard to achieve something, that commands respect. But you shouldn't treat someone with less respect just because the person cleans the street. Maybe as a human being, he's much better than the president of a bank or of a big company. It is important to be respectful of everyone.

Being respectful is also about making the world around you a better place for you yourself to live in. This may sound a little *egoísta*, egoistic. However, if you respect others, if you're nice, if you smile, if you're good, if your actions are good, you will also be treated with respect by others. That's where harmony comes from. It's really about being happy with yourself. Then, that happiness enables you to be good to others and that respectful treatment is returned to you.

I completely agree with Benito Juárez when he said *"El respeto ajeno es la paz."* If you pay attention to someone, if you really hear someone, if you're someone worthy of respect and give respect, that is peace, that is love. Respect is the most important thing because out of respect comes believing in yourself and believing in others. Honesty comes out of respect. Respect is the most important virtue.

An important part of respect is self-respect, because you cannot give what you do not already have.

Honor is also a part of respect. It is a quality that has great meaning in the Hispanic culture.

Hector Elizondo
Actor

When I was growing up, dishonoring the family was about as bad a thing as you could do. There are certain elements of that notion that are so old-fashioned but, to me, my father's words resonate with me as clearly as if I heard them yesterday. There is also a great contradiction. What is honor? Who ever hears that today? It sounds corny, but honor was a big deal for my father. What he taught me has helped me whenever I came to a crossroads where I might have gotten into trouble.

When I was in my early twenties, I had hair that stuck up a few inches above my head with my comb stuck in it and goo dripping down my neck. I was a baby-faced kid who could box, and I was a good athlete. I was part of the stable of boxers at a gym. My dad liked that I was boxing, but he didn't like the fact that it automatically meant I had to make friends with the guys who hung around there, guys with questionable morals.

One of the things a guy did if he got into the stable was run little errands, earning your keep, in a sense, and earning some spending money. You were asked to take a package here and there. You'd dress nice, and you'd deliver the package. At first I would not deliver the package, but one day, I succumbed. I dressed nice. "Why you dressing nice?" my dad asked. "I don't know, I dress nice." I delivered the package. The package was about a hand's length in each direction. It was in a neighborhood with walkup apartments. There were five flights of stairs, those wooden steps of New York that I know so well. I could smell the urine in the hallway. I sat by the door of the apartment, waited a minute.

The guy came to the door, said, "Stay here, thanks." He shook my hand and slapped a couple of bills into it. Fifteen dollars! I wasn't making fifteen dollars a week. So I went back to Tony, shall we call him, and he said, "Thanks, you did a good job." Wow, I could make two or three deliveries a week, and make more than my father makes by delivering packages. But I never delivered a second package because I kept hearing my father saying, "What kind of man does that? You have other options," and his advice over the years was part of me.

I told my dad about it, and he said, "First of all, you're right." He continued, "You're lucky. You could have come out looking like Uncle Charlie and Cousin Joey. Your face could pop out looking any way." He understood the situation. And once again he said, "You shouldn't do that. You have other options."

That's why I never delivered another package. I didn't want to dishonor my family. What he taught me also affects the way I do business. I realize that the only thing I have that's of any value is my good name. That is really what makes business for me, my reputation. More and more, I become like my father in some ways, less and less in others. He'd be laughing now if he could see me. I try to do it his way.

Honor is an important part of respect. We are called upon to defend our honor, as individuals, as a nation. Simón Bolívar was one of the liberators of Latin America. He envisioned an "America fashioned into the greatest nation in the world, greatest not so much by virtue of

It's All in the Frijoles

her area and wealth as by her freedom and glory." He saw the people
of Latin America as worthy of respect and urged them to take the path
of honor and defend their freedom.

Simón Bolívar (Venezuela)
(1783–1830)
Statesman and Leader of the Revolution Against Spain

Those wretched Spaniards who are superior to us only in wickedness do not excel us in valor, because our indulgence is what gives them their strength. If they appear great to us, it is because we are on our knees. Let us avenge three centuries of shame. War alone can save us through the path of honor.

Anthony Stevens Arroyo
Professor of Religion, City University of New York

The biggest influence on my morals and my values were my grandparents. My parents, who immigrated from Puerto Rico, were very busy trying to become Americanized and to become successful in this country, so my grandparents were a tremendous source of wisdom and morality for me.

My grandfather taught me the importance of maintaining one's honor, *dignidad*. I remember the point of survival was not economic survival. My father was fortunate in business. The point of survival was the issue of honor, *dignidad*. I remember the time I received the second Eagle Scout award in my Boy Scout troop. I was the youngest boy to receive it. One person from each troop was selected to go to the

Boy Scout Jamboree, and I was chosen. Some of the others were jealous and tried to alter the selection. Someone accused the Scoutmaster of being my lover. My parents took this as an opportunity to teach me the value of *dignidad*. I was told to never give people a cause to say this is true, and I was told to be very polite.

I was carefully coached not to sink down to their level. It was a real message for survival that, no matter what they do, they can't take away your *dignidad*. This idea of not insulting them back, this idea of turning the other cheek, never left me.

This farewell song, sung throughout Latin America, can also be played as a game. For the first verse, children hold hands and walk around a child in the center of the circle. For the second verse, the circle stops moving, and the center child picks another for handshaking and for a farewell hug. For the third verse, the first child joins the circle, waving good-bye to the second child, who stays in the center. The game continues this way, teaching good manners as children play.

Naranja Dulce	Sweet Orange
Naranja dulce,	Sweet honey orange,
limón partido,	a slice of lemon, dear,
dame un abrazo	if I could hug
que yo te pido.	if could have you near.
Si fueran falsos	Time to shake hands now,
mis juramentos,	a hug for farewell,
en otros tiempos	Adios amigo(a),
se olvidarán.	I wish you well.
Toca la marcha,	The march is playing,
mi pecho llora,	I'll part tomorrow,
adiós, señora,	Good-bye my dear friend,
yo ya me voy.	I leave with sorrow.

It's All in the Frijoles

Pepe Aguilar

Performing Artist

My parents (actress Flor Silvestre and singer Antonio Aguilar) were raised the old way, as they say. They are very traditional, *muy mexicanos*. My father is a *charro*, and I was raised in this tradition. *Charrería* is something very beautiful. It is passed from generation to generation. It is the only Mexican sport that keeps alive a time-honored tradition. It reminds us of what we were like at an earlier time in our country's development, how we were raised and from what people. It is a belief system, a way of living and thinking. In a way, it is like a religion in that it demands that a man be a gentleman, a person who respects his family, who respects God above all things, who deeply believes in his country. A *charro* is the descendant of the men who defended the ideals of liberation and who fought with the insurrectionists and who gave freedom to the Mexican people. That was the real *charro*.

So, my father taught me to respect everybody and every living thing. Each living thing—human beings, a little dog, a plant—is here for a reason and a purpose. I believe in respecting people, their privacy, their manner of thinking, their customs. Respect for the dignity of each human being—the poor person as well as the Nobel Prize winner—for the folklore of each country, for laws, is essential. You have to have respect. It is the basis for society. Imagine if we all treated each other with respect, loved our parents, loved each other, if we lived responsible, balanced lives, if we had faith. We would all be very happy!

Respect for women is an important part of engendering respect within the family. In the following poem Rodolfo Díaz captures the love and appreciation he feels for his mother. After all, respect is the highest form of love.

Rodolfo Díaz

Mother of My Soul

Beloved mother, you were my first love;
although the years have passed, I still adore you
with all my heart.

Beautiful white-haired *mamita*,
your prayers are always in my soul,
The advice you gave me
is forever imprinted in my mind.

For all the affection and love you gave me
with such motherly tenderness
I give you thanks.

For the grief and sadness I have caused you,
I ask a thousand pardons.
Today receive from me, my precious *mamita*,
the kisses and embraces I never gave you.

Dichos

Lo mismo es irse que huirse, que irse sin licencia.
It's all the same whether you leave in flight or simply without permission.

Si respetas a tus mayores, te respetan tus menores.
Respect your elders, and youth will respect you.

Honra a tus mayores y aprecia a los menores.
Honor your elders and appreciate your young.

El hombre debe ser feo, fuerte y formal.
A man should be homely, hardy, and honorable.

Hijo de bien, todos lo ven.
A well-mannered kid will never be hid.

Favor publicado, favor deshonrado.
A favor made public is without honor.

Favor referido, ni de Dios ni del diablo agradecido.
A spoken favor pleases neither God nor the devil.

La buena educación conviene para usarla con quien la tiene.
Good manners are handy if you come upon good-mannered folk to
use them on.

Haz bien a los presentes y habla bien de los ausentes.
Do good to those present and speak well of those absent.

Cortesía de boca mucho consigue y nada cuesta.
Courteous words gain much at little cost.

Lo cortés no quita lo valiente.
Courtesy doesn't take away from valor.

Una cosa es prometer, otra es cumplir.
It's one thing to promise; it's another to fulfill your word.

Quien pregunta lo que no debe, le responden lo que no quiere.
If your question is out of bounds, you won't like how the answer sounds. (Use a little tact.)

Nunca preguntes lo que no te importa.
Never ask what is none of your business.

Cada perico a su mecate y cada chango a su metate.
Every parrot to its perch and every monkey to its task. (Mind your own business.)

Chisme averiguado jamás es acabado.
Gossip once begun will never be done.

La ropa sucia se lava en casa.
Dirty linen is washed at home.

3

Hard Work
Trabajo Duro

La ociosidad es la madre de todos los vicios.
Idleness is the mother of all vice.

To work is to pray.

—St. Benedict

Trabaja para más valer, estudia para más saber.
Work to be worth more, study to know more.

Mamá worked very hard to support our home. She was a sample maker and finisher in the garment district of Los Angeles working for Helga Oppenheimer, whose fine detail work made the stylish, beautifully tailored suits and coats produced by Helga, Inc. so distinctively stunning.

I never once heard Mamá complain about having to get up early to walk to the bus stop in the rain, about conditions at the garment factory where she spent her days, or about bringing home extra work to meet a production deadline for her boss. Instead, she took pride in her contribution to the line of clothing she helped produce.

Looking back, I believe she saw work as an opportunity, and her gifts as a fine seamstress as a gift from God. Mamá started working as a young girl in her teens to help support her family of seven brothers and sisters, and to buy the things that her parents couldn't afford. Back then, she worked in canning and meat packing plants close to home on the east side of Los Angeles.

Somewhere along the way, she discovered her gifts were in her hands and, by the time I was born, she was earning money part-time at home by making beautiful ceramic flowers for ashtrays, candy bowls with lids, and other accessories. She also made lifelike flowers out of small, colorful silk squares of fabric, which were bundled in neat stacks on the kitchen table. She would spread out the colorful fabric along with the wire and fabric greenery and, almost magically, create magnificent flowers. She told me she worked at home because she thought it important for a mother to care for her children until they were five, after which they went off to kindergarten.

My father, although educated and a writer for the Spanish-language daily La Opinión, did not earn a lot of money, so Mom also worked to provide the necessities. I don't think she knew how not to work. She kept our home spotless, line-dried the clothes which had to be manually wrung through the old fashioned washing machines of the times, and cooked fabulous meals to perfection, hand-chopping all the ingredients more efficiently than any food-processing machine. She also made the majority of our clothes, often from remnants she purchased for pennies or brought home from the shop.

On Saturdays, she would clean house. She would wash the windows and polish and wax the furniture, only passing the chore of polishing the silver on to me when I was old enough to muster a rag and elbow grease. "El trabajo de los niños es poco y él que no lo aprovecha es loco" (A child's work is little, but anyone who fails to cultivate it is crazy) must have been one of her favorite dichos.

Sundays were considered days of rest, but still Mamá would create wonderful dinners after church when we would be joined by various family members.

For these weekly celebrations we would eat pollo con arroz, frijoles de la olla, calabacitas con maíz, and tortillas de harina, along with a homemade apple, cherry, or lemon-meringue pie. These Sunday meals were always served family style on her best china, accompanied by her best crystal and fine damask cotton table linens which, of course, she washed and ironed by hand.

"A woman's work is never done" was a favorite saying of hers. But it was said with an air of pride in accomplishment, rather than defeat.

How did she manage to work two jobs with such grace? It was in her gratitude for the opportunity to work, to be good at her craft, and to maintain a beautiful home for her family. She took pride in her work and made an effort to do the best job possible in everything she did.

Mamá also took time to rest at the end of a long day. Del trabajar nace el descansar. *Rest is born from work. Like the* dicho, *she lived a life in balance. Evenings, she would read a book—she preferred autobiographies of famous people—watch an educational television program like* Masterpiece Theatre, *or read the newspaper out loud to improve her English pronunciation. Even at rest, she did things to improve herself.*

The phrase laborare est orare, *"to labor is to pray," written by St. Benedict some 1,400 years ago, is still a powerful thought: that our work is a kind of prayer and, thus, like prayer, charged with meaning. In the Bible, the dignity of work stems from the earliest chapters of the book of Genesis, where human labor is modeled on God's labor. We are called to be the stewards of the Creator and "tend the earth." Mamá truly believed that work, in and of itself, embraces inherent dignity, and all her work reflected this deeply held conviction.*

Loretta Sanchez
Member of the U.S. Congress

My parents were not afraid of hard work. My brothers, sisters and I saw that on an ongoing basis. My dad had a business in the plastic industry. He took my brothers to work with him on the big machinery. Some people would ask him why, and he said, "Because I want them to learn that it's much better to work with their brains than it is to work with their backs." They learned the lesson—none of four boys wanted to take over his business!

We also learned about doing the best job you could in every situation. My dad was a Cubmaster, and all my brothers were Boy Scouts. I remember in the Scout book there was a project by which you could turn two orange crates into a bench. Well, my father was a machinist and a carpenter, and he scoffed at the idea of orange crates. "It's not the way you make something that's worth investing your time in." He taught the boys to make it right, even if it meant going to the lumberyard and paying a little extra for real wood, then taking the time to show them how to put it together—how to make the corners line up and everything. To this day, thirty years later, I have one of those little stools in my garage. My dad always cared more about how well you could do something, not how quickly. I was a Girl Scout, and my mom was the same way. She wanted us to learn to do things the right way.

My mom taught us teamwork. We always helped her make fried shrimp. We would help shell, devein, and clean them. My sister and I would batter the shrimp, and my mom would fry them. It would take us an hour or two to do it right. Each of us had our own little specialty. I think my brother Frank had the worst job—he was kind of the black sheep of the family for a while, and I always attribute that to all those shrimp he had to clean. But he wanted them the most, so he had to do the biggest job. My mom taught us that if you wanted something, you had to work to get it. It wasn't just going to be given to you without any effort. All seven of us learned that lesson. We also learned that things are easier if everybody helps. That's how we won the election against a well-financed incumbent. I first asked my family to get involved, then we expanded our network of supporters. All of us worked together to achieve victory.

⟫⟫⟫

Luis Jimenez
Sculptor

My father was a very ambitious immigrant from Mexico. He was a sign painter who eventually bought the relatively large company where he worked. I grew up working in his shop, and listening to the stories told by my grandmother, my father, and the other workers. When I started writing them down, I realized that work was the most common theme. They told me *"Camarón que se duerme se lo lleva la corriente,"* which, of course, means the shrimp that sleeps is carried off by the current. Growing up along the border with constant contact with those in Mexico, I heard stories about how hard the people across the border in Mexico had to hustle to make a living. The closest thing to a compliment I received from my father was *"Tengo un hijo que no le pide nada a Dios, no más que le ponga cerca"* (I have a son that doesn't ask anything of God, only that he be close to him). Another one of his favorite sayings was *"El flojo trabaja doble"* (The lazy man works twice). A lot of his *dichos* were work related.

He used to tell me a children's story about the pious man who tried to cross the river. As the story goes, the pious man went to the river and his ox cart got stuck at the side of the river in the mud. The man fell down on his knees and prayed.

Another man came along and tried going around the ox cart. He, too, got bogged down in the mud, but he grabbed a stick and started whacking the oxen. Then he got behind his cart and started pushing it as he let out a tirade of abusive words and curses—*Chinga* this, and *chinga* that, taking the Lord's name in vain along with everything else. Pretty soon his ox cart started moving across the river.

The pious man in the meantime, still sat there praying. At this point, he hollered towards the heavens. He said, "I'm a pious man. I've always lived an upright life. I just don't understand how you can help this cursing *pelado,* peasant, that just crossed here and not help me." The voice of God booms down from above, *"Sí, pero no estaba ayudando* (Yes, but you weren't helping).

To read Victor Villaseñor's classic novel Rain of Gold *is to appreciate the essence and importance of work, not work as drudgery, but work as the ultimate act of creation. This attitude of work as one of the miracles of life was passed on to the author by his father at an early age.*

It's All in the Frijoles

Victor Villaseñor
Author, Rain of Gold

I think that, in my family, hard work was one of the most important virtues. My father would tell us stories over and over, showing that he had no right to have children or a family if he was not hard-working. Then he would give us the example of the *burro*. He would tell us that the *burro* will carry a huge load for its size and weight—the *burro* isn't that big—and if you came into a camp and there wasn't food there, the *burro* would be willing to go on to the next camp. Now, a lot of horses and mules will swell up their backs, get back sores, and deliberately sabotage themselves, break down, because they don't want to go on to the next place without food. So, he explained, a man had to be a *burro*. That's where the word *macho* comes from, it refers to a *macho burro*. That is, a man that is hard-working, responsible, and willing to go beyond what is necessary to get the job done. In this context, *macho* was always a positive word.

My father insisted on telling us stories because he was preparing us to survive. He would tell us that a boy of fifteen, sixteen, or seventeen who is well prepared can be dropped anywhere on the planet and will be able to survive. "Within thirty days, he will be doing well."

The boy doesn't need to speak the language, he told us; he needs no money. All he has to do is not be lazy and bitter. My father would say, "If you are dropped off somewhere and are willing to work, just start washing dishes. You'll get fed. Start cleaning up and you'll be given a place to sleep. As soon as people see you are willing to wash dishes and you are willing to work, people will start liking you, because most people go around being arrogant, lazy, and not willing to work."

There is a wonderful story about three men working at a construction site in Mexico. A passerby walks up to the first man and asks, "What are you doing?" The man looks at him blankly and says, "I'm digging a trench." Then the stranger walks up to the second laborer and asks the same question. The second worker responds with the same bored attitude. "Why, can't you see? I'm pouring cement." The stranger walks a few yards further along to where a third laborer is very hard at work. He stops and asks the third laborer, "What are you doing?" The laborer pauses from his work and smiles broadly. "Don't you see?" he asks, motioning his arms up towards the sky. "I'm building a beautiful cathedral."

Jesus Treviño

Director, Chicago Hope

One *dicho* that comes to mind that I heard as a child is *"El flojo y el mezquino andan dos veces el camino"* (The lazy man and the miser have to walk the same road twice). It's basically about doing things right the first time. I think that early on when I was growing up—this was before *chicanismo,* Chicano power, and all that—I had an inferior sense of self. Because I felt inferior, I thought the only way I could succeed was to try extra hard to make up for what I lacked. Of course, at that time, I could not articulate any of this. All I knew was that I wasn't very good, I wasn't very smart, and I wasn't very intelligent. I didn't know if it was just me or all Mexicans, but I felt that the only way to succeed was to try doubly hard.

I developed this sense of quality, this reaching for high goals, setting high standards, and trying extra hard to meet them, by being very disciplined. A lot of this has carried over into my adulthood in terms of what I do as a director of *Chicago Hope.* You have to approach directing with a degree of perfectionism. You have to set high standards and goals, and ask your actors, and your camera crew, and everyone working on the set, to come along for the ride to see if we can really make this thing look terrific.

So a little bit of that *dicho,* that if you are lazy or if you pull back and don't give it your all, you're going to have to do it over again, has encouraged me to work harder to do things right the first time.

Joe Kapp
Football Superstar

My mother, Florence García, would always say, *"Si vas a hacer algo, hazlo correcto"* (If you're going to something, do it right). It's not a profound message, but I have always remembered it. That message carried me through hours of football practice and school. She also taught me that there is a price for everything; that is to say, you must concentrate on your goal. I learned there is a price you pay for focusing on being an athlete—you give up art or you give up a musical instrument. You develop certain other skills. You have to maintain academic skills in order to play, so you have to work very hard on both the mental and physical front. And always, spoken and unspoken, is the message that if you want to be good at something, then you gotta keep doing it and doing it. The honest effort of spending the time to perfect certain aspects of the game is necessary. Since I was doing something I loved, it didn't seem like work at all.

We moved a lot, like a lot of families in rural farming communities. I went through kindergarten to the third grade in San Fernando, from third grade to tenth grade in Salinas, and finished the eleventh and twelfth grade in Newhall. I learned to live with change. The only constant was football.

From my mother, I learned to eat all the *frijoles* on the plate. Translated to football, that means you never leave the plate empty. If you have a talent, use it. Fulfill your promise. My mother made tremendous sacrifices to even allow me to go on to college with three younger sisters and a brother still at home. She worked hard to allow me the luxury of getting that college education and participating in the crazy game of football.

A lot of people say, "Joe Kapp made it." In other words, I wasn't such a gifted natural, but I chose to work at football. I chose to work at it, and I chose to say, "Okay, you want to go to college? Okay." And I would tell myself, "If I play sports, I can go to college, and that's where I've gotta go."

You choose to pay the price of what it takes to be the best in your chosen position. You compete. I haven't paid the price for learning how to play the guitar, so the result is that all my friends get to hear me play badly.

However, in my chosen field, I've paid the price of time and effort and focus and discipline. It's the same with everything else. That's how you work through certain fears and weaknesses. You just work at it. We also have to work to improve ourselves in other ways.

When I was growing up I wouldn't speak to the public, although I was captain of every team I ever played on, and the captain usually does the talking. Behind the scenes, I always made arrangements not to talk in public. Finally, in Canada, I saw that speaking was an opportunity, but I realized I was afraid, *tenía miedo,* so to speak.

So I said to myself, "I can't do this anymore. I'm gonna look this fear in the eye and I'm gonna change. I'm gonna conquer this fear." I started speaking to kids, not twelve-year-olds, but third graders, Cub Scouts. I learned to speak to them, I graduated to the seventh graders, and so on. And, in the end, by working at it, I got over the fear of speaking in public. I spoke to a thousand people here recently. Imagine, the young man who was afraid to speak in public delivering motivational speeches. But I had to work at it.

Danny Villañueva is another football player turned businessman, and entrepreneur, and one of the wealthiest Latinos in the U.S. It has been said that he did more with his talents than any player in his league. He

It's All in the Frijoles

was short and not too fast, but he had heart. And he was willing to work very, very hard, which has made him a success at everything he has attempted.

Danny Villañueva
Entrepreneur

I never thought about it until this moment, but when I was playing football and we lost, my mother would always ask, "Is there anything you could have done to win the game?" She would bait me, "*¿Que no tienes vergüenza que perdieron?*" (Aren't you ashamed your team lost?) She never asked me, "How did you play?" She did ask, "Did you do everything you could have to help the team win? Did you work hard enough?" That was very important to her. She had a strong work ethic and sense of discipline. She had me out cutting lawns, working, and sweeping the basketball courts from the time I was ten. I always had a job. She always encouraged me to have a job and she encouraged us to pool our money—to put it in the family pot. My eleven brothers and sisters did that willingly. I'd keep a little bit for me and all the rest went in the pool, for mom. All of the families we knew pooled the efforts of their labor. As soon as school was out in the summer she would say, "*Vamos por arriba,* let's go up to Northern California." We worked each summer in Salinas because it was cooler there than in Calexico, where we lived.

After working all summer, people would come back to Calexico with new clothes, or a car. For us, the end of every summer meant a bigger decision. Do the kids go back to school and give up their jobs? That was a very tough time for everybody, but Mom absolutely did not hesitate. She pushed us back into school, pushed us into sports, pushed us into the church. Those were three legs of her strategy. The fourth leg of "the stool" was the family. So you had the family, the church, the school, and work.

Dad did it all by example. We were always amazed. He was a minister and a handyman. I remember he was always working, always doing something for somebody. I remember he was very sad and cried a little when he had to retire. He saw that as a defeat. It was really strange, because my father-in-law looked at retirement as the ultimate reward for a life of hard work. Dad saw it as an absolute defeat. *"Ya no sirvo, estoy muy viejo, me echaron afuera,"* "I'm useless, I'm old, they threw me out." He took it very, very, hard. It was a rejection because he could no longer do the job and he went downhill very quickly. Two things, my mom's illness and his obligatory retirement, hurt him deeply, and it was all downhill from there. I know . . . I saw him. They gave him pills and he wouldn't take them. He would put them in his jacket. He wanted to die. He kept telling me this.

When I came to see him, they told me they were taking him to the hospital. He told me, "I'm very tired." I went to the doctor and told him, "No life-saving equipment. When he goes, he goes." I returned to work in Los Angeles. When my family called me to tell me that he'd died, I jumped on a plane to go down to Calexico for the service. Then I flew back straight from the funeral because we were having a business event here in Los Angeles that I had promised to attend. Some of my brothers have never forgiven me for attending a work-related event on the day of the funeral, but I guarantee you my dad would have told me to do that. He would have said, "Don't stop doing things. Keep working, keep serving."

These were the basics: You had an illiterate woman who never set foot in a school laying down the law and giving us the rules of life—the *virtues,* as you call them—and a man living the virtues. I don't know of any other combination that would have worked with twelve kids in that setting, in that place. They kept us incredibly focused by using the family, the church, sports, and work. Those four things kept us going.

Moctezuma Esparza

Film Producer

My father loved work. He said there was fulfillment in it. From him I learned that work gives our life meaning: It's how we learn, it's how we perfect our will. How can we achieve anything without building our will, strengthening our will to get up every day to work and to complete something?

If somebody came to visit, my father would put them to work, every chance he had. When my friends came over, he would put them to work. He'd say, "Okay, let's go pull these weeds, let's go move these boxes and cans, let's go harvest some corn." What I remember is that everybody got into it, everybody liked it. Work wasn't a chore in the way my father presented it. It wasn't a burden. There was satisfaction and fulfillment in achieving and completing something. I did learn that from him.

I have this image of him, at seventy-nine, carrying a ninety-pound roll of roofing material up a thirty-foot ladder to the roof of my house. I was driving up and I saw him do this. My heart almost jumped out of my mouth. I didn't even know he was going to do it. He told me, "The rains are coming and it's time to re-roof the house."

Phil Roman followed a dream by working toward it every day. His story of his career and how he started his own production company is a roadmap for success. The key is hard work.

Phil Roman

Animator and Producer

My folks taught me that you have to try, you have to work hard, because nobody's going to give anything to you. They said if you work at what you want, you can make it happen.

At age eleven, I saw the film *Bambi*. I decided right then that I wanted to become an animator. The movie affected me so much that I started drawing. At first I'd copy pictures, then I started drawing other things. I'd buy books on drawing because there were no art schools and our school didn't teach art. I would practice and practice and practice.

I started doing drawings for the school paper. We didn't have much money, so when I decided I wanted to go to art school in Los Angeles, I had to work for a year at a theater in Fresno to save a little bit of money. I was still contributing to my folks—we were all chipping in—so it took a while to save some for myself. When I saved sixty dollars, I decided to travel to Los Angeles. In September of 1949, I just got on a Greyhound bus to Los Angeles to attend art school. I didn't know anybody here. I didn't know if I was going to find a job. I didn't know where I was going to live. But I found a job, thanks to my theater experience—two, actually—I found a place to live, and I enrolled in art school.

In 1950, I quit and joined the Air Force. I was stationed in Paris and in Germany, which were great experiences. When I returned, I started going to school at Art Center on the GI Bill. I also worked at night at the school. The night job led me to another opportunity. Disney was hiring. I prepared a portfolio very quickly and made an appointment. Now, this was the place I considered to be like the Holy Grail, a place I'd always dreamed about. When I went there for my interview I walked on Mickey Mouse Avenue and Dopey Drive. I

It's All in the Frijoles

showed my portfolio to someone who said, "Fine. We'll call you." And they did.

I started at Disney at ninety-nine cents an hour for a one-month trial period. I was told that after a month that if you passed your qualifying exam, they would assign you to a project and boost your wage twenty-five cents an hour, but I would have paid them to go work there.

The fact that they were giving me ninety-nine cents an hour, who cared? I just wanted the opportunity to do what I wanted to do. The reason I left for a small commercial studio in San Francisco was that I wanted to animate and I needed more experience than was available at Disney.

That turned out to be another good decision because, on the new job, I got to do storyboarding and camera work. I was visiting ad agencies and talking with them about ideas, so I was getting a complete idea of how to put a film together. That was a tremendous opportunity which came from my desire to work and to be an animator, which as it turned out, became much bigger than that.

I never analyzed anything. I never looked at the odds against me. I just applied a lot of efforts to go after what I felt I wanted in my heart and guts. I never thought what I wanted was impossible because, if you think something can't happen, it won't, because you've already set your mind against it.

Amalia Mesa-Bains

Artist; Recipient, MacArthur Foundation Genius Award

There was never any idleness around my home when I was growing up. You were always kept busy. I was taught that there are many things you can make and do. When I was young, people were always building machines to make things easier, or training dogs or horses, so we could see even the animals' behavior could be improved. So I grew up with this quality of inventing and solving problems—with the idea "I think it could work this way or that way." Thus, work was an enjoyable thing, and being productive was a wonderful thing. Being creative was part of being productive.

Some of my uncles were gifted wood carvers. One of them was working on a set of four-inch soldiers of the Roman Legion. You know how many different kinds of Roman soldiers there were? This was sort of a life work for him. He was constantly carving them, one at a time, painting their little shields. This was a man who never even went past grade school, yet he got books and he studied images of the soldiers, so that his figures would be exact. He kept them in rows so that we could see whatever legion he was working on at that time.

I had a *gran tío*, great uncle, who was an artist in Fresno. My parents used to tell stories when I was a child about how he invented a steam engine when he was nine or ten years old. It's very similar to a story I read about Diego Rivera making a little steam engine when he was seven or eight. I grew up with the idea that making things, working hard to do something, was important. We were taught to develop our own standards all the time and we were taught that there is a right way to do things and to learn how to do them correctly. It didn't matter if you could get away with less—we knew this wasn't right for us, because we were taught to do our best.

––––––––––––––

Anthony Quinn was born in Chihuahua, Mexico, in 1915. He began his acting career at the age of twenty as a means of improving his speech and has worked steadily ever since. His intimate and candid biography, One Man Tango, *captures the importance of work to a man's identity, and the pride and joy Quinn felt when he was able to accompany his father in the fields.*

It's All in the Frijoles

Anthony Quinn

Actor

We lived in a small hut on a knoll about a mile from the grove, and the secret was to reach the shade of the trees before the sun was too high. God, it was hot, but under the trees it was tolerable. I scrambled to keep pace with my father on the long walks to work each morning, trying to beat the sun. His strides were tremendous next to mine, but he did not slow to accommodate me. Either I kept up or fell back.

In the walnut grove, each man worked an area of ten or twenty trees, and it was my father's job to shake the nuts from our trees with a long hook. It was a tricky business. He had to drive the hook into the limb of the tree and shake with everything he had, or the nuts would not fall. When they did, we took cover, and then quickly collected the droppings. It was my job to separate the nuts from their peels and bag them. My hands were browned by the juice and blistered by the tugging. It was awful work, but I loved this time with my father. I was only five years old, but I imagined myself a young man, sharing the burdens of our family. I fashioned myself in his image and hoped he would notice. My mother and grandmother helped, when they were finished with the cleaning, and with Stella, but these long days were remarkable for the ways they let me see my father, and for the ways I let him see me.

My father liked the work, and the lifestyle, and soon he had us following the seasons. We moved from one plantation to the next, wherever there was work and a place to stay. In this, my father was nearly alone. Most migrant workers worked the same crop, one season to the next, but he had us moving everywhere, picking everything: tomatoes, nuts, lettuce. We picked grapes in the north, between Oxnard and the Napa Valley, and lemons and oranges in the citrus groves of Southern California.

Hard Work/*Trabajo Duro*

After a while, we developed our preferences. A day in the cotton fields was the worst. We had to pull the flowers from the ground and rake them with our hands; whatever was left in our hands we put into the sack. We wore no gloves, and I was torn and bloodied by the drill. String beans were less painful, but just as bad. We stood behind a huge threshing machine, picking the beans with one hand and shielding our faces from the dirt and debris with the other.

The most pleasant jobs were among the fruit trees, out of the sun. We picked peaches, apricots, apples, pears, quinces. These jobs were harder to come by, but my father somehow managed to land us in the better fields before the positions were all taken. He made friends wherever we went, and people told him things. The plantation owners liked him because he looked whiter than most Mexicans, and because he spoke English. The other pickers liked him because he was a hard worker, and a great storyteller, and because his English helped them to stay one step ahead of everyone else.

It was a marvelous, rambling existence. Like gypsies, we vagabonded from one home to the next, but one stop was much like another. We carried our home on our backs and in our routine. I will never lose the feeling of waking before the sun, and tromping down to the fields with my father, of wanting to please him, and helping him provide for our family. It was a magical thing. It did not matter where we were, or what we were picking. What mattered was that we had a job to do, together, and that he needed me. What mattered was that we were finally making a life out of no life at all.

Gloria Molina
Los Angeles County Supervisor

My father used to work very hard. There were ten of us, so he worked two jobs to support his family. During the day he

It's All in the Frijoles

worked in construction as a laborer. In the evenings he worked in the steel mills in Maywood.

He got his work ethic from the woman who raised him. His parents died when he was very young and, when he was three years old, he was sent back to Mexico to live with the woman who would act as his mother, and her brother. They owned a working ranch in Casas Grandes, Chihuahua. I remember visiting "Grandma" every summer and being amazed by how she managed her numerous responsibilities on the ranch.

She would get up at four o'clock in the morning—I'd get up with her—fix her hair in a bun, put on her dress and lipstick, recite her prayers at a small altar in the home, then go outside, cut wood, draw water from the well, and tote it all back to the house. Then she would start a fire, grind the corn, and begin making *tortillas.* She would make stacks of *tortillas,* then make *burritos* for the ranch hands to eat for lunch.

At six o'clock in the morning she would get everybody else up, and serve breakfast. There would be coffee, eggs, tortillas, beans, salsa. She had everything organized in that tiny kitchen. She even collected her eggs early in the morning. Sometimes she would gather herbal teas, *yerba buena* and *manzanilla,* from her little herb garden by the *asequía,* a creek near the house.

When the men went to work, she cleaned up the kitchen, washed clothes, and ironed. She even ironed the sheets! This was every day. She also fed all the animals, gave the pigs their slop, and the horses their feed. She was amazing! She prepared lunch, served all the men and the children, then did more work.

In the afternoons, she would take the bedding outside and hang it in the sun to air. Everything was aired daily. We used to sleep on *colchones,* and she would lay those out in the sun, too. She would make the beds. Then she would make more *tortillas,* stacks and stacks of them, and prepare dinner. She did everything by herself.

Every third day she would clean the floors. They were dirt floors and there was a special process to maintaining them. Grandma would take a bucket of water and get the floors all muddy. Then she would make beautiful semicircular designs with her bare hands to keep the dirt down. I used to love helping her create the designs in the mud. She would do this in every room. Her home was always neat and clean. All the sheets were hand embroidered.

After dinner, she would sit by a lantern and mend and embroider. Then she would go to bed and get up at four o'clock in the morning and start again. She did the same thing every day, except Sundays, when she went to church. On Sundays, she would prepare a big meal and lots of family and friends would come over. After church, the other women would help, too. Again, there were stacks of *tortillas*. I was always amazed watching those stacks of *tortillas* grow.

My father admired her, and so he also worked very hard. He worked his two jobs, then worked at home, where he was always fixing something or working in the garden. He would tell me you could take pride in working for your things, because in fact, you earned your possessions by working hard. He was never negative about work. Never said, "Oh, God, another miserable day." Working is what made him happy. He never complained about having too many kids and two jobs. On Sundays, we would go to church, then to the park. We went to every park in east Los Angeles.

For me, it was a tremendous source of pride when I got my first job. I was only thirteen when I started working. I said I was sixteen so I could get a job as a telephone solicitor for $1.25 an hour. This was a very important thing to share with my parents. Really important. I always felt the same kind of pride in working as my father did. I've never had a problem with hard work. So, when I had to work twice as hard as a man to be considered equal, I never looked at it as a negative thing.

Internationally renowned Oaxaca artist Laura Hernandez began painting at age six, and started selling her work at age nine, when one of her teachers asked Laura to draw a portrait of her. Laura didn't particularly like the teacher, so she charged her. Highly creative, independent and resourceful, she learned the importance of hard work from her parents and grandparents. By spending summers on her grandparents' ranch, she also learned that necessity is the mother of invention.

It's All in the Frijoles

Laura Hernandez
Artist

Since my daughter Sabina was five years old, I have always answered her in the same way when she says, "Mamá, I want this or that." "Ah," I reply, "And what are you going to do to get it?" In this way she has come to understand that you cannot get everything you want. I wanted her to learn that life and getting what you want require effort. A child can learn how to create her own reality and live life on her own terms.

When I was a child, I didn't always have enough money to buy what I wanted, especially the usual painting materials. Therefore, I had to invent my own paints. This fascinated me. I used to go into the kitchen and experiment with everything I could paint with. My brown pigment was real coffee. I continue to make my colors from natural elements and mix them with sand.

In Oaxaca, you can observe how the people are in touch with the earth, how they work with their hands. It would not be satisfying for me to simply take a paint brush and only squeeze paints from a tube, which would be the same for me as having to eat sausages from the supermarket every day. Consequently, I enjoy working with soil. I turn it into a ritual. I have thereby developed a few techniques which may seem strange, but are like life itself. I always look for the most complicated techniques possible in order to experience something intensely, just as one does when one cooks. You heat something, wait, knead something and stir it for a while over a small fire. I like that experimentation. Necessity has made many of the local artists and artisans in Oaxaca very inventive and has resulted in wonderful art.

San Ysidro is the patron saint of farmers. A devout farm laborer who worked outside of Madrid in the twelfth century, his feast day is cele-

brated on May 15. This lovely poem is from Aunt Carmen's Book of
Practical Saints by *Pat Mora.*

Pat Mora

San Ysidro Labrador

May our work enrich the earth. Hear our request.
A worker like us, but all day the Lord you'd address.
This night and at our death, in peace may we rest.

Early to the fields, but soon you'd lose interest,
Angels to your aid, reward for daily prayerfulness.
May our work enrich the earth. Hear our request.

We'll carry you in procession, our faith attest,
Sing and pray this evening that our fields you'll bless.
This night and at our death, en paz may we rest.

You see the dry land needs rain. Quick, send a tempest.
Enjoy your canopy but hear the need we express.
May our work enrich the earth. Hear our request.

Good life is rhythms as we poor workers know best.
To wake to this gold land, now that's true wealthiness.
This night and at our death, in peace may we rest.

Corn and trees glow in the sunset, grace manifest.
Send one of those hard-working angeles to my address.
May our work enrich the earth. Hear our request.
This night and at our death, en paz may we rest.

It's All in the Frijoles

Dichos

El trabajo es virtud.
Work is a virtue.

La diligencia es madre de la industria.
Diligence is the mother of industry.

El trabajo hace la vida agradable.
Work makes life more pleasant.

Pereza, llave de pobreza.
Laziness: key to poverty.

Los premios del trabajo justo son honra, provecho y gusto.
Rewards for honest labor are honor, good health, and joy.

Arrear que vienen arreando.
Keep things moving.

Sólo Dios sabe para quién trabajas.
Only God knows for whom you work.

A quien es trabajador le pesa que se haga noche.
A good worker regrets the coming of night.

Al mal trabajador no le viene bien ningún azadón.
To a bad worker, no tool works right.

Garañón que no relincha, que lo capen.
The stallion that does not neigh should be castrated.
(Get rid of a worker who does not perform.)

Antes trabajaba y ahora es trabajoso.
He used to work, now he's a lot of work.

El trabajo es sagrado, no lo toques.
Work is sacred, don't touch it.

Mucho ruido, poco trabajo.
Big noise, little work.

No hay atajo sin trabajo.
There is no shortcut without work.

Los platicadores y los desocupados son el azote de los ocupados.
Chatterers and the idle are the scourge of the industrious.

De bajada hasta las piedras ruedan.
Downhill, even rocks roll.

Aprendiz de todo, oficial de nada.
Apprentice of all, official of nothing.
(Jack of all trades, master of none.)

Si el ocio causa tedio, el trabajo es buen remedio.
If idleness causes boredom, work is a good remedy.

Trabajar como esclavos para vivir como blancos.
Work like slaves to live like whites.

Al que le ven caballo, le ofrecen silla.
Whoever looks like a horse will be offered a saddle.

En el modo de cortar el queso se conoce al que es tendero.
How the cheese is sliced tells you who the shopkeeper is.

It's All in the Frijoles

El que primero va al molino, primero muele.
First to the mill, first to grind.

Antes de cazar, tener casa en que morar y tierras que labrar.
Before going hunting, make sure you have a house to live in and land to toil.

Lo que de noche se hace, de día mal parece.
What is made by night, looks bad by day.

Tejado de un rato, labor para todo el año.
A temporary roof means year-round work.

Lo bien hecho ni trabajo da venderlo.
The well-made product isn't hard to sell.

Más vale una yunta andando que cien paradas.
A yoke of oxen is worth more than a hundred untethered.

El trabajo ennoblece pero también envejece.
Work ennobles but it also ages.

Camarón que se duerme se lo lleva a la corriente.
Shrimp that sleep are carried off by the current.

4

Loyalty
Lealtad

El que es ciego de nación, nunca sabe por dónde anda.
Who is blind to his own nation will never know where he
is traveling.

Know therefore that the Lord thy God, he *is* God, the
faithful God, which keepeth covenant and mercy with
them that love him and keep his commandments.
—DEUTERONOMY 7:9

What does your mind seek?
Where is your heart?
If you give your heart to each and every thing,
you lead it nowwhere: you destroy your heart.
Can anything be found on earth?
—NEZAHUALCÓYOTL,
from *Mexican Songs*

Loyalty is faithfulness to one's oath, commitments, or obligations. It is the feeling of devotion that one holds for one's country, creed, family, and friends. As such, it is one of the most beautiful virtues.

In Latin countries, we see loyalty manifested when men and women die to save family or country, or when friends seek to protect each other from mishap or danger. Male friends often protect each other in difficult situations, such as when someone is trying to take advantage of a friend, or if one of the group is incapacitated, when his friends literally pick him up and take him home to safety, rather than leave him behind to be mugged, robbed, or worse. This loyalty, this sense of protectiveness and commitment, is a marvelous quality, but it is only a part of this virtue.

Like so many of the virtues, which are interconnected, one to another, like so many perfect links in a beautiful gold chain, loyalty is tied to obligation, or responsibility. It is also tied to honesty. A man is a loyal son, a woman a faithful wife, a soldier a loyal supporter of his captain and country. Ultimately, one must be loyal to God, and to oneself and one's own truth, integrity, and highest ideals. This is a definition of loyalty that is often ignored.

The opposite of loyalty is faithlessness, or treachery. It is helpful to look at all the virtues in terms of their opposites, because, when we are not moving towards a desired goal, we are, indeed, moving away

It's All in the Frijoles

from that desired virtue and towards its opposite. Are we loyal? To whom or to what do we give our loyalty?

Hector Elizondo
Actor

When I was young, somebody suggested that we go to the west side of New York to beat up Jews. "That's a great idea, right?" said one guy. "Yeah, that's cool," said another. You're ten or eleven years old. It's Halloween. You fill the socks with powder and you bop somebody on the head. There were some bad boys in the group, really racist kids. I realized this was wrong. I wasn't going to do it. But how could I get out of it? And if I went along, I could just hear my father. I could just see him stringing me up and letting the crows peck my eyes out. Either way, I would not survive this.

So, I decided not to be loyal to my friends in that situation. I said, "Yeah, let's go. I'll go this way. I'll meet you over there." I never went.

It was a choice. My loyalty wasn't to a gang but to my family, my bedrock, my cornerstone.

Sometimes loyalty costs us dearly. It is when we are asked to put ourselves at risk that loyalty is really tested, as Anthony Quinn tells us in this story from his autobiography, One Man Tango.

Anthony Quinn

Actor

Normally, the trip from Chihuahua to Juarez took hours, but we traveled for days as the train moved slowly north through enemy lines. *[This was during the Mexican Revolution when thousands of soldiers were missing and families uprooted.]* It was a tiring journey, but my mother was a tireless woman. The only food she had to eat was an occasional bite of a tortilla offered by the engineer, and she was barely able to make enough milk to feed me. We pulled into town tired, and hungry, and black as the coals we rode in on.

There is the taste of a hot breakfast—eggs—made for us by a benevolent stranger, who put us up on our first night in Juarez. My mother did not know a soul in town, and she was grateful for the kindness, but those eggs almost cost me my career. The woman called my mother over forty years later, looking for help. She remembered our name, and tracked my accomplishments. Her grandson, a boy named Levas, was one of twenty-one kids charged with first-degree murder in a famous Los Angeles gang killing. It was in all the papers. The Sleepy Lagoon case. I was under contract to 20th Century-Fox at the time, and my mother looked to me for help.

"Mama," I said, "what the hell do you want me to do?"

"The eggs, Tony," she said. "Remember the eggs."

I remembered the eggs, so I agreed to raise money for the boy's defense. This was no easy decision, but as my mother reminded me, there was no other decision to make. I got my friends involved. Orson Welles helped us out, and George Raft. I even asked Eleanor Roosevelt to look into the matter, and tried to hire a former judge named Brandt, whose brother was one of the heads of 20th Century-Fox, to represent the boy. I was accused of being a communist, and a knee-jerk Mexican, back when it was not a smart thing for any actor to be accused of the former, or for this particular actor to be accused of either. I might have been blackballed from motion pictures, were it not for the empathy of Darryl F. Zanuck. He called me into his office, and I told him about the eggs. He understood what I had to do.

Many people incorrectly view loyalty in an almost blind fashion as something which commands "my friend right or wrong" or "my country right or wrong." Indeed, some of the most heinous crimes of abuse or incest against women and children have been hidden by family members not wanting to be "disloyal" by reporting the crime to authorities. However, there is another loyalty which operates on a higher level. It is to that loyalty that Marta Monahan speaks.

Marta Monahan
Author, Strength of Character and Grace

My father taught me that the first loyalty is, of course, to God, then to your own truth. From that one comes the loyalty to everybody else's truth.

I learned that loyalty is more than fidelity. Loyalty is a tremendous sense of respect and belief and support for the truth in another person. However, while I always support and respect the truth of people I am loyal to, I do not have to approve of what they are doing or participate in it, if it is not in keeping with my own higher truth.

The standard is this: if I wouldn't do it and I wouldn't approve of it for myself, then I would not support it in anybody else. I don't tell them, "Don't do it." They are free to do it, but I don't want to hear about it, and I don't want them to ask me to come along and be part of it. It is painful to me to see a friend in a situation where they are losing their dignity and I see they are not willing to change. Sometimes, a friend will get angry and call you disloyal; sometimes, you lose a friend over such a situation.

As a child, if I did something wrong, my father would have a conversation with me for two or three hours. He would have me look at what I had done and have me appraise it myself. He didn't say, "You did this" and "You did that." Instead, he would ask me, "What do you think you did? Why do you think that was not intelligent?"

That's how I learned not to repeat mistakes. I discovered that he had certain standards that were very strict. I knew if I violated a rule a second time, there would be another talk and a warning. The third time, you lost big time. But, I tell you, I never got talked to about the same thing twice. That was a standard I created for myself. I was humiliated enough the first time. That's how I absorbed the sense of loyalty to my highest truth.

During our conversation, Marta Monahan made the essential distinction between loyalty to one's own truth and to a higher truth, versus a false sense of loyalty to a person no matter what they do. That misinterpreted loyalty is often what gets people in trouble. A person should not help a friend rob a bank. Nor should they support the wickedness of a parent, as in the pre-Columbian story of "The Trees of White Flowers." The key here is to develop loyalty at the highest level.

The Trees of White Flowers

Over five hundred years ago, the young, handsome King Cosijoeza was crowned king of the Zapotecs in the city of Juchitán, which is now known as Oaxaca. Cosijoeza was greatly loved by his people, for he was gentle, kind, and wise. He was also a brave warrior, which was important, since the Aztecs, who lived not too far away, continuously tried to conquer the Zapotecs through battle or through deceit.

Late one afternoon, Cosijoeza walked through the palace gardens to enjoy the blooms of the trees of white flowers. It was that time of day when the flowers opened, petal by petal, sending their delicate fragrance throughout the city. As he turned a corner, he came upon one of his servants and some Aztec emissaries.

"What is it you want?" Cosijoeza asked the emissaries.

"King Ahuizolt would like you to send him some of the trees of white flowers. He wishes to grow them in the gardens of his palace and along his canals."

Cosijoeza thought about the request for a few moments. He knew Ahuizolt had longed for these trees for many years. He also knew Ahuzolt had tried for years to conquer Juchitan so that he could rule both Tenochtitlán and Juchitán.

His reverie was interrupted by one of the emissaries. "If you do not send the trees, my king will send thousands of warriors to conquer your land. Then he will own all the trees."

"Go back and tell your king I refused his request," replied Cosijoeza calmly.

After the emissaries had gone, Cosijoeza gathered his warriors around him. "Once more the Aztecs have promised to come and try to conquer our beautiful city. Please fortify the city and prepare the poisoned arrows for battle."

The warriors, intensely loyal to their king, promised to obey his every command. They knew how wise he was. Thus it was that, several months later, when a large group of weary Aztec warriors arrived, tired from their long journey, they were quickly defeated by the Zapotecs.

When King Ahuizolt heard of his army's defeat once again, he was furious. "There must be some way I can win this battle and gain Juchitán for my own!" he declared. After spending a few hours deep in thought, he called his daughter, Coyolicatzin, to his side.

Coyolicatzin was a most beautiful young woman, with long, straight hair, dark as the night, and eyes that glowed like the evening stars. Ahuizolt loved her dearly, and she returned his love. When her father asked her to help him carry out his plan, she agreed immediately.

Several days later, in the early hours of the morning, before the sun reached the tops of the mountains, Coyolicatzin left the city, hidden in a cloak, accompanied by a handful of servants. The journey was long and difficult but, by nightfall, the group had reached a forest just outside Juchitan, where they spent the night.

Early the next morning, Cosijoeza took a stroll through the forest, as was his habit. Imagine his surprise when a beautiful young woman appeared in front of him!

"Who are you, my dear?" he asked. "You have the face of a goddess, and I don't think we have ever met before."

"I am destined to travel through unknown lands in search of my happiness, which has for so long eluded me."

The king did not reveal who he was. "I am a powerful man in Juchitan. Perhaps I can help you. Please let me know what you seek."

Coyolicatzin merely smiled demurely.

"Come, let us return to my palace. My mother will care for you as if you were her own."

Coyolicatzin appeared reluctant to accept the offer. Accompanied by her servants, she spent several enjoyable days in the company of Cosijoeza. When she was sure he had fallen completely in love with her, she told him, "It is time for me to leave. I thank you for your generous hospitality, but I now must return to my own country."

Cosijoeza took the young woman's hand. "Please do not go. Stay here and be my wife. I would follow you to the ends of the earth, no matter how dangerous the journey."

Coyolicatzin pretended to be sad. "My father is the Aztec king, Ahuizolt. How can I then be your wife?"

Cosijoeza loved the beautiful young woman so much that he could not bear her parting. He felt love could conquer all problems. He replied, "My dear, if it is your wish to return to your father and your home, then you must go. I will send emissaries in a few days to ask your father for your hand."

It's All in the Frijoles

Coyolicatzin journeyed home, happy that she had successfully completed the first part of her father's plan, while Cosijoeza sadly remained in his city. True to his word, the emissaries arrived a few days after Coyolicatzin's return, bearing valuable gifts and asking for the princess's hand in marriage. They returned in joy with Ahuizolt's consent, not suspecting the evil plans in store for their king and his kingdom.

Coyolicatzin prepared for her journey. That night, her father came to her and said, "You must learn how the city of Juchitán is fortified, and find the formula for the poisoned arrows. You can pass these secrets on to my emissaries, who will visit every moon. With this information we will be able to conquer the city, and you can return home again."

The wedding of Coyolicatzin and Cosijoeza was very joyous. Cosijoeza felt he was the luckiest of men, and treated his beautiful wife with great tenderness and respect. He did not suspect the plan against him.

Time passed, and Coyolicatzin slowly gathered information on the fortifications of Juchitán. Eventually, she discovered the secrets of the poisoned arrows. But she also discovered something else. She now loved her young husband and his people with all her heart, and knew she could never betray their trust.

One morning, tears in her eyes, she ran through the gardens to find Cosijoeza. Sobbing, she took his hand and told him of the plan.

Cosijoeza, with great tenderness, forgave his wife.

Soon thereafter, in gratitude for his wife's love and loyalty, Cosijoeza sent some trees with white flowers to Ahuizolt. Even today, these trees can be seen in Tenochtitlán, which is now Mexico City.

Antonio Caso was an early twentieth century Mexican philosopher-humanist, a moral educator who left behind a rich legacy of writings. A supreme patriot, Caso believed that the best way for the individual to "serve the race"—meaning to improve the condition of the Latin American people—was to be a good patriot. If you were loyal to your country, you were loyal to your people. "In everything we do," he said, "one of our primary responsibilities is to make sure that it is for the good of us all." My mother shared this belief, and she took this charge of "improving the race" very seriously where I was concerned. Indeed, I can recall her using those exact words, whenever she felt I was going to make a decision without this goal in mind.

Caso was optimistic that man could be good if he could free himself from himself—from the persistent demands of his brutal animal instincts and his egocentrism. To this end, he pleaded for Mexicans not to be content with seeking pleasure and possessions, but to have the courage and enthusiasm to seek unselfishly for the good of all. The excerpt below is from his essay, "Mexico! Show Them Your Worth!" It is his call to his compatriots to fulfill their responsibilities to their homeland.

Antonio Caso (Mexico)
(1883–1946)

The Obligations of a Citizen

. . . The enormous majority of Mexicans do not distinguish themselves because of the exceptional gifts of a powerful psychic individualism but for the absurd wealth of profound and vehement emotions that leap like wild horses over the unyielding prerogatives of reason.

That is why we all want the first place and condemn those who occupy it. That is why we struggle endlessly in formidable public and private disputes. That is why we wound ourselves and tear ourselves to pieces without accepting a truce, while other more fortunate nations love themselves and assert themselves. Nietzsche has said: "Over the doors of our time is written 'show them your worth.'" Mexico show them your worth! In the school, in the shop, in the church, in the laboratory, let us replace passion with compassion; the traditional antipathy with sympathy, offenses with intelligence and forgiveness; because if we do not love ourselves, Holy God, who shall love us?

Translated by Yolanda Nava.

José Martí (Cuba)
(1853–1895)

Two Countries

Two countries have I, Cuba and the night.
Or are they both one? His majesty the sun,
With long veils and a carnation in the hand,
Refuses to set. Silent Cuba
Appears to me as a sad widow.
I know this bloodstained carnation
That trembles in her hand! My breast
Is destroyed, empty
Where my heart once was. Now is the time
To begin to die. Night is a good time
For farewells. Light obstructs,
As do human words. The universe
Speaks more clearly than man.
The red flame
Of the burning candle flutters
Like a flag that invites to battle.

The windows of my soul
Open, bringing me ever closer to her.
Silently breaking the petals of the carnation,
Cuba, widow, passes
Like a cloud that obscures the sky.

Translated by Yolanda Nava.

Henry Cisneros

President and Chief Operating Officer, Univisión,
former U.S. Secretary of Housing and Urban Development,
and Mayor of San Antonio, Texas

My grandfather was an activist in Mexico in the teens. He was involved in the Mexican Revolution as an organizer of unions and a printer. Some say he was a radical, even a communist. He came to the United States from Puebla in 1924 because he had been targeted for assassination. A group of friends went to his business one afternoon and said to him, "Don't go home by your usual route, because you're going to be captured and executed."

So, instead of going home he left for San Antonio, Texas, that day and arrived there with twenty-nine cents in his pocket. My mother has framed postcards in her living room that he sent to my grandmother from San Antonio saying, "I've arrived, will send for you soon, love to the children," all in Spanish. But he never gave up wanting to go back to Mexico.

He had seven children, five of them boys. Although all of his sons served in the armed forces of the United States in World War II, he never became a U.S. citizen because he was tied to Mexico. I always thought of him as one would General Charles de Gaulle of France, not as *from* Mexico, but, because he carried himself with such dignity, his bodily demeanor told you that he *was* Mexico.

I remember going with him as a boy to the *Diez y Seis de Septiembre* events [celebrating Mexico's independence from Spain] and standing next to him. He was a distinguished gentleman. All the younger men and the political activists in the community called him Don Romulo. He was so proud of being a Mexican that his body would shake, and he cried as they played the Mexican national anthem that day.

Although he wasn't in public life as a Mexican in the *colonia mexicana* of San Antonio, he was, nevertheless, the essence of a public man, with deep political and intellectual values. Because he was such a respected figure, mayors and members of Congress visited him.

My grandfather was a hard-working man. He built a print shop, published local and influential newspapers, and worked up until his death, at 93 years of age. He would go home every day for lunch, take a nap, and go back to work.

He was a stellar person and a devoted family man, and I think his sense of obligation to the community, of loyalty to the people, of patriotism, of country, and of roots, all of those values he embodied, were transferred to the rest of our family.

Cruz Bustamante
Lieutenant Governor of California

It was the interactions within our loving family that taught me unforgetable lessons about respect, loyalty to family and about creating family. I remember as a new legislator going to Sacramento and telling the entire state Latino Caucus about the kitchen table in the Bustamante family. I told them at our table, we could say anything. We could fight, argue about politics, listen to family gossip. We learned about everything at the kitchen table. That was the center of activity in our home, the place where we all interacted.

And I told them I remembered that even if we disagreed, we were still family, still united. I told the Latino Caucus, "I want to build a political family, here," a family like the one I grew up in, where they would cover me when someone was coming around behind my back.

And little by little, we did become very close knit, like a family, despite the fact that there was no basis for agreement on issues between someone from urban east L.A. and someone from rural Fresno County. How was it that people from completely different backgrounds got along? How was it that we became good friends? Could it have been the common bond of our culture?

When we legislators meet as family we recognize the need to work together on issues of mutual concern affecting the Latino community. We then find many more parallels in terms of public policy than we ever thought possible. It's because we had a chance to become a family. Sometimes we represent highly diverse districts, but we come to the table as members of the same family and community.

As a family we worked, ate, partied and slugged it out together. We covered each other's backs. Whenever we saw harm coming toward one of the members, we made sure that person knew it was coming. We were united.

It is amazing that a small group of four—then eight—members in an eighty-member legislature could become the nucleus of a much larger group of people that would elect me Speaker of the Assembly. Key chairmanships went to other members of the Latino Caucus. All of a sudden, members of the Latino Caucus were the leading decision-makers for the entire state—not just the Latino community. All because we organized our group like a family, just like I experienced at the kitchen table. We united around those same principles of respect, common interest and loyalty.

Loyalty to patria y persona, *to country and person, is a beautiful virtue. It is one to which some of the greatest poets have dedicated some of their most superb verses. Jaime Torres Bodet (1902–1974) once wrote that the poet is the "subtle educator" of democracy.*

It's All in the Frijoles

Jaime Torres Bodet (Mexico)
(1902–1974)

My Country

This profound piety is my own country.
Here, if I advance, what I touch is my country;
a presence where I feel with each instant
a harmony of body and soul.

This is my voice. But I hear it
in different mouths. And although nothing
of what it says can surprise me,
to listen to it charms me because in it
sings a heart always distinct
which explains it all to us without words.

Here, if I advance, the world stops.
Everything is original and spontaneous truth:
day, until death, made of dawn!
life, until the end, made of childhood!

Translated by Yolanda Nava.

———————

During his time abroad César Vallejo travelled to Spain from France where he worked with Pablo Neruda and others to raise support for the Republican cause. This excerpt from "Spain, Take This Cup from Me" reflects his compassionate commitment to and participation in the agonies of humankind, as well as his loyalty to his principles and the fate of the Republic in the Spanish Civil War.

César Vallejo (Peru/France)
(1892?–1938)

XIV. Spain, Take This Cup from Me

Children of the world,
if Spain falls—I mean, it's just a thought—
if she falls
from the sky downward let her forearm be seized,
in a halter, by two terrestrial plates;
children, what age in those concave temples
how early in the sun what I was telling you!
how soon in your chest the ancient noise!
how old your 2 in your notebook!

    Children of the world,
mother Spain is with her belly on her shoulders;
our teacher is with her ferules,
she appears as mother and teacher,
cross and wood, because she gave you the height,
vertigo and division and addition, children;
she is with herself, procedural fathers!

    If she falls—I mean, it's just a thought—if Spain
falls, from the earth downward,
children, how are you going to stop growing!
how the year is going to punish the month!
how you're never going to have more than ten teeth,
how the diphthong will remain in downstroke,
    the medal in tears!
How the little lamb is going to continue

It's All in the Frijoles

bound by its leg to the great inkwell!
How you're going to descend the steps of the alphabet
to the letter in which pain was born!

Children,
sons of warriors, meanwhile,
lower your voice, for Spain is right this moment
    distributing
energy among the animal kingdom,
little flowers, comets and men.
Lower your voice, for she is
with her rigor, which is great, not knowing
what to do, and she has in her hand
the talking skull and it talks and talks,
the skull, the one with the braid,
the skull, the one with life!

Lower your voice, I tell you,
lower your voice, the song of syllables, the crying
of matter and the minor rumor of the pyramids, and even
that of your temples which walk with two stones!
Lower your breathing, and if
the forearm comes down,
if the ferules sound, if it is night,
if the sky fits into two terrestrial limbos,
if there is noise in the sound of the doors,
if I am late,
if you don't see anyone, if the blunt pencils
frighten you, if mother
Spain falls—I mean, it's just a thought—
go out, children of the world, go and look for her! . . .

Translated by Clayton Eshleman.

The most famous poet of Latin America, Neftalí Ricardo Reyes Basoalto, later known as Pablo Neruda, is the poet who inscribed Latin American experience into the world's consciousness. This poem is a testimony to the country of his birth.

Pablo Neruda (Chile)
(1904–1973)

Ode to César Vallejo

The stone in your face,
Vallejo,
the creases
of the dry sierras:
I remember them in my song:
your enormous
forehead
over your delicate body,
the black twilight
in your eyes,
freshly unearthed,
those harsh
uneven
days, each hour held
different bitternesses
or distant
tendernesses,
the keys
of life
trembled
in the dusty light

It's All in the Frijoles

of the street,
you returned
from a slow
journey, from under the earth,
and in the heights
of the scarred mountain ranges
I pounded on the doors,
to make the walls
open,
to make the walls
open,
to make the roads
unroll,
just arrived from Valparaíso
I disembarked at Marseille,
the earth
broke open
like a fragrant lemon
in fresh yellow hemispheres,
you
stayed
there, subject
to nothing,
with your death,
with your sand
dropping,
measuring you
and emptying you,
in the air,
in the smoke,
in the defeated alleys
of the winter.
You were in Paris, living
in the misfortunate
hostels of the poor.

Loyalty/*Lealtad*

Spain
was bleeding.
We left.
And again
you remained
once more in the smoke,
so that when
suddenly you were not any longer,
it was not the earth
with its scars,
it was not
the stone of the Andes
that held your bones
but the smoke,
the frost,
of Paris in winter.
Exiled twice,
my brother;
from the earth and the air
from life and death,
exiled
from Peru, from your rivers,
absent
from your clay soil.
I never missed you in life,
only in death.
I seek you
drop by drop,
dust by dust,
in your land,
your face is yellow,
your face is craggy,
you are full
of old jewels,
of failures,

It's All in the Frijoles

I climb
the ancient
terraces,
perhaps you have
gotten lost,
entangled
among threads of gold,
covered
with turquoise,
silent,
or perhaps
in your village,
in your race,
a grain
of corn spread out,
seed
of a flag.
Perhaps, perhaps now
you are transmigrating,
and you are returning,
you are coming
to the end
of the journey,
so that
one day
you will find yourself in the middle
of your native land,
insurgent,
alive,
crystal of your crystal, flame in your flame,
beam of purple stone.

Translated by Yolanda Nava.

———————————

Mexico has always had a precarious relationship with the United States. I remember growing up with my father saying to me, "Pobre México. Tan cerca de los Estados Unidos, tan lejos de Dios." Poor Mexico, so close to the United States, so far from God. In this poem addressed to President Franklin Delano Roosevelt, poet Rubén Darío speaks as a loyal Latin American as he addresses the tension and the mixed feelings of loyalty, respect, and concern which color relations between the two countries.

Rubén Darío (Nicaragua)
(1867–1916)

To Roosevelt

The voice that would reach you, Hunter, must speak
with Biblical tones, or in the poetry of Walt Whitman.
You are primitive and modern, simple and complex;
you are one part George Washington and one part Nimrod.
You are the United States,
future invader of our naive America
with its Indian blood, an America
that still prays to Christ and still speaks Spanish.

You are a strong, proud model of your race;
you are cultured and able; you opposed Tolstoy.
You are an Alexander-Nebuchadnezzar,
breaking horses and murdering tigers.
(You are a professor of Energy,
as the current lunatics say.)

It's All in the Frijoles

You think that life is a fire,
that progress is an eruption,
that the future is wherever
your bullet strikes.
No.

The United States is grand and powerful.
Whenever it trembles, a profound shudder
runs down the enormous backbone of the Andes.
If it shouts, the sound is like the roar of a lion.
And Hugo said to Grant: "The stars are yours."
(The dawning sun of the Argentine barely shines;
the star of Chile is rising . . .) A wealthy country,
joining the cult of Mammon to the cult of Hercules;
while Liberty, lighting the path
to easy conquest, raises her torch in New York.

But our own America, which has had poets
since the ancient times of Nezahualcóyotl;
which preserved the footprints of great Bacchus,
and learned the Panic alphabet once,
and consulted the stars; which also knew Atlantis
(whose name comes ringing down to us in Plato)
and has lived, since the earliest moments of its life,
in light, in fire, in fragrance, and in love—
the America of Moctezuma and Atahualpa,
the aromatic America of Columbus,
Catholic America, Spanish America,
the America where noble Cuauhtémoc said:
"I am not on a bed of roses"— our America,
trembling with hurricanes, trembling with Love:
O men with Saxon eyes and barbarous souls,
our America lives. And dreams. And loves.
And it is the daughter of the Sun. Be careful.

Long live Spanish America!
A thousand cubs of the Spanish lion are roaming free.
Roosevelt, you must become, by God's own will,
the deadly Rifleman and the dreadful Hunter
before you can clutch us in your iron claws.

And though you have everything, you are lacking
  one thing: God!

Translated by Lysander Kemp.

Dichos

El que es ciego de nación, nunca sabe por dónde anda.
He who is blind to his own nation will never know where he is traveling.

El que sirve a dos amos, no queda bien con ninguno.
He who serves two masters, disappoints both of them.

Pueblo dividido, pueblo vencido.
A people divided, a people conquered.

Cada uno jala pa' su lado.
Everyone pulls toward his own side.
(Everyone looks after his own interests.)

Uno para todos y todos para uno.
All for one and one for all.

It's All in the Frijoles

El pueblo unido jamás será vencido.
A people united will never be defeated.

O todos hijos o todos entenados.
Either we are all children or all stepchildren.

5

Faith

Fe

Dios es Principio.
God is the Beginning.

— SPANISH SAYING

You live in heaven;
you uphold the mountain,
Anáhuac is in your hands.
Awaited, you are always everywhere;
you are invoked, you are prayed to.
Your glory, your fame is sought.
You live in heaven;
Anáhuac is in your hands.

— AZTEC POEM

For verily I say unto you, That whosoever shall say unto this mountain, Be thou removed, and be thou cast into the sea; and shall not doubt in his heart, but shall believe that those things which he saith shall come to pass; he shall have whatsoever he saith. Therefore I say unto you, What things soever ye desire when ye pray, believe that ye receive *them,* and ye shall have *them.*

—MARK 11:23–24

God will provide the means.

—SPANISH SAYING

Desire is prayer.

—CONSUELO CHAVIRA SEPULVEDA

The cornerstone of Hispanic life is faith. Faith in God, faith in miracles, faith in the ongoingness of life and faith that God will provide. Culturally, faith is manifested through a deep-rooted Catholicism that took hold in Latin countries during the fifteenth century following the Spanish conquest. The rituals and celebrations of the church define family and social life throughout the Spanish-speaking world. And yet, long before the arrival of the Spanish, the indigenous people of the Americas had a highly evolved belief and moral system which is still in evidence today. Whether Catholic, Protestant, Jew, or spiritually eclectic, Latinos are highly spiritual people, believers in God whose faith permeates all aspects of daily living.

Mamá's life was centered in faith. As a result, my belief in God became the foundation for my life. This was her greatest gift to me. My earliest memories are of my mornings in Sunday school, followed by visits to the park and to family gatherings after church with my parents. I also remember accompanying my mother and her two sisters, Mary and Agnes, to Aimee Semple McPherson's Four-Square Gospel Temple in Echo Park as a young girl, as well as joining them at tent revival meetings in east Los Angeles and El Monte. When I saw the film Elmer Gantry, I recalled those joyful prayer meetings where people young and old put down their crutches and walked, or experienced other "miracles."

Mamá and her two sisters had left the Catholic Church during the Great Depression, but they were spiritual seekers who finally adopted Christian Science as their religion of choice.

Mamá lived her faith. I can remember waking up very early one morning when I was in junior high school and wandering upstairs to our kitchen. There I found Mamá reading in the early morning light. She was studying the lesson from the Bible and Science and Health with Key to the Scriptures by Mary Baker Eddy. She did this every day before getting ready for work. I realized then that she had a very private life apart from her role as my mother. Her conversion to Christian Science was a powerful influence in our lives. Her religion taught that God is all-in-all and that through God all things were possible. These words, the "Scientific Statement of Being," are indelibly imprinted on my consciousness: "There is no life, truth, intelligence, or substance in matter. . . . Spirit is God, and man is His image and likeness. Therefore man is not material; he is spiritual."

How can I explain the profound impact of her belief system on my life?

I understand now that all of my mother's virtues flowed from her faith in God's goodness and in her awareness that Christ lived so that he might be the Wayshower for all humankind. She taught me that Christ is the Light of the World, and always told me I was to follow our Lord's example in my everyday life.

From my mother's and my own experience, I learned that faith is the source of courage, charity, justice, honesty, humility, and temperance. There can be no fortitude without faith, nor prudence, because prudence requires that we listen to a higher voice, as does loyalty and honesty. All of the virtues are interconnected, and the foundation, the basis for them in Latino life and culture is faith.

When I questioned God's bounty in providing for us, Mamá would quote these words from Jesus: "Therefore I say unto you, Take no thought for your life, what ye shall eat, or what ye shall drink; nor yet for your body, what ye shall put on. Is not the life more than meat, and the body than raiment?" And she talked of the lilies of the field: "Do you think God would take any less care of you, His child?"

Mamá also taught me to pray, to turn to God for my every need. She taught me the Lord's Prayer and the Twenty-third Psalm, still one of my favorites, and a source of strength amidst any challenge.

Just as she did when I was a young girl, Mamá always encouraged me to turn my burden over to God whenever I felt overwhelmed by circumstances as an adult. "You are trying to do it all alone, mijita. *Let God help you. Don't you know that of ourselves we can do nothing? God will lighten the load."*

Mamá also taught me that desire is prayer. That there is nothing we desire in our heart that God does not want us to have. It is not a question of begging or beseeching, but a matter of accepting God's bounty and following His guidance. I never understood that concept as a child, but I know it to be true as an adult. "Dios pondrá los medios, God will provide the means, always remember this."

The ancient civilizations of Meso-America also understood the importance of faith. Many of their ritual practices, including the criticized practice of offering up human blood to the gods, were done to help keep order in the cosmos, so that the precious sun would always rise.

Faith has played a powerful role in the lives of Latinos, whether in the practices of the ancient indigenous people of the Americas, or among Catholics following the conquest by the Spaniards. Indeed, along with the Spanish language, the central unifying force for all people of Hispanic descent is the Catholic Church. But whether we are Catholic, Protestant, Jewish, or have developed other spiritual practices, Spanish-speaking people are among the world's most faithful.

It is very common to find a large crucifix or a shrine to the Virgen de Guadalupe or another revered saint in homes throughout Latin America and the southwestern United States. Although I an not a Catholic, I, too, have an antique wooden carved Virgen de Guadalupe in my bedroom, along with a wooden painting, a retablo, *of the Black Madonna and Child. The Madonna is a model of faith and, whatever our religious practice, many of us are drawn to her.*

Faith has been a major element of the Indo-Hispano culture for centuries. In this creation myth from the Popul Vuh, first written in Quiché Maya and translated by Father Francisco Ximénez of the order of Santo Domingo, we discover that man was created to praise and honor the gods.

How People Came to Be

A Story from the Mayan People of Guatemala

In the very beginning, there was silence and emptiness. The sky did not ripple with birds. There were no people, no animals or fish, no mountains, or lush green grass, or gently waving trees. There was only the sky and calm, unmoving water.

Tepeu and Gucumatz, the creators, decided there must be more. They sat beneath a dome of light. "Let there be earth!" they cried. Instantly the water receded, mountains grew, and valleys formed. Currents of water flowed from the mountains towards the seas. But the land was barren and brown. They looked at each other and smiled.

"Let the land be green and lush, filled with a thousand kinds of plants." And it was done. Huge forests carpeted the mountains. Valleys became lush and green, filled with multicolored flowers. Deserts grew cactuses and grasses.

Then they created the animals, giving each its special place to live. Birds were given trees and vines to nest in, and the dome of the skies in which to travel. Animals each had their special place. And all were given their own special voices.

"Speak then, praise us," commanded Tepeu and Gucumatz. But the response was a cacophony of squeaks, whistles, grunts, and howls. None were able to make words.

"They cannot worship and adore us." said the gods. They told their creations, "Because you cannot speak, we shall create others to worship us. You shall be their food."

It's All in the Frijoles

Then Tepeu and Gucumatz created figures out of mud, red, yellow, brown, and black. But these creatures were soft, and melted in the warmth of the day. Disgusted, the gods smashed them flat.

Then Tepeu and Gucumatz took wood sticks to Ixpiyacoc, Grandfather of the Day, and Chiracan Xmucane, Grandmother of the Dawn. With their blessings the gods turned these sticks into men. The sticks could walk and talk. They could multiply, and soon covered the earth. But they did not have souls, neither could they think nor remember their creators. The gods were angry, and they destroyed these first men, first by sending a great flood upon them, then by loosing the eagle to gouge out their eyes. All the animals were set loose to destroy these men. However, a few escaped by climbing into trees, where they remain to this day and are known as monkeys.

Tepeu and Gucumatz once again came together, pledging to create new people with intelligence, flesh, and bones. In the dark of night, just before the sun, the moon, and the stars appeared, they created the first men. They ground corn, mixing water into it to create a soft dough, from which they formed their bodies. They used weeds as the structure of the bones to give the bodies strength. Only four men were created: Balam-Quitze, Balam-Acab, Mahucutah, and Iqui-Balam.

"Look at the mountains, the valleys, the rivers. What do you see?" the gods asked them.

The new men understood. "We thank you for the gift of our lives," they said, "and for all that surrounds us."

The gods asked many questions, and they answered them well. These men knew their purpose in life was to praise and honor the gods. Then the gods created women so the men would not be alone. Soon children blessed their world, and these children grew into adults to whom other children were born, and so on until they covered the earth. And the gods were pleased.

This is how people came to be.

Faith. It is a part of the genetic memory from centuries past. It is woven into the fabric of our lives as Spanish-speaking people. As you

*read the stories of faith shared by the remarkable people interviewed,
I hope you will understand how directly God works in our lives, guiding us lovingly to fulfill our purpose and potential.*

Lalo Guerrero
Songwriter, Performer

After I received the Medal of National Merit for the Arts and Humanities in 1997, I appeared on the "María Conchita Alonso Show." When I saw the video of my life as a young man and realized what I had accomplished and done over the years, I thought to myself, "What am I doing here? How did I get here? How did this young Mexican-American boy from the *barrio,* from a lower-middle-income family, get up here to the White House to receive a medal from the President? How did it happen?"

And then I realized that I don't know how I got there. I didn't plan it that way. I just wrote and I sang and I looked for a job to get ahead in my music. But there was no master plan, no "I want to do this and now I'm going do that." It just happened. It's as if God took me by the hand, guided me in the right direction, and gave me a talent for music and lyrics.

I got where I am because I can write good music and I am a good lyricist. And I got behind the right projects to further the causes of Mexican-Americans. I helped all I could by writing songs for them. This is part of my faith, my upbringing. I feel that I am on this Earth to do some good, not just to go through life having a ball.

My mother, who taught me to play the guitar, was a wonderful person. I've never met anyone like her. At home, she played the guitar and she sang all the time. She'd talk about God and tell me to pray. After I made my First Communion, I would go to confession every Saturday and mass every Sunday. I would go to the priest and say,

It's All in the Frijoles

"*Acúsame, padre.*" What sins could I have committed at that age? And he would say "*¿Qué hiciste?*" "*Fue malcriado con mi papá*" (I was a bad boy with my father). The priest must have known. "*Ah, pues, no debe hacerlo.*" (You should not do that).

And he'd say, "What else?" "Well, I lied." "To whom did you lie?" "To my little friend, so-and-so, *dije mentiras.*" "*Andale, pues. Vaya y reze veinte Ave Marías, y diez Padre Nuestros.*" (Go on then. Go and pray twenty Hail Marys, and ten Our Fathers). I was such a holy little guy, but all that was part of the training that gave me a strong faith, that will and that belief in God which continues to this day.

It's amazing—and I don't mean to brag—but I think God has something to do with the fact that I'm eighty-one years old and completely healthy. I have normal blood pressure, no high cholesterol, no inflammation of any kind, except a little bit of arthritis in my knees.

And I am still performing, still working, doing well both economically and professionally. And I feel marvelous. I'm in very good health, in good spirits, and I love to travel. I'm always happy. It's as if God took me under his wing and said, "Hey, you're my kind of kid. I'll bring you along."

Edward James Olmos
Actor

Prayer was an important part of my upbringing. My great-grandparents were American Baptists. My great-grandfather was the person who opened the church and took care of the church, the altar, and the baptismal bath—he took care of the entire church.

I distinctly remember they prayed out loud on their knees for hours, both in the morning and at night, every single day, seven days a week. It was an integral part of our life. They would do prayers that were like poetry, all done from the heart, all done in direct communication with God. They would switch off verses. One would talk for maybe four, five, or ten minutes, then the other one would carry it forward and elevate it to the highest level of commitment and understanding. It was, now that I reflect on it, probably one of the most extraordinary environments I could have been raised in. It was an entire involvement with prayer. I've never discussed this with anyone . . . that prayer was the centerpiece of where I came from and the way I was brought up.

I was also exposed to many spiritual traditions. There was the Baptist faith of my great-grandparents, augmented by both the Catholic philosophy that my father brought into the home and by the Jewish philosophy that my mother exposed us to. Then there were the Jehovah's Witnesses that I was exposed to as they stood on the corner handing out their publication, *The Watchtower*, or running into the Mormons who used to come by our home asking if anyone had passed away. They did this so they could baptize the dead person's soul into the Mormon church. I have also learned from Buddhism because they believe in all that is good and all that makes us what we should be.

I continue to use spirituality as the central point of my existence. Spiritual energy is the source of all life. And spirituality is as essential for people as food. It is a vital form of nourishment. It's as necessary as putting gasoline into your car. It helps you remain balanced and provides you with the strength to go on and move forward.

We are surrounded by many good things. But we are also bombarded by negative and destructive energy, which can knock us off balance unless we are grounded spiritually. Spirituality keeps you balanced and keeps you humble, because it reminds you that we are part of a larger whole. For me it is the key.

It's All in the Frijoles

Moctezuma Esparza
Film Producer

My father was not a very religious man in the conventional sense, yet he used to take me to church three or four times a week. He would always tell me it didn't matter what religion the church was, so I say he wasn't religious. It didn't matter what church presented itself, he would say, that's where we can go to pray to God. What he emphasized to me was a personal relationship with God and the power of prayer. What he taught me about prayer was not to pray for God to pull me out of a particular problem or to give me things, but to pray for wisdom, judgment, and guidance. There was to be no praying for new houses, clothes, money, or for deliverance from a jam or problem. He would say, "God helps those who help themselves." "Knock and the door shall be opened." He emphasized prayer and was consistent in what he taught me.

He opposed all religions' claims to be the only door to salvation. He wanted me to hear all that was said by different religions, so I would know they were the same things. He also wanted me to know that all of them fought each other.

He talked about religion as being something that produced jealousy, and as a human institution subject to the problems, vices, and failings of humans, including the human desire for earthly power. He told me not to focus on these institutions, but on the spiritual teachings they had in common.

It didn't matter who came to the door, a Jehovah's Witness, a Methodist, an Episcopalian, or a Mormon . . . all of them came to convert those of us in the *barrio*. Dad would bring them in and engage them in conversation, both because they had come to the door and it was proper and right to invite them in—it was hospitable to invite them in—and to hear what they had to say. He would engage them in conversation about their beliefs.

Dad believed in an afterlife. He gave me a clear understanding that the body is not the person, that we all have an eternal spirit that is working its way back to God. He taught me that we are here on earth to learn and to advance. He was hopeful that humanity would rise to the level of the angels. The afterlife was very real. He also spoke of dreams. The spirit world was real to our family. His mom and dad would visit him, as did my mother, who died when I was one-and-a-half years old.

As I grew older, it became harder to follow his beliefs due to my formal Western education. Yet in the study of physics and philosophy, I could understand that energy is never destroyed, only transmuted. With this I was able to understand what he taught me, what he shared with me as a child.

My father taught me that birth and death are passages, so we shouldn't fear death. We are not to look for it, but also not to fear it. He said to me that we mourn the dead not because they die, but because we're left behind. That became very real to me when he passed on. I have no doubt that my father continues on his own journey, his own path. I remember understanding my sorrow and sadness at his death was for myself at being left behind, at our separation. And, just as he talked about visitations of family and friends in his dreams, there have been a few moments in my life when I have felt visited by him in my dreams.

These charming children's songs of faith are from the anthology of Mexican children's songs Naranja Dulce, Limón Partido, *published by El Colegio de México. They are often sung as a prayer before going to sleep.*

Children's Bedtime Songs

Pájaros de mayo,	Birds of April
pájaros de abril,	birds of May
háganme la cuna	make me a cradle
en un toronjil.	that calms.

It's All in the Frijoles

Toronjil de plata,	Balm of silver,
cuna de marfil,	cradle of ivory,
cántenle a mi niño	may you sing to my child
que se va a dormir.	so he goes to sleep.
Angel de la Guarda	Guardian Angel
que vas a venir	that is going to come
cuida a mi niñito	watch over my big boy
que se va a dormir.	that is going to sleep.
Este niño lindo	This precious child
por fin se durmió,	at last went to sleep,
que lo cuide el ángel	may the angel sent by
que le manda Dios.	God watch over him.

Oremos, oremos,	We pray, we pray
angelitos somos,	little angels we are
del cielo	from the sky
bajamos	we come down
pidiendo limosnas;	asking for alms;
si no nos las dan,	if they are not given us
puertas y ventanas	doors and windows
nos las pagarán.	will pay.

Suzanna Guzmán

Mezzo-Soprano

My father and my mother separated when my mother was sixty-one, and she completely cut herself off from the world. For two years, she never left the house. It was a very difficult period for all of us. We were living in New York at the time. I remember speaking to her one day and she said, "I'm thinking of getting a job." She had no vibrancy in her voice and I said, "Mom, you have to get out of the house to get a job. You have to go look at and talk to people. Talk to friends and maybe you'll find something." I said, "You think someone is just going to call and offer you a job?" And she said, "If God wants me to have a job, he'll find me a job."

That's when I heard a little bit of the spark coming back into her voice. Then one day she called and said, "Ha, ha, ha, ha haaaa!" I said "What?" She said, "The phone rang. It was the beauty college. They needed a receptionist and I got the job."

At that moment, she shook off two years of grieving and being closed off and she went back into the world. Not only did she go back into the world—she hadn't had a job for years—but it was a job she was perfect for.

Faith works miracles. The following two stories demonstrate the power of prayer. Like actor Luís Avalos, I, too, nearly drowned when I was nine years old. At the same age my son Joaquín fell off a bicycle and suffered a head injury, which required five hours of delicate cranial surgery. I know it was faith and a mother's prayers which saved me, and years later, saved my son.

Luis Avalos

Actor

For me, faith means having a sense that there is a God and another world that we can't materially or physically address. This nourishing, spiritual universe is God. I have this sense that man is so finite, and know there is so much more beyond all our aspirations and everything else we think is so important.

It's All in the Frijoles

When I was in college, I went to Brazil with a friend to stay with his family. The weather was mild but, because it was winter, no one went to the beach to swim, even though it was eighty degrees outside.

Because it wasn't winter for me, I wanted to go swimming anyway. My friend warned me against it, saying "You shouldn't go in the water because of the winter currents." I went in anyway. I dove in the water, and came out, and dove in again. Before I knew it I couldn't touch bottom because the current started taking me out. After a while, the buildings that are on the other side of the beach on Copacabana—buildings that are 20 stories high—looked like they were three or four inches tall. I was way out in the ocean.

I was wearing a gold chain around my neck, a gold ID bracelet, and a ring. I was desperately trying to get those things off me and throw them into the ocean, because I felt that they were weighing me down and that I was going to drown.

I prayed. I repeated the Lord's Prayer and I said "Dear God, I think I'm going to die, and I don't want to die. If I can be of any use to you, let me live."

I thought about how I was supposed to be back in the school of the arts the following year. I thought about my parents and how the next time they would see me, I'd be in this coffin, and they'd be looking down on me. And I saw myself looking at them and smiling and saying, "Listen, I'm okay."

At that moment, a huge wave came and I thought, "That's it." The wave took me and I started spinning as if I were inside a washing machine. I remember opening my eyes at that moment and just seeing swirling, swirling sand and salt. When my lungs were absolutely about to burst, I stood up. I was able to stand up. My head was above the water, and I was standing on sand.

My throat was absolutely scratched from spitting up all the salt water and everything else and from yelling for help. And I was positive that I was dead, but I was fine.

I finally found my way back to the other guys I was with. My friends gave a party. I stayed another week in Rio de Janeiro and then I went to visit a friend in Peru for another week. All this time I had never called home. Two weeks after nearly drowning, I arrived home in New York City.

My mother was waiting for me at the entrance to our building. She came running to me, and she was crying. She said, "I had a dream two weeks ago that you had drowned. I went to see Santa Barbara"—our patron saint—"and I prayed for her to save you."

Amalia Mesa-Bains
Artist

I come from a very religious family. My grandmother kept a home altar and my *madrina,* my godmother, had a little *capilla,* an outdoor shrine. My mother was orphaned as a young girl and raised by an order of Italian nuns, so she, too, had a great deal of faith and prayed a lot.

I rejected much of that religious upbringing when I was eighteen or nineteen because I had a very serious auto accident. I killed a young boy on a motor bike. It had rained, they were working on the road, and the road just crumbled. It was a freak accident and I was never ever charged with anything, but I was devastated. The church gave me no answers then. All that the church represented to me seemed so very false, so I left the church.

However, over the years, I've come to realize that my artwork has a spiritual dimension influenced by the religion of my childhood. A friend of mine who is a Christian Brother once told me, "Amalia, your art is the aesthetic doorway to the spiritual world." It's been my mother all along who has really fostered that in me. She prays for me and she sends me little religious things. Even when I'm doing artwork she finds me these unpainted kitschy little nuns at these ceramic shops and buys them. My mother has really been the connection I've had with an active faith.

About five years ago, I became very, very ill with an often-fatal

It's All in the Frijoles

pulmonary condition. But it wasn't fatal for me. I'm very sure that my mother's prayers and the prayers of others, along with changes I've made in my way of life, account for the return of my health.

Throughout my life, I've been tested several times over this issue of faith. I've come to realize it isn't about a church. It's really a belief in an afterlife and in a higher being. Many people struggle with challenges far greater than mine. I believe their faith makes them strong, resilient, and capable of living through really difficult situations.

Luis Valdez

Director, Writer, Founder El Teatro Campesino

I learned from my mother that religion is not just a tool for crisis, but a daily practice. It's something that we live every waking moment. In our home, we had an *altar de esperanza,* an altar of hope, where she said her prayers. She was a spiritual counselor, and people would bring her their problems. She would put them at ease, and always give them a larger context for their lives, saying, "Life is what you make it," "You must live with effort," and "It is up to you to improve your life, to be psychologically strong." She would talk to them about their problems. She was always telling people to be wary of *los elementos negativos,* negative elements, which were the devil, doubt, self-hatred, and anything else that prevented one from believing in the spiritual dimension.

My mother taught me that religion is not for convenience nor sociability. It's an affirmation of a larger scope of all our lives. It allows us to penetrate the darkness of not knowing. It's a leap of faith, not unlike the leap we make when we get into a car each day. When it's a part of you, there is no single moment when you can turn it off.

Our lives should have magic in them; to deny magic is to deny much of our human nature. Religion and ritual provide us with the magic. I light a candle every day. I have an altar in my house. The *altares,* altars, and the burning candles are symbols of our faith. When I light a candle, it's a manifestation of my belief in God. Ritual is part of my essential experience, a cosmic reference point I've inherited from my mother.

She would say a healthy mental state comes from being conscious, thinking good thoughts, watching unguarded comments, not saying cruel things, and banishing negative thoughts from the brain. Mental acuity allows you to interact positively, and it is a part of spiritual training. We don't live in a society which teaches us that. We live in a material universe. This is not good. We must reassess our vision of life. The scientific view doesn't do this. Only the spiritual track can take you there. The spiritual path you choose is not important—all of them lead to God. These are the key lessons my mother taught me, the legacy of faith she left me.

Alfonso Cortés (Nicaragua)
(1893–1969)

Great Prayer

Time is hunger, space is cold
Pray, pray, for prayer alone can quiet
The anxieties of void.

Dream is a solitary rock
Where the soul's hawk nests:
Dream, dream, during
Ordinary life.

Translated by Thomas Merton.

It's All in the Frijoles

People seek God in many ways. As Luis Valdez said, all pathways, all religions, lead to God. In this excerpt from Brazilian author Paulo Coelho's book By the River Piedra I Sat Down and Wept, *Coelho talks about the spiritual life.*

Paulo Coelho (Brazil)
Author, The Alchemist

"Tell me what you know about the spiritual life," asked the priest. I didn't respond for a moment. "I'm not sure. There are people who leave everything behind and go in search of God."

"And do they find Him?"

"Well, you would know the answer to that, Padre. I have no idea."

The padre noticed that I was beginning to gasp with exertion, and he slowed his pace.

"You had that wrong," he said. "A person who goes in search of God is wasting his time. He can walk a thousand roads and join many religions and sects—but he'll never find God that way.

"God is here, right now, at our side. We can see Him in this mist, in the ground we're walking on, even in my shoes. His angels keep watch while we sleep and help us in our work. In order to find God, you have only to look around.

"But meeting Him is not easy. The more God asks us to participate in His mysteries, the more disoriented we become, because He asks us constantly to follow our dreams and our hearts. And that's difficult to do when we're used to living in a different way.

"Finally we discover, to our surprise, that God wants us to be happy, because He is the father."

"And the mother," I said.

The fog was beginning to clear. I could see a small farmhouse where a woman was gathering hay.

"Yes, and the mother," he said. "In order to have a spiritual life, you need not enter a seminary, or fast, or abstain, or take a vow of chastity. All you have to do is have faith and accept God. From then on, each of us becomes a part of His path. We become a vehicle for His miracles."

"He has already told me about you," I interrupted, "and he has taught me these ideas."

"I hope that you accept God's gifts," he answered.

"Because it hasn't always been that way, as history teaches us. Osiris was drawn and quartered in Egypt. The Greek gods battled because of the mortals on earth. The Aztecs expelled Quetzalcoatl. The Viking gods witnessed the burning of Valhalla because of a woman. Jesus was crucified. Why?"

I didn't answer.

"Because God came to earth to demonstrate His power to us. We are a part of His dream, and He wants His dream to be a happy one. Thus, if we acknowledge that God created us for happiness, then we have to assume that everything that leads to sadness and defeat is our own doing. That's the reason we always kill God, whether on the cross, by fire, through exile, or simply in our hearts."

"But those who understand Him . . ."

"They are the ones who transform the world—while making great sacrifices."

Saint Teresa de Avila was a great saint and mystic in sixteenth-century Spain who referred to herself as "a pencil in God's hands." She wrote familiarly but passionately of her mystical experiences in her master-piece, The Interior Castle, *written in 1588. She had a marvelously straightforward approach to spirituality that my mother liked to quote: "God is in the pots and pans." Perhaps it was Saint Teresa who inspired my mother's everyday struggle to subdue our defects of character and increase our goodness of heart.*

It's All in the Frijoles

Saint Teresa de Avila (Spain)
(1515–1582)

You know that God is everywhere, it is clear that where the King is there is his court; in short, where God is, is heaven. You will allow that where His Majesty is, there is all glory. St Augustine says that he sought him everywhere and found him in himself. Do you think it a matter of small importance for a soul who wants to open her heart to understand this truth, to see that she has no need to go to heaven to speak to her eternal Father and enjoy his presence, that it isn't even necessary for her to raise her voice? She has no need of wings to go and seek him: all she needs is to be alone and contemplate him in herself.

———————

Another great mystic and master of literature during the Golden Age of Spain was Saint John of the Cross. A contemporary of Saint Teresa de Avila, he met her during the time when she was establishing her reformation of the Carmelites. Saint Teresa admired his spirit and told him that God had called him to sanctify himself in the Order of Our Lady of Mt. Carmel and head her newly founded reformed home of men. He took up the call to serve. His book The Dark Night of the Soul *is a classic among spiritual literature.*

Saint John of the Cross (Spain)
(1542–1591)

The Dark Night of the Soul

Once in the dark of night
when love burned bright with yearning, I arose
   (O windfall of delight!)
   and how I left none knows—
dead to the world my house, in dull repose;
   There in the lucky dark,
in secret, with all sleepers heavy-eyed;
    no sign for me to mark,
    no other light, no guide
except for my heart—the fire, the fire inside!

Alfonso Cortés (Nicaragua)
(1893–1969)

Space Song

The distance that lies from here
To some star that never existed
Because God has not yet managed
To pull the skin of night that far!

And to think we still believe greater
More useful world peace

Than the peace of one lone savage . . .
This relativity craze
In our contemporary life: There's
What gives space an importance
Found only in ourselves!

Who knows how long we'll take to learn
To live as stars—
Free in the midst of what is without end
And needing no one to feed us.

Earth knows nothing of the paths it daily travels—
Yet those paths are the conscience of earth. . . . But if
This is not so, allow me just
One question:—Time, you and I
Where are we,
I who live in you
And you who do not exist?

Translated by Thomas Merton.

———————

I discovered this poem among my notes, but it was untitled. I translated it because it is so simple yet so profound that it must be shared. It makes me recall the magnificent painting by Michelangelo on the ceiling of the Sistine Chapel in Rome that shows God's fingers reaching out to touch the fingers of man and give life to His creation.

Anonymous

There are not words that are more clear; and none, I believe, that are
more assuredly heard.

> In prayer the heart
> extends itself as a hand
> beyond
> the entire system of
> time and space we can imagine
> and joins its fragile humanity
> with the curative hand of God.

Prayer moves beyond poetry. Its grace lies not in its art but in the
humility and honesty
honesty of an isolated soul.

Jorge Luis Borges (Argentina)
1899–1986

Everness

There is only one thing that is not. Oblivion.
God, who saves the metal, saves the dross,
And his prophetic memory guards from loss
The moons and those of evenings past.
Everything *is:* the thousands of reflections
Which in between the two twilights of the day

Your face left behind on mirrors of glass
And those you will continue to leave still,
And everything is part of that diverse
Crystal clear memory, there is
No end to the arduous corridors of the universe;
The doors close as you go by;
Only on the other side of the setting of a star
Will you see the Archetypes and Splendors.

Translated by Yolanda Nava.

Amado Nervo (Mexico)
(1870–1919)

The Gift

Life, are you by chance reserving a gift for me?
(Late afternoon. Prayer sounds from the tower.)
Life, are you by chance reserving a gift for me?

The mournful wind laments in the dry branches;
twilight breaks apart on a lively stream . . .
life, tell me what will be your last remaining gift?

Will your best gift be a great love?
(Some blue eyes, some lips in bloom?)
Oh, what luck! What luck if it were a great love!

. . . Or will it be great peace: that my poor
soul needs after its misfortunate pilgrimage?
Yes, perhaps peace, infinite peace.

. . . Or, better still, will the enigma of my journey
become clear, lighting up like a star in the
deep heavens, until, at last I find God.

Translated by Yolanda Nava.

Jaime Sabines (Mexico)
(1925–1999)

Me encanta Dios

I really like God. He is a magnificent old man not to be taken seriously. He enjoys playing and he plays, and at times, with a stroke of
the hand he breaks one of our legs or he flattens us altogether. This
happens because he is a bit blind and his hands rather clumsy.

He has sent us exceptional types such as Buddha, or Christ, or
Mohammed or my aunt Chofi, in order for them to tell us we should
behave ourselves. This doesn't preoccupy him much: he know us. He
knows that the large fish swallows the smaller one, that the big lizard
eats the little one, that one man preys on the other. And because of this
he invented death: so that life—neither you nor me—life, exists always.

Now the scientists come out with their theory of the Big
Bang . . . but what difference does it make if the universe is endlessly
expanding or contracting? This is of concern only to travel agencies.

I love God. He has made order in the galaxies and artfully regu-
lates the movement of the ants on the road. And he is so playful and
mischievous that the other day I discovered that he had—in the face of
the attack of antibiotics—created mutant bacteria!

Old wise man or boy scout explorer, when he stops playing with his little toy soldiers made of lead, of flesh and bone, he makes fields of flowers or paints the sky in such an incredible way.

He moves one hand and makes the ocean, he moves the other and makes a forest. And when he passes over us: The clouds remain, bits of his encouragement.

They say that, at times, he gets angry and makes earthquakes and orders storms, huge fires, destructive winds, churning waters, punishments, and disasters. But this is a lie.

It is the earth that changes—and it shakes and grows—when God draws away.

God is always in good humor. For this he is the favorite of my parents, the chosen of my children, the closest of my brothers, the woman most loved, the dog and the flea, the ancient rock, the most tender petal, the sweetest aroma, the unfathomable night, the beam of light, the spring which I am.

I really like, I really love God. May God bless God.

Translated by Yolanda Nava.

Dichos

Hasta el diablo fue un ángel en sus comienzos.
Even the devil was an angel when he began.

El infierno está lleno de buenos propósitos y el cielo de buenas obras.
Hell is filled with good proposals and heaven with good acts.

Dichosos los que creen sin haber visto.
Blessed are they that have not seen and yet have believed.
— JOHN 20:29

Quien cree en todos, yerra; y quien cree a ninguno, acierta.
Whoever believes in everyone errs, and whoever believes in no one is mistaken.

Créanse del aire.
Believe in the air.

Ver para creer.
Seeing is believing.

Hasta que lo veas, no lo creas.
Until you see it, don't believe it.

Santo Tomás, ver y creer.
Saint Thomas, seeing and believing.

Flor marchita y fe perdida, nunca vuelven a la vida.
A withered flower and lost faith never regain life.

De hombre sin fe no me fiaré.
A man without faith, I will not trust.

Orar sin parar.
Pray without ceasing.

6

Honesty
Integridad

Dura la mentira hasta que llega la verdad.
The lie lasts until the truth arrives.

Finally, brethren, whatsoever things are true, whatsoever
things *are* honest, whatsoever things *are* just, whatsoever
things *are* pure, whatsoever things *are* lovely, whatsoever
things *are* of good report, if *there be* any virtue, and if *there
be* any praise, think on these things.
—PHILIPPIANS 4:8

You must always tell the truth," my mother told me. "Don't ever lie." Like many children, I sometimes wanted to hide the fact that I was up to some forbidden mischief, but I was terrified at the consequences of lying to my mother. I think the fear of her disfavor, or worse yet her punishment, kept me from violating more of her rules. Todo saldrá en la lavada, *everything will come out in the wash,* she would tell me when I was caught in a lie.

I wondered how she always seemed to know what I was up to, even when I was away from her. "Mothers have eyes in the back of their heads," she would tell me. "We see and know everything about our children."

Telling the truth is vital to all human relationships, which is why honesty is taught in all good families. Since Mamá saw her primary role as developing my character, she would remind me of the reasons we must tell the truth, often using dichos *to make her point:* La mentira es hija del diablo; la verdad es hija de Dios, *the lie is the devil's daughter; truth is God's daughter. And whether we are Catholic, Protestant, or Jew, Mamá always told me, it is our responsibility to do God's work and to express Godliness.* "Remember, mijita, 'siempre digas la verdad.'" *Mamá would use the story of the boy who cried wolf, to make her point that if one is not consistent in telling the truth, one might not be believed at a critical time.*

In Spanish, the word mentiroso, *liar, also means false. If we are* to be true and authentic we cannot lie, not to ourselves, and not to others. Even the word mentira has a harsh, almost vulgar, sound to it. It is an insult to be called a liar, because it cuts to the core of the person's character. Without truth there is no word which can be trusted, no honor, no integrity. In the Hispanic world, one's honor, one's word, is all important.

Another component of honesty is honor. Honor means having integrity and honesty in one's beliefs and actions. Honor is also respect manifested in action. Because my mother worked away from home all day, she had to trust me to behave. I was on my honor to accept personal responsibility for my actions. Furthermore, she knew she had to trust me to do the right thing. Honesty and trust go hand in hand, like most of the virtues. In the business world, honesty is also vital. There can be no deceit or fraud or the relationship cannot function. The fact that the United States is the most litigious nation in the world speaks to the breakdown of honesty—of honor—in the personal and business world. There is never honor among thieves.

Honor is also tied to the chastity or purity of a woman, as in a "woman of honor." To be on one's honor is to accept and to acknowledge personal responsibility for one's actions. Indeed, honor refers to the highest moral principles and the absence of deceit or fraud. Honor also speaks to the worship of a supreme being; to show courteous regard or respect, to honor one's father and mother as set forth in the Ten Commandments. Indeed, honor is synonymous with honesty and integrity, and it is interesting to note that the Spanish word for honesty is integridad, integrity.

There is also another side to truth. Because the truth often hurts, Mamá told me that I could invoke the "little white lie" to avoid hurting someone's feelings. These softened words were acceptable under certain conditions. "Al decir las verdades se pierden las amistades," "In telling the truth, friendships are lost," she said. As a child, I always found it difficult to live with such contradictions.

Many of the dichos listed at the end of this chapter address the impact of always telling the truth. Certainly Victor Villaseñor's story about the little foxes shows that even "little white lies" can cause seri-

ous harm. Our goal should be to always speak the truth and to live our lives with integridad, *integrity.*

Victor Villaseñor
Author, Rain of Gold

When I was very young my father started telling me stories. There was never any baby talk. As soon as we started talking, my father began teaching us and showing us things on the ranch. He would say "Look at the trees, look at the grass, look at the horses." I particularly loved to hear his stories about the little *zorritos,* the little foxes and the coyote.

There was a female fox who was coming down a hill one morning. As she was trotting down, a big male coyote was going up the hill. They bumped into each other and he asked, "How's life so far?" The *zorrita* said, "There isn't much to eat up there, so I'm going to go down to the lowlands where the ducks are." The coyote said, "I'm going to go up into the mountains and see if I can find anything up there."

The *zorrita* said, "Well, when you go up there, just be careful you don't eat up my kids."

"How will I know they are your kids?" The *zorrita* said, "The cubs are very pretty. There are four of them and they are right under that rock over there."

"OK," said the coyote, "I won't eat them." They went their separate ways. At the end of the day they passed each other again and the coyote said, "How'd you do?"

"Oh, I found a duck. How'd you do?"

"Oh, I did real well. I came around this clump of bushes and I found these four ugly, monstrous, smelly things." And the *zorrita* said, "Oh, no! Those were my kids!"

It's All in the Frijoles

"Why didn't you tell me they were ugly? Then I would have known they were yours."

My father always said, "It's the responsibility of the mother to be truthful with her kids, not try to fool them and tell them things that aren't true."

Another story my father loved to tell was about an old couple who had one last child. The husband asked, "Why does this kid look different from all our other kids? Did you have an affair with someone?" She said, *"Déjale, viejito, todo está bien,"* "Leave it alone, old man, everything is fine." "No, no, I want to know why this kid looks so different than the other kids." And again she said leave it alone, fantastic things happen, this and this and that, even the Virgin Mary had a child. Now the husband got really mad and said, "I demand to know right now why this kid is different than the other kids." And she said, "Okay, I'll tell you. This one is yours."

Then there's a story from my novel, *Rain of Gold*. Tía Sophia's husband gets shot in the Revolution and he is dying. She's very pretty and he says to her, *"Júrame que nunca te vas a casar otra vez,"* "Promise that you will never remarry." And she said, "How can I promise you that? I'm nineteen, I've got kids, and life is going to go on." He's gargling up blood, and says, *"Júrame* at least, that you'll never be in love again." "Well, how could I marry someone and not be in love again? You're really not being very realistic, or helpful so that I can go on in my life." And he died. But she never lied to him. My father said she was right not to lie to him, that he was stupid. He said many men bully women for answers when they don't really want to know the truth, so they shouldn't ask.

Loretta Sanchez
Member of Congress

One day, my father sent my brother and me to the store. He gave us a dollar and told us to get a head of lettuce. Well, once we were at the store we bought ourselves some candy bars along with the lettuce. When we returned home, my dad said, "Where's the receipt?" My brother said, "We lost it." "Well, where's the plastic over the lettuce package?" "It didn't come with the plastic over the package." And Dad said, "Are you sure this lettuce cost $.39?" "Yeah, dad, this lettuce cost thirty-nine cents." I was quiet up to this point. My dad looked at me and said, "What do you think, Loretta?" "We just bought the lettuce," I lied, because my brother told me not to tell my dad we bought candy bars.

Obviously, my dad realized we had bought something else. He said, "Let's walk down to the store together and we'll ask for the receipt." My brother said, "Oh, no, we can't do that!" Finally, we broke down and told dad we had bought candy bars. My father said, "I knew you had bought something, but I wanted to make sure you bought something for your sister, too."

My father told us, "You see, once you start telling one lie you have to tell other lies to cover the first lie up." This lesson about why you shouldn't lie has always stuck with me because telling the truth is much easier. You don't have to remember the last story you made up.

It's All in the Frijoles

Gloria Bonilla-Santiago, Ph.D.

Professor, Rutgers State University; Author

My parents always taught us that you had to be honest. Integrity was something very important to them, even when people were doing bad things in the *barrio*. There were some families who would give up their strong values about right and wrong in order to make quick money.

Where we grew up, people often resold stolen items to get money, often to buy drugs. My parents knew these things were stolen. "No, we're not interested," they would say, even if the items were things we needed. Their message to us was "We're not going to support that dishonest behavior. We're going to work for the things we need." Their lessons about honesty and integrity have really made me who I am.

———————————

Baltazar Gracián was one of the greatest thinkers of the seventeenth century. He was an adviser to royalty and friends with Saint Teresa de Avila and Saint John of the Cross. He was a favorite of Arthur Schopenhauer, Friedrich Nietzsche, King Philip IV of Spain, and Voltaire. This selection is from a book of his writings, A Pocket Mirror for Heroes, *published by Currency Doubleday. Perhaps Mamá had read Gracián when she talked to me about dressing up the truth a bit so I wouldn't hurt someone's feelings.*

Baltazar Gracián (Spain)
(1601–1658)

Truth Applies Her Makeup

Truth was the lawful wife of Understanding; but Falsehood, her great rival, attempted to expel her from her bed and pull her from her throne. What ruses he invented! What slander! She began by calling Truth gross, unkempt, hard, and simple. And sold herself as courtly, smart, stylish, and gentle. And although she was naturally ugly, she was very good with makeup. She took Pleasure as her go-between, and before long had overthrown the noblest part of the mind.

Scorned and persecuted, Truth went to Wit to tell of her travails and inquire about a remedy. "Listen, my friend," said Wit, "in times like these, no food is more unpalatable than raw disillusionment; nothing more bitter than a mouthful of naked truth. Light that strikes the eyes directly can torture an eagle or a lynx. What do you expect from people whose vision is ill? This is why clever doctors of the mind invented the art of gilding truths, of sweetening disillusion. Take this down: you'll thank me for this advice.

"You ought to be more of a politician. Dress the way Deceit does, borrow some of her jewelry, and I promise you success." Truth opened her eyes to artifice, and has never been the same. More inventive now, she devises stratagems, makes the distant appear close, speaks of the present in the past, ponders in one person what she wants to condemn in another, aims at Bill to bring down Jack, ravishes the emotions, counterfeits affection, draws on sweet and easy fables, and through ingenious meanderings like this one, comes to rest just where she wants to.

It's All in the Frijoles

To seek truth, to seek wisdom, was the major pursuit of the ancient peoples of Meso-America. They believed that the purpose of education was both to give shape and meaning to the human personality and to humanize the heart and will of man. The wise men in the Calmécac, *the schools of the Aztecs, taught their pupils "to assume a face" and "to humanize their will." They believed that only men with an authentic "face and heart" were able to escape the dream world of Tlaltícpac. In this manner each man might arrive at his own individual truth, and thus be able to follow the path leading him to the "only truth on earth."*

> He makes wise the countenances of others
> he contributes to their assuming a face;
> he leads them to develop it. . . .
> Before their faces, he places a mirror;
> prudent and wise he makes them;
> he causes a face to appear on them. . . .
> Thanks to him, people humanize their will
> and receive a strict education.

For film director Gregory Nava, developing our face, our personality, continues to be an important part of being honest with oneself, as well as others. Like many prominent, well-educated Latino professionals, he draws from the wisdom and traditional beliefs of the ancient Meso-American peoples, who built highly advanced civilizations on this continent centuries before the arrival of the Spaniards.

Gregory Nava

Film Director, Mi Familia, Selena

I am a very firm believer in the Toltecs' pre-Columbian view of honesty. They believed you have to make your heart your face, to be honest, live honestly and truthfully. And when you do that, then you can see your path. The Toltecs also believed you find your way when you have eyes and can see clearly, honestly from the deepest part of yourself. When you find your way, you find your calling. And if everybody finds their calling, then everything that needs to be done will be done. Everybody who's a poet will be a poet. Everybody who's a farmer will be a farmer. Everybody's who is meant to be a warrior, will be a warrior. I think this means that you find God within, in a sense and, when you do, you see your path and fulfill your destiny. The Toltecs had a more proactive and less fatalistic view, which I share. Everybody needs to find their way.

We also have to allow people to be honest. It's hard these days for young boys to find their path. First you have to have faith in yourself. We need to teach children that. You have to have faith in your ability; that faith is there if you look for it. When you look within yourself, you will find what you need to find in order to find out what you must do.

Marta Monahan

Author, Strength of Character and Grace, Speaker

My father used to say to me, "If you tell the truth and you live with the truth, you have the right to be believed every time." My father didn't lie. He was known—and this is a fact—as the most honest man in El Salvador. That was his title. People would send him letters from all over the world addressed to "Don José León Flores, The Most Honest Man in El Salvador, Better Known Than Many Presidents, San Salvador, El Salvador," with no address. He was very proud of this. He would never take a penny. And, when he was in positions of power— he was a diplomat, who held one of the highest positions in the diplomatic corps in the country, and was appointed to various positions by the President—he would not allow anybody, even people who were his friends, to do things to get extra money for their services beyond that for which they were getting paid.

Towards the end of his life, my father worked throughout Central America to organize banks. One one trip he audited the Bank of Nicaragua and prepared a report to be submitted to a world banking organization. In truth this was not the Bank of Nicaragua. The bank was personally owned by the dictator Somoza.

When my father returned home, bank officials sent him a printed copy of the annual report they had submitted to the banking organization. He knew his numbers in the report had been changed because Somoza did not want to admit that he owned the bank.

My father was furious. He went back to Nicaragua to face Somoza. My mother panicked and told us, "If we haven't heard from him in three days, he is dead." My father knew he was risking his life, too. However, he also knew he couldn't live with himself if he didn't confront Somoza, so he left for Nicaragua.

As it turned out, Somoza was in awe of my father's courage and his commitment to honesty. Somoza changed the figures. He agreed to put the report back the way my father had it. We knew my father was alive when we saw a picture of him having a drink with Somoza, on the front page of the San Salvador newspaper.

Dichos

La verdad es hija de Dios y heredera de su gloria.
Truth is the daughter of God and heir to His glory.

Burla, burlando, verdades soltando.
Tease, teasing, truth goes fleeing.

Realidades son verdades y no esperanzas falsas.
Realities are truths and not false hopes.

La verdad no peca pero incomoda.
Truth does not sin but it can make you uncomfortable.

Si dices la verdad no pecas, pero no sabes los males que suscitas.
You do not sin if you tell the truth, but you don't know the troubles you cause.

Los borrachos y los niños siempre dicen la verdad.
Drunks and children always tell the truth.

La verdad es amarga.
The truth is bitter.

La verdad, aunque severa, es amiga verdadera.
The truth, no matter how severe, is a truthful friend.

La verdad, como el aceite, siempre queda encima.
Truth, like oil, always stays on top.

La verdad no se viste de muchos colores.
Truth does not dress up in many colors.

It's All in the Frijoles

Mas verdades se han de saber que decir.
More truths should be known than said.

Quien mucho jura, poca verdad dice.
Whoever swears much, offers little truth.

La verdad sale como el maíz.
The truth comes out like maize.

La verdad padece pero no perece.
Truth suffers but never dies.

Todo saldrá en la lavada.
Everything will come out in the wash.

La mentira es hija del diablo; la verdad es hija de Dios.
The lie is the devils' daughter; truth is God's daughter.

Embustero conocido, ya nunca es creído.
Known liars are no longer credible.

La mentira no tiene pies.
A lie doesn't travel on its own.

Mentira general pasa por real verdad.
A general lie passes for gospel truth.

Los que dicen mentiras deben siempre tienen buena memoria.
Those who tell lies should always have good memories.

Antes se atrapa al mentiroso que al cojo.
It's easier to catch a liar than a cripple.

El que engaña con aparencia de verdad es impostor.
He who deceives with a truthful appearance is an impostor.

En boca de mentiroso, lo cierto se hace dudoso.
In the mouth of a liar, the truth becomes doubtful.

El derecho nace del hecho.
Right is born from the fact.

Por las acciones se juzgan los corazones.
Our hearts are judged by our actions.

El que sirve a dos amos, no queda bien con ninguno.
He who serves two masters, disappoints both of them.

La mentira presto es vencida.
The lie is soon found out.

La confianza también mata.
Trust also kills.

En la confianza está el peligro.
In trust is the danger.

El método ideal para engañar a la gente es decir la verdad.
The best way to deceive people is to tell them the truth.

Hacer caravana con sombrero ajeno.
Don't greet people wearing someone else's hat.
(Don't take another persons's thought, opinions, or ideas.)

Fingir no es mentir.
Pretense is not lying.

7

Courage
Valentía

Haz más altas cosas que cazar mariposas.
Do some things more highly prized
than merely chasing butterflies.

Courage is the atom of change.

—BETTINA R. FLORES,
Chiquita's Cocoon

Necesidad y oportunidad le dan valor al cobarde.
Necessity and opportunity give the coward courage.

You don't get to choose how you're going to die. Or when.
You can only decide how you're going to live. Now.

—JOAN BAEZ, *Daybreak*

Courage is an admired virtue. Fearlessness, fortitude, daring, heroism, pluck, and gallantry are synonyms for courage. But it is the quality of spirit and conduct that permits one to face extreme dangers and difficulties without fear that we think of in defining this word. However, courage is not something that is only required under circumstances of extreme duress or challenge. The ability to live with firmness, faith, and without fear is a quality to be developed in both young and old alike.

Every time we try something new it involves a risk. We're required to move beyond what has been comfortable for us up to that point. Entering new situations, occupations, and challenges requires courage. This is why rites of passage are so important. They teach young people to master needed skills and to overcome fear. Children must be taught to live with courage and not to be victims of fear.

Mamá felt that courage came from having strong convictions: "Right makes might." For her, courage meant moral courage. As a woman of tremendous faith, her convictions about right and wrong came from the Bible. She believed that we develop moral courage by exercising the virtues in order to choke out their opposites—we are what we give our attention to. Thus, hatred is held in abeyance by kindness; lust is conquered by chastity; revenge by charity; and deceit by honesty. So, Mamá was always looking for ways to help her rambunctious daughter weed out those bad little habits from an early age. "Whatsoever a man soweth, that shall he also reap," she would say.

If we develop the habit of moral courage through practicing right actions, we will be able to make quick choices consistent with our sense of good and evil, right and wrong. It takes courage to admit that you are wrong. One day I took a candy bar from the grocery store without paying for it. My mother not only gave me a lecture about honesty, starting with "Thou shalt not steal," she forced me to return to the store, apologize for my bad behavior, and pay for the candy. She forced me to move beyond my own comfort level, break through the barrier of fear, confront the wrong, and do the right thing.

When my junior high schoolmate Eddie shoved me into the muddy street, spoiling my new red plaid coat, my mother did not ignore the situation. She contacted the school principal, and called the boy's mother. Eddie was a bully who had to be stopped. Mamá invited Eddie and his mother to our home to rectify the situation. He was quite contrite. He brought me chocolates and a popular record to make amends. I was surprised, but Mamá understood the young man's character flaw.

"A dog that barks doesn't bite," "El perro que ladra no muerde," she quipped. Since that time, I've come to understand bullies as cowards and, as such, I am not afraid of them. We must teach children to stand up for themselves and not allow themselves to be abused by anyone. This was the strength that enabled me to question a junior high teacher who incorrectly gave me a B+ instead of an A− and, years later, as an adult, to challenge my boss's decision to hire a man for a promotion that should have been mine. I received the A− I earned, and also won the promotion.

The story "Pinocchio" is a wonderful example of how cowardly, weak choices deform our character. When Pinocchio went off with the bad carnival boys to get into mischief, not only did his nose grow, but he also grew a donkey's tail and ears. He was literally making an ass of himself by his weak choices! Like so many of the stories Mamá read to me, there was a moral to be gleaned from the tale. This one taught me to behave in such a way that I wouldn't grow a tail of my own!

Mamá would often remind me that what separates humans from beasts is living our virtues, our higher consciousness. "No te portes como un animal" (Don't behave like an animal). It is a harder sell today, since so many of today's movies and television programs seem to reinforce exactly those qualities we should avoid, and the images children see on the screen make a strong impact on their young minds.

Courage is like a muscle. It needs to be strengthened until doing the right thing becomes an innate part of who we are and what we do.

Hector Elizondo
Actor

As a young boy I was a weak, scared, sickly kid. I realized I didn't want to live like that, so, using my own initiative , I overcame my fears and reinvented myself physically—totally—by working out. Prior to that I was not the essence of courage—standing up to the bad guys, doing the right thing, or laying my cards on the table.

The turning point in my life was a rite of passage. I was constantly being humiliated by some very, very large kids in our neighborhood, part of a large Irish family, the Matthews. They were a very rambunctious fighting group, right out of central casting, and they hated everybody. They were looking for somebody who was a little lower than they were in class, so to speak. And there we were, some Latins.

One day they came looking for the Quintanas. But the Quintanas weren't around, so they came after me. I had a fight for the fourteenth time and ran home crying because Micky had chased me around the block. Dad was thoroughly disgusted. One morning, on the way to church—I'm all dressed up in a little hat, coat, shirt, and stupid tie, like a little man—we saw one of the Matthew brothers with

It's All in the Frijoles

his father across the street. I remember I used to practically defecate at the sight of those boys, and I was shaking inside, thinking "Oh God, my nemesis." My father said, "Take off your jacket."

"What are you gonna do?"

"Take off your jacket. Loosen your tie. Go over there and just sock him, that's all." I was scared to death. My little *cojones* were on the line. I walked across the street and stood in front of my tormentor crying, *chillando*. I said, "My father said I have to sock you." I swung at him with everything I had. I missed. "Run!" I thought to myself. But we started tussling, holding on to each other. I was still crying, but I hit him. Then I felt my father's strong hand pull me away and Mickey's dad pulled his son away, too. Fathers do what fathers do. My dad and I walked back across the street. I was still sniffling. Dad said, "Well, that's it. Now he won't bother you anymore." I calmed down and we walked to church.

You would never see that today. I learned that you had to be brave and that sometimes someone had to force you to be brave. Nobody got hurt. Everybody was healed, in a way. And the fathers knew what was going on. Courage was everything.

We have to be taught to confront at the appropriate time and to not allow people to step on us or intimidate us. But another thing my father used to tell me was, "Never be a bully. You might as well be a coward."

By the way, years later, I met Mickey Matthew. I was in my early twenties and running a gymnasium. By that time, I was a weightlifting coach built like an apple on a stick, about one hundred ninety pounds with a thirty-inch waist. I saw this tall Irish guy with a toolbelt come in. It was Mickey. And, you know, I didn't want to deck him. I didn't want to break his neck, nothing. But I could have. I felt nothing. "You want to look around?" I asked and introduced myself. We never spoke of any acrimony. I never said, "You remember how you used to chase me around, you son-of-a bitch?" I never said anything. He didn't remember our fight, because he fought all the time. He just remembered the good times.

Nely Galán

President, Galán Entertainment

What my mother taught me about having the best of both worlds gave me courage. When I came home upset and crying because I had been called names and ridiculed for being Cuban, my mother said, "They're ignorant and don't know that you have it better than they do." So, I grew up thinking I had it better because I had two languages and two cultures. When I stand up for something I believe in, it comes from that place. How could anyone be told that knowing more is less?

When I was a sophomore in high school I learned a big lesson about courage. I wrote a story for a class requirement and was accused of plagiarism and suspended. I didn't know how to fight it. My parents couldn't go into school and fight for me because they didn't speak the language.

My story was about being a child of immigrants and it was very sad. The school decided that it was something a fourteen-year-old couldn't have written. Inspired by this incident, I wrote an article for *Seventeen* magazine on why you shouldn't send your daughter to an all-girl Catholic school. It was the only magazine I read at the time. Meanwhile, my problem at school sort of blew over.

Two or three months later, the article was published and I was expelled. It was very humiliating. I was the only Latina in the school and my parents had struggled to send me there. I told my mother, "I'm not putting up with this. I'm going to the Board of Education and I'm fighting it. They can't expel me because I wrote the article." My mother said, *"No. Es sacrilegio. No puedes combatir con las monjas. Tenemos que ir a pedir perdón."* (No. It's a sacrilege. You can't have your way with the nuns. We have to go and ask for forgiveness.) I said, "No way am I asking for forgiveness. I didn't do anything wrong."

So, I went to the Board of Education of New Jersey and talked to

It's All in the Frijoles

the person in charge, a black man. I asked him, "Can nuns expel me because I wrote an article against them?" He said, "No way." He told me, "It could be really bad, but I'll take the case." My parents told me, "No, don't do it. Don't do it."

But I felt as though, if I didn't do it, I was going to really be disappointed in myself for the rest of my life. So I took the case on and I won. We settled out of court, and the nuns graduated me early. I always say that one experience was my metamorphosis. It made me realize that when you're afraid of being courageous, you must do the thing you fear, because it's something you need to learn to overcome.

One of the early advocates of democracy in Mexico, Benito Juárez was orphaned at three years of age. He later pursued an education and became an attorney at a time when there were gross abuses of law and of power by the wealthy and by clergy of the Catholic church. A Zapotec Indian, who later became President of Mexico twice, Juárez was a man who followed his convictions. He made administrative decisions which benefited the people and challenged injustice wherever he saw it. It was Juárez who decreed that the Church and state were separate, and that, while religious freedom was to be protected, religion was not to challenge state prerogatives. When French troops surrounded Puebla in 1863, Juárez's forces fought back, holding out for so long that they were reduced to eating dogs and cats. By the end of 1865, Juárez had been driven out of Mexico to El Paso, Texas, and was threatened by a rival for the presidency. The French were weakened, and French and reactionary forces retreated. Harsh reprisals began. Juárez returned south and barely escaped capture in 1865 while parading about in front of his troops. These words were written to Porfirio Díaz following his near-capture.

Benito Juárez
(1806–1872)
President of Mexico

I have received the sermon on what seems to have been my tomfoolery on January 27 at Zacatecas. [But] there are circumstances in life in which it is necessary to risk everything, if one wishes to go on living physically and morally, and it is thus that I see the circumstances of that day. I got away with it, and I am happy and satisfied with what I did.

It takes courage to do the seemingly impossible. If we can get out of our own way, take risks, and move forward with our good intentions and plans, we can accomplish things that impact society in a significant way. This story, by the founder of the Mexican American Opportunity Foundation, which appears in his autobiography, A Life in Two Cultures, *is a perfect example.*

Dionicio Morales

A Life in Two Cultures

Two years of trying to raise money for the foundation proved fruitless. To complicate matters, the ten people who had been with me through this struggle decided to give it up. It was the consensus that we had exhausted our resources.

I didn't think so. Like any good leader, I faced either retreat or advance. I pleaded for just one more chance.

Frank Terrazas gruffly asked, "What do you propose to do?"

"We haven't talked to the President of the United States yet," I answered.

We had not yet had the opportunity to present our case to John Fitzgerald Kennedy. They all burst out in laughter. My team wondered if I had lost my marbles. To them it all seemed beyond our reach.

Someone asked, "How do you propose to get in touch with him?"

I could feel my blood pressure rising. I got lightheaded. My heart was pounding. It now, was do or die. My answer struck my associates like a bombshell. In a trembling voice, I said, "Why not call him on the phone?"

At that moment, it was noon in Pico Rivera and 3:00 P.M. in Washington, D.C. The idea of calling J.F.K. personally seemed like mission impossible. Even that was some relief to the general malaise of the meeting, which some thought would result in dissolving our ineffective organization. All we had left to show for our struggle was $22 in the treasury and two copies of our constitution and bylaws. In a moment of desperation and in the presence of ten skeptical board members, I picked up the phone, dialed the White House, and spoke to a woman on the switchboard.

"To whom do you wish to speak?" she asked.

When I said, "To the President, please," there was a pause.

At this point, ten stunned board members were staring at me, blankly. She asked the nature of my call.

I said that I was from a Mexican-American group in Pico Rivera, interested in talking about doing something about the employment problems of our people.

She referred me to the Mexican Embassy in Washington and gave me the number. She kindly advised me that the ambassador might resolve my problem.

At this point it almost seemed like the end of the road. I dialed again. The ambassador's secretary heard my story and said, "I think that the ambassador is meeting with Vice President Lyndon Johnson at this moment about the concerns you have expressed." She then advised me to call the vice president and gave me his number. I called once more and was referred to one of L.B.J.'s chief deputies. When I asked to speak with Mr. Johnson, he was pleased to hear from a person with my interests. He told me that there would be a Conference on Equal Employment Opportunity and that Mr. Johnson was the Chairman of the President's Committee on Equal Employment Opportunity. I was further informed that L.B.J. would be glad to talk to me personally before the conference to discuss Mexican-American employment issues, as they were looking for someone from the west coast to participate in the conference.

As a result of the phone conversation, I received a formal telegram of invitation repeating the offer of a special audience with the vice president.

Of course, I had no money for the transcontinental trip. But our committee of ten, now with renewed hope, got together the price of the ticket. I was left to worry about the specifics of my out-of-pocket expenses along the way. With about $15 in my wallet, I arrived in Washington, D.C., the day before my appointment and spent the night in an all-night movie house watching and rewatching *Fort Apache,* with John Wayne. The satchel-style briefcase I carried was borrowed for the occasion to carry my proposal. Inside the satchel, my wife had packed a toothbrush, a pair of shorts, and some socks. I had added two bananas. When I went for my mother's blessing, she added to the briefcase three burritos wrapped in Weber's Bread waxed paper. In the morning, after a shave in the Pickwick bus station, I announced my presence to the vice president from a phone booth. When asked where they should pick me up, I asked a man shining shoes what hotel was nearby. He said, "The Capital Hilton." That is where they picked me up.

Before the conference started, I had the opportunity to meet with L.B.J. I recall two memorable features of the man; the first was his firm, powerful handshake and the second his very marked Texas drawl. I asked him for just seven minutes of his time. He greeted me with that unforgettable Texas-style handshake and said, "You can have seventeen!"

L.B.J. opened the conversation with an expression of his concern that Mexican-American people rarely sought him out, even though his position as Chairman of the President's Committee on Equal Employment Opportunity put him in a position to help.

I told him, "I have a proposal for the Department of Labor. I've been sent all over the place and nothing happens. They tell me in Los Angeles to go to the Urban League. Will you help me get it funded?"

L.B.J. asked, "May I see it?"

Of all the times to go through an embarrassing predicament! I couldn't open the briefcase. Mr. Johnson's secretary tried to rescue me with the aid of a letter opener. Meanwhile, L.B.J. took it all in with patience and grace, smiling. Suddenly, the briefcase flew open. Out rolled my socks, the three burritos, the bananas, and my underwear. The cascade of personal items rolled across the office floor and under the vice president's desk. When I crawled under the desk to retrieve them, the secretary joined me and whispered in my ear, "Please don't be embarrassed. He's used to this sort of thing!" Despite my embarrassment, I was finally able to hand the vice president of the United States my proposal. It got to the Department of Labor and it got funded.

This was the beginning of my long friendship with L.B.J. On various occasions L.B.J. called on me. When the time came for the U.S. to return the disputed El Chamisal to Mexican sovereighty, Mr. Johnson invited me to join the official delegation which restored the title of the land to Mexico. He was always gracious and attentive and seemed to intuitively appreciate the depths of frustration which lay behind my emotional appeal for help.

. . . . When Johnson visited Los Angeles at my invitation, he dropped a bombshell. He asked, "My fellow Americans, can you guess how many communications I have received from the total Mexican-American and Hispanic population of the United States during the several months I have been in office as Chairman of the Presidential Committee on Equal Employment Opportunity? How many do you think? One thousand? Ten thousand? Twenty thousand?"

There was a pause. Many thought that L.B.J's daily mail must be heavy with reports from the millions of Mexican Americans specifying conditions of discrimination and unfairness in employment. Then came the bombshell.

Johnson answered his own question: "Sixty-five!"

Burt Corona
Activist

My grandmother used to tell us a story about her family, who had a very rich gold-and-silver mine outside Parral in Minas Nuevas, Chihuahua. The U.S. Army had made a deal with Geronimo that, if he would leave the Southwestern states alone, they would give him repeater rifles so he could go into Mexico and clean out the rich Mexican mine owners. So, the Comanches invaded Chihuahua with Geronimo.

Eventually, they attacked the mine at Minas Nuevas. At the time, my grandmother was twelve years old. She and her family were in the house, where they stored the gold and silver. Geronimo tried to capture the house. Two of my grandmother's brothers were killed in that battle. Grandmother told me of lying on the ground next to her other brother, loading the single-shot guns the Mexicans had to fight with against the Indians' repeater rifles.

Not long ago, I was in Chihuahua and visited Minas Nuevas, now an abandoned mining town, and the family's house, which is still there. I could see the holes next to the windows that my grandmother described using to shoot at the Indians during the attack. When I saw the town and the house, I understood how brave my grandmother had been.

This was the folklore of the people I grew up with: the fights against the Americans, the fights against the French, the fights against the Indians, and the fights against Porfirio Díaz. The film *La Longitud de la Guerra* depicts these towns in the mountains of Chihuahua in Northern Mexico where there have been three hundred years of battle against the injustices of the Spanish, the Jesuits, the Americans, and the French. There was a tradition of resistance and fighting for liberty in Northern Chihuahua. Many of the heroes of the revolution came from those towns in the mining areas where my family lived.

César Chavez, the founder and president of the United Farm Workers union, is recognized as one of the most important labor leaders of this century. He was a man of tremendous courage, often risking his life for the principles he stood for. His lengthy fasts to protest injustices and his emphasis upon nonviolence, while demanding better treatment and wages for campesinos, *produced significant victories for the people who labor to put the food we eat on our tables.*

César Chavez
(1927–1993)
Founder and President, United Farm Workers (UFW)

When we are really honest with ourselves we must admit that our lives are all that really belong to us. So, it is how we use our lives that determines what kind of men we are. It is my deepest belief that only by giving our lives do we find life. I am convinced that the truest act of courage, the strongest act of manliness, is to sacrifice for others in a totally nonviolent struggle for justice.

Courage is usually evoked in the defense of some higher principle or right. Such was the case among the surviving Nahuatl native chiefs and wise men in the face of an attack on their religion by the first twelve Spanish missionary friars in 1524, three years following the conquest and destruction of the Aztec culture and religion. Contrary

to general belief, the Aztecs were neither submissive nor passive. Indeed, the Third Dispatch *sent to Charles V on May 15, 1522, said*
"The Aztecs said that by no means would they give themselves up, for
as long as one of them was left he would die fighting, and that we
would get nothing of theirs because they would burn everything or
throw it into the water."

In the following passage, the Nahuatl wise men confronted and
defended the Spanish friars with full knowledge that the defense of
their religion could cost them their lives. It is important to note the extreme courtesy and prudence of their words, which show they were
aware of the subordinate position of a conquered people.

Our Lords, our very esteemed Lords:
great hardships have you endured to reach this land.
Here before you,
we ignorant people contemplate you. . . .

And now, what are we to say?
What should we cause your ears to hear?
Perchance, is there any meaning to us?
Only very common people are we. . . .

Through an interpreter we reply,
we exhale the breath and the words
of the Lord of the Close Vicinity.
Because of Him we dare to do this.
For this reason we place ourselves in danger. . . .

Perhaps we are to be taken to our ruin, to our destruction.
But where are we to go now?
We are ordinary people.
We are subject to death and destruction, we are mortals;
allow us then to die,
let us perish now,
since our gods are already dead.

It's All in the Frijoles

But calm your hearts . . .
Our Lords!
Because we will break open a little,
we will open a bit now
the secret, the ark of the Lord, our god.

You said
that we know not
the Lord of the Close Vicinity,
to Whom the heavens and the earth belong.
You said
that our gods are not true gods.
New words are these
that you speak;
because of them we are disturbed,
because of them we are troubled.

For our ancestors
before us, who lived upon the earth,
were unaccustomed to speak thus.
From them have we inherited
our pattern of life
which in truth did they hold;
in reverence they held,
they honored, our gods.
They taught us
all their rules of worship,
all their ways of honoring the gods.
Thus before them, do we prostrate ourselves;
in their names we bleed ourselves;
our oaths we keep,
incense we burn,
and sacrifices we offer.

It was the doctrine of the elders
that there is life because of the gods;

with their sacrifice, they gave us life.
In what manner? When? Where?
When there was still darkness.

It was their doctrine.

WE'RE UNACCUSTOMED TO SPEAK THUS.
FROM THEM HAVE WE INHERITED
OUR PATTERN OF LIFE
WHICH IN TRUTH DID THEY HOLD.

––––––––––

Emiliano Zapata was a hero of the Mexican Revolution. This famous quote speaks to self-respect as much as to courage.

Emiliano Zapata
(1879–1919)
Hero of the Mexican Revolution

It is better to die on our feet, than to live on our knees.

Ginny Mancini
Singer, Philanthropist

We need courage to use whatever gifts and talents we have to maximize our life experience. I know that music was my conduit—it's gotten me here. My family was very musical. My mother played the piano and the violin, and her brothers played instruments, so I was raised around music from day one. I was encouraged to sing and dance and play the piano. I remember the first piece my mother taught me on the piano was called "Zacatecas," the Mexican revolutionary march. I laugh about that today because it's a very stirring, wonderful march, and there's not a mariachi band in town that sees me that doesn't start to play "Zacatecas."

I must have been nine or ten when I started performing. I was winning contests when I was eleven, and started teaching young children how to dance tap at that age. I started earning $2.00 a week when I was twelve. Before that, I had to stand up and perform for my family, who loved to show me off. I was the family pride and joy. Later, I started to sing professionally, and that opened up all kinds of doors to a different life.

This passage, from the novel By the River Piedra I Sat Down and Wept *by Brazilian author Paulo Coelho, speaks to the courage to live life to its fullest, the same courage Ginny Mancini referred to when she grabbed those magic moments and shared her talents.*

Paolo Coelho (Brazil)
Author, The Alchemist

You have to take risks, he said. We will only understand the miracle of life fully when we allow the unexpected to happen.

Every day, God gives us the sun—and also one moment in which we have the ability to change everything that makes us unhappy. Every day, we try to pretend that we haven't perceived that moment, that it doesn't exist—that today is the same as yesterday and will be the same as tomorrow. But if people really pay attention to their everyday lives, they will discover that magic moment. It may arrive in the instant when we are doing something mundane, like putting our front-door key in the lock; it may lie hidden in the quiet that follows the lunch hour or in the thousand and one things that all seem the same to us. But that moment exists—a moment when all the power of the satyrs becomes a part of us and enables us to perform miracles.

Joy is sometimes a blessing, but it is often a conquest. Our magic moment helps us to change and sends us off in search of our dreams. Yes, we are going to suffer, we will have difficult times, and we will experience many disappointments—but all of this is transitory; it leaves no permanent mark. And one day we will look back with pride and faith at the journey we have taken.

Pitiful is the person who is afraid of taking risks. Perhaps this person will never be disappointed or disillusioned; perhaps she won't suffer the way people do when they have a dream to follow. But when that person looks back—and at some point everyone looks back—she will hear her heart saying, "What have you done with the miracles that God planted in your days? What have you done with the talents God bestowed on you? You buried yourself in a cave because you were fearful of losing those talents. So this is your heritage: the certainty that you wasted your life."

Pitiful are the people who must realize this. Because when they are finally able to believe in miracles, their life's magic moments will have already passed them by.

Dichos

Valiente de boca, ligero de pies.
Bold mouth, fast feet.

It's All in the Frijoles

El valiente vive hasta que el cobarde quiere.
The valiant one lives as long as the coward wishes.

Sólo los valientes tienen miedo.
Only the brave have fear.

El hombre a quien muchos temen a muchos ha de temer.
A man who is feared by many has many to fear.

El valor no necesita anunciarse.
Courage needs no announcement.

Las ratas son las primeras que abondonan el barco.
The rats are the first to jump a sinking ship.

Quien oye trueno no teme al rayo.
Who hears the thunder will not fear the lightning.

Más vale mearse de gusto que mearse de susto.
Better to pee for delight than to pee from fright.

Pones un espantajo y luego te espantas.
You make a scare and scare yourself.

Perro ladrador, poco mordedor.
All bark, no bite.

Cargado de fierro, cargado de miedo.
Weighted down with gear—weighted down with fear.

El cobarde de su sombra tiene miedo.
The coward is afraid of his own shadow.

8

Humility
Humildad

Para saber mandar es preciso saber obedecer.
To know how to give orders one must know how to obey.

It is the humblest of you who are the most perfect.
> —Saint Teresa de Avila,
> Seventeenth century Spanish mystic

Humility . . . is to live and act from an attitude and an altitude of Being.
> —Rafael Catalá, author,
> *Mysticism Now*

In this day and age, humility is in danger of becoming a lost virtue. However, in my mother's time, it was a cherished quality to be practiced and developed. True humility requires an accurate assessment of oneself and one's strengths and weaknesses. Unfortunately, humility has come to mean a putting down, a devaluing, or even a rejection of the self. Humility is better seen as a virtue to be developed in opposition to pride. Mystics and Mamá accurately describe humility as an attitude of serving God. It is an attitude of acceptance, of knowing one's worth, and appreciating the worth of others. Humility also allows us to act from a place of strength and commitment.

Mamá was a master of simplicity and humility because she lived the words of Saint Teresa de Avila: "The Lord is to be found among the pots and pans." She sought to perfect each daily action, like making the perfect pot of frijoles. Mamá read the Bible and prayed daily. She constantly referred to the Bible as a sacred scripture and teaching tool.

She taught me that true humility comes from a life of prayer and from the love of God working within. She always encouraged me to do better, to be better, to be kinder, more loving, because "that is what God wants for us, mijita."

As a child, of course, I didn't register Mamá's constant comparisons between base, vulgar human behavior and the behavior of of animals. "We are different from animals, mijita, because we think and can choose how we will behave. We can learn to control our human impulses. Our behavior must always be in keeping with our higher self." Many years later, after reading Saint Teresa de Avila, I realized what Mamá was telling me. Fortunately, by the time my daughter Danielle was born I had discovered a charming little book that teaches examples of the "little" me and the "great" me. The book encouraged children to blow out the "little" me—those outbursts of anger and the like—and breathe in the "great" me. I loved reading it to her and took particular delight when, a few years later, she would breathe in reverse of the book's recommendation, breathing in the "little" me—just to be difficult. I knew then that she knew the difference, and that she realized she could control her temper and other behaviors which were not in keeping with her "great" me. In that moment of awareness, as she teased me, she accepted responsibility for her actions and behavior and has been a delight ever since.

If humility comes from an attitude of strength, conviction, and love; conceit, fear, and pride are its opposites. It is important that we strive toward becoming better human beings. If we've fallen short of our potential, humility helps us pick ourselves up and realign ourselves with our higher truth . . . our essential nature.

Mamá would say that humility means taking to heart these words from Romans 12:2: "Do not imitate the way of this world, but be transformed by the renewing of your minds, that you may discern what is that good, acceptable, and perfect will of God."

Toney Anaya grew up in a one-bedroom adobe house in northern New Mexico. His family were among the earliest settlers there. The family was extremely poor. The floor was dirt, and there was no electricity or telephone. A wood-burning stove was the only heat and wood had to be chopped daily to keep a fire going. He learned early the virtues of hard work, respect, faith ("we used to visit church twice a week and said the stations of the cross each time"), and humility.

Toney Anaya
Attorney, Former Governor of New Mexico

We were dirt poor, yet proud and respectful. From our parents and grandmother we learned not to be boisterous, not to brag. We were told that as long as you tried your best, you would do fine. We were also told we shouldn't attempt to put others down in order to raise ourselves up. My grandmother used to say that every human being can make a contribution. Even though my parents had little formal education—Mom went only as far as second grade and spoke little English, Dad as far as the third grade and spoke broken English—education was strongly emphasized. We were encouraged to do our best, to work hard, and to apply ourselves in school and elsewhere. My grandmother used to say, *"Te pueden quitar la ropa, te pueden quitar la casa, te pueden quitar la vida, pero la educación que tienes no te la pueden quitar"* (They can take away your clothes, they can take away your house, they can take away your life, but they can never take away your education).

This was the message drummed into us which I have repeated to my children and grandchildren: As long as you always do your best, as long as you don't think you are better or worse than anyone else, as long as you do the best you can do, you can hold your head high.

Lucille Roybal-Allard
Member of Congress

I've had some tremendous role models in my Mom and Dad. The opportunities we did have because of my father's position as a member of Congress, such as going to hotels, going to banquets, things other kids in our neighborhood didn't do and couldn't do, also instilled in us a sense of humility. I remember my dad saying to us, "Never forget where you came from and remember these opportunities you have are a result of my office. Don't ever confuse the opportunities you receive because of the position your dad holds with who you are and who your father is."

For myself, I've learned when I get to go to the White House, or when I receive special recognition, it isn't because I am Lucille Roybal-Allard. It's because I am a congresswoman. It is the position that provides me with the opportunity to do certain things. We have to keep the two separate, and not confuse them. The minute you confuse them is when you end up in trouble. My dad always reinforced this. He always used to say, "The day I lose all these privileges, friends will disappear and these headquarters will be the loneliest place." That was one of the best messages he gave us. I never dreamed I'd be in politics but, since I am, it's helped keep me grounded.

I can see where it would be very easy to get caught up in the glory of Washington. It's really important to remember who you represent and why you are there.

Lee Baca

Sheriff, Los Angeles County

For me, humility falls under the realm of humor. Being humble means not taking yourself too seriously. During a recent parade honoring Dr. Martin Luther King, I did a "pump it up" gyration as my car passed the (largely African-American) crowd. "Pump it up" is a hip-hop gesture where you hold your palm shoulder high, pushing up as if you are "pumping it up." It's a teenage dance form that says you're trying to do better and aiming as high as you can. Culturally, the gesture is more black (than Latino), so to see a Mexican-American Sheriff "pumping it up" was a real crowd pleaser.

The idea behind humility it to make others feel as important as you are, to feel connected to you. Spiritually, I feel connected to the world and all living things. We are all part of something which is so huge. We are each just one piece of the puzzle of life. This is very humbling.

We are taught by the Bible to "become like children" before the Lord, that is, to be open, innocent, loving, and accepting. Humility also requires strength—as does love—as author and internationally renowned lecturer Rafael Catalá explains in this excerpt from his inspiring and instructive book Mysticism Now, The Art of Being Alive.

Rafael Catalá (Cuba)

Humility is Not Humiliation

One of the most important dimensions of the spiritual life is humility. Most people think that the word humility means to accept being a doormat. They usually repeat the Biblical phrase from the New Testament, "turn the other cheek," as Jesus did before his tormentors.

What they do not realize is that Jesus "turned the other cheek" on very firm ground. His action conveyed this awareness: You can kill me and I will do nothing to defend my body but what I have said remains. I will not take back one single word of what I have taught. I will not recant from a single one of my actions. "For truly I say to you, till heaven and earth pass away, not an iota, not a dot, will pass from the law until all is accomplished." (Matthew 5:18)

Humility then, is to live and act from an attitude and altitude of

Being. Out of this conscious awareness we live and express Life. This appears as teaching. What we do out of this awareness stands firm. We may go to prison, be made fun of, or be killed, but we do not recant or disavow our position, our actions, or our words. This is humility.

This principle works in our daily lives as well. How many of us give in to social pressure? How many of us give in to the maneuvering of our children or our relatives and let the principles we live by fall by the wayside? How many times would we rather give in than be an example to our neighbors, our children, and our other relatives?

Jesus turned the other cheek from a position of great strength and love for humanity. Humility is strength, not weakness. Humility is love, not servitude or bondage. Humility is not humiliation.

———————

Saint Teresa de Avila saw God in the simplest of things, and was one of the writers who inspired Mamá. Saint Teresa is considered the greatest of the Spanish mystics and an extraordinary example of Christian humility.

Saint Teresa spoke about the sanctity of everyday life, acknowledging that to be heroic in danger is not the most difficult of achievements. At those moments, the greatness of the circumstances temporarily arouses the will. However, to be perfect each day, in humble ways, to do well what one does, to treat all those with whom we work with a sense of equality, even with love, there is sancity indeed.

Knowledge of self and humility go hand in hand. For Saint Teresa, true humility makes us aware of our smallness as well as of the presence of God in man.

Saint Teresa de Avila

(1515–1582)

Spanish Mystic

If I had understood, as I do now, that my soul's tiny palace contained so great a King, I shouldn't have left him there so often alone. I should have stayed with him from time to time and, moreover, I should have made an effort to keep his house in less dirt and disorder.

Humility is to keep within the bounds of truth. The truth is magnificent: we are nothing, but God swells in us and God is everything. Worse than the beasts we are. We don't understand our soul's great dignity and we insult it by bringing it down to the level of the vile things of this world. . . . Let us beware of the false humility which refuses to recognize the gifts which God has so generously bestowed upon us: Let us understand clearly, absolutely clearly, about this. God grants them to us without any merit on our part and therefore we should thank His Majesty. . . . The richer we find ourselves, knowing all the time that we are really poor, the more progress we make in true humility.

Humility is also living in awe of all of creation and our part in it. Amado Nervo, diplomat, journalist, fiction writer, and biographer of Sor Juana Inés de la Cruz, and one of the great Latin-American poets of Mexico, captures this spirit of wonder in his poem "Ecstasy."

It's All in the Frijoles

Amado Nervo (Mexico)
(1870–1919)

Ecstasy

Each gentle rose that bloomed yesterday,
each dawn that appears between blushes,
leaves my soul in heightened ecstasy.
My eyes never tire of looking at
the perpetual miracle of Life!

It's been ages that I contemplate the stars
in the diaphanous nights of Spain
and I find them more beautiful each time.
For years, alone with myself by the sea,
I listened to the lament of the waves,
and still the wonder of the waves overwhelms me.

Each time I find Nature
more supernatural, more pure and holy.
For me, all is beautiful around me;
and everything equally enchants me:
the mouth of the mother, when she prays;
the mouth of the child, when he sings.

I want to be immortal with a thirst that is intense,
because we are gifted a marvelous panorama,
by a creation that is immense;
because each star demands of me
telling me in its sparkle: "Here there is also
thought, here there is struggle, here there is love."

Translated by Yolanda Nava.

Humility/*Humildad*

Joan Baez
Musician, Activist

I was born gifted. I can speak of my gifts with little or no modesty, but with tremendous gratitude, precisely because they are gifts, not things which I created, or actions about which I might be proud.

It has been said that pride goeth before a fall. Pride, of course, is the opposite of humility. This delightful story about what can happen when we become too full of ourselves is often sung, accompanied by a drum. Children often clap along as the story is told.

The Alligator and the Dog

Many years ago, on the island of Cuba, there was a very vain alligator. He loved to spend hours admiring himself in the river. He would turn his head this way and that, admiring his reflection, saying, "What a handsome fellow I am! Look at those beautiful white teeth. Look how green my scales are. And talented—no one else can play the drum and sing the way I do!"

One day, however, Dog was passing by and heard Alligator drumming and singing. "That looks like fun," he thought to himself. "Maybe I should try it." So up he walked to Alligator. When Alligator finished his song, he said, "Oh, you sing and play so well. I know I could never hope to play as well as you. But it looks like so much fun! Please, old friend, may I borrow your drum, just to try it out?"

Alligator was flattered. "Of course you may borrow my drum—but only for a few minutes." As he handed the drum to Dog, he thought, "He'll never play or sing as well as I do. What's the harm?"

Dog began to pat the drum with his paws. Soon, he had a nice rhythm going and began to sing:

"Tata nue
bom, bom, bom
findecabon
san, san, san."

Alligator was very surprised. Dog had a beautiful, melodic voice that rose and fell to the rhythmic beat he was pounding. "He sounds awfully good," he thought. "I'd better get that drum back quickly."

"Dog, *Perro,* old friend, I need my *tambor* back now."

"Oh, it's only been a minute, *Caimán.* Please let me play for a little while more. I promise I will give it back soon."

"Okay," said Alligator reluctantly. "But just for a few more minutes."

Dog again began to play and sing. The rhythm was so persuasive that he rose to his feet and began dancing as he played.

"Tata nue
bom, bom, bom
findecabon
san, san, san."

Dog looked as though he was having the time of his life. Alligator began to get upset. "*Perro,* give me my drum back this instant. I need it."

"Oh, *Caimán,* please, let me play it one more time. You are so talented and handsome. I am just a poor dog and could never hope to be as good as you. Just one more time and I promise I will return it. I also promise not to ask you for it again."

"All right, just one more time." Alligator was sorry he had ever let Dog play the drum. Dog started to play. As he did, he rose to his feet, dancing, and once again began to sing

"Tata nue . . ."

Dancing, he moved further and further away, breaking into a run. Alligator tried to catch him, but Dog was much too swift for him.

Soon Dog had become famous. Everywhere he went, people asked him to perform his song. He was happy to oblige:

"Tata nue
bom, bom, bom
findecabon,
san, san, san."

One day the king went to Dog. "My daughter, Princess Lana, has died. I have heard of your fine playing, and would be honored if you would play for her funeral."

Dog agreed. On the day of the funeral, Dog played and sang his song as people throughout the town marched in time to the beat. Everyone like his music, and he continued traveling throughout the land, performing for everyone he passed.

Alligator, knowing he would never see Dog again, finally bought another drum. But no matter now much he practiced, he never became as good as Dog—or as famous, either.

———————

Meso-American myths contain profound lessons for proper behavior, in addition to being sacred accounts of the origins of the world. Interestingly, arrogance and greed are the most commonly mentioned vices which bring disaster or defeat. In Aztec mythology it is the humble yet brave Hanhuatzin who eventually becomes the sun, not the vain and wealthy Tecuciztecatl. In the Popol Vuh, *the outstanding Quiché doc-*

ument of Maya religion, the monster bird Vucub Caquix is slain by the hero twins because of his excessive pride and bragging. A great deal of the preserved mythology provided models for royal conduct with vices common to high office being arrogance and avarice. In the Popul Vuh, the gods create the present race of humans, the people of maize, to supply sustenance to the gods in the form of prayer and sacrifice. While the necessity of human sacrifice to continue the world continues to be the most vilified aspect of ancient Meso-American religion, human sacrifice arose out of a basic premise, a recognition of the active role and responsibility of people for the maintenance of cosmic balance.

Humility is an attitude of peacefulness and respectfulness. In the following Nahuatl metaphor, the attitude desired is one free of arrogance. In many cultures throughout the world, it is a sign of respect to lower one's head when passing or greeting someone, out of respect. In this country we speak of someone who is full of himself as one whose "nose is stuck in the air." So, we also have the dicho, "Cuando más alto se sube, más fuerte es la caída," "The higher you climb, the harder you fall." We are not talking about success, but the arrogance that sometimes accompanies an inflated sense of self, that is to be eliminated.

Nahuatl Metaphor

Iuian, yocuxca ximonemilti: ma totolol, ma momalcoch, in tetloc, in tenaoac.
Live tranquilly and peacefully with others, and with others keep your head lowered, your head bowed.

This was said to the nobles or children of nobles. They were told: "You must live tranquilly and peacefully with others and beside others. You must not be arrogant, you must not be presumptuous; arrogance is not proper, it is not right. One does not live with others in this manner. It is proper to live with one's head bowed, one's head lowered."

———————

Humility is knowing who we really are. This point of view is clearly stated in this brief passage from Don Miguel Ruiz's The Mastery of Love: A Toltec Wisdom Book.

Don Miguel Ruiz
Healer, Teacher, and Author

When you know that the power that is Life is inside you, you accept your own Divinity, and yet you are humble, because you see the same Divinity in everyone else. You see how easy it is to understand God, because everything is a manifestation of God. The body is going to die, the mind is going to dissolve also, but not you.

———————

When I read and reread in English and Spanish the words of Violeta Parra, "Here's to Life," a song made famous by singer Joan Baez, I wept. I felt such immense gratitude for my life, for all life, for its joys and travails, for a God who has given us so much love and beauty.

Violeta Parra
(1917–1967)

Here's to Life

Thanks to life that has given me so much.
It has given me two eyes, when I open them
I can distinguish black and white clearly apart
and the star-covered depths of the lofty sky
and the man I love from among the crowd.

Thanks to life that has given me so much.
It has given me hearing that in all its breadth
records night and day crickets and canaries;
hammers, turbines, bricks, gusts of wind and rain,
and the tender voice of the one I love.

Thanks to life that has given me so much.
It has given me sound and the alphabet,
with it the words that I think and declare,
mother, friend, brother and light that brightens
the way of the soul of the one I love.

Thanks to life that has given me so much.
It has given me the stride of my tired feet.
With them I walked around cities and puddles,
Beaches and deserts, mountains and plains
And your house, your street, and your courtyard.

Thanks to life that has given me so much.
It has given me a heart that becomes excited or disturbed
when it sees the consequences of the human mind,

when it sees good distanced from evil,
when it sees the depths of your bright eyes.

Thanks to life that has given me so much.
It has given me laughter and it has given me tears,
So I can distinguish good fortune from despair,
The two elements that form my song,
and your song that is my selfsame song
and the song of all that is my own song.

Translated by Yolanda Nava.

Dichos

El Fray Modesto nunca llegó a prior.
Friar Modest never became prior.

Nadie diga de sí nada, que sus obras lo dirán.
Nobody speaks for himself—his words speak for him.

¿Con esa boca comes?
You can eat with that mouth?
(To someone who uses coarse language.)

Los últimos serán los primeros.
The last will be the first.

Cuando más alto se sube, más fuerte es la caída.
The higher you climb, the harder you fall.

9

Temperance
Moderación

Los tres estados de la embriaguez son:
león, mono y cerdo.
The three stages of inebriation are:
lion, ape, and pig.

En la duda, abstente.
When in doubt, abstain.

Add to your faith virtue; and to virtue knowledge; and to
knowledge temperance; and to temperance patience; and
to patience godliness; and to godliness brotherly kindness;
and to brotherly kindness charity.
—II PETER 1:5-7

Seneca was one of the first Roman sages to speak about moderation. Mamá would often remind me of his wisdom. She would quote him when I was about to make a glutton of myself by eating too much ice cream or some other favorite food. "It's okay to have a little bit of everything but not to overdo it. It's important to learn to be moderate in all things. Avoid excess." "How can there ever be too much of a good thing, Mamá?" "Well, if you eat too much of that ice cream, you can make yourself sick. It's like that with everything. It's important to be moderate in the way we live." Of course, I had to learn this the hard way. One day I ate an entire half-gallon of ice cream. I was stuffed to the gills and, when I complained, the first thing Mamá asked was "What did you eat?" I pointed to the empty container and she just looked at me. "Ah, mija, te dije, oh, my little one, I told you, your eyes are bigger than your stomach." She once again tried to explain the lesson of moderation.

Temperance is moderation, self-restraint in action or statement. It is self-control, balance, mastery, and as such is one of the key building blocks of character. "One must learn to control oneself," Mamá would say, meaning one should control one's passions and appetites. As I got older, she explained that it was all right to wear a little makeup, but not to overdo it. "Don't overdo it" was one of her favorite phrases. It was all right to play, but not to exhaust myself by not getting adequate rest or nourishment. It was all right to express my being upset, but not to lose my temper or raise my voice. *Displays of temper were not tolerated in our home.* Indeed, I rarely saw my mother lose hers, despite the fact that she lived with a rambunctious, precocious child who preferred to run free and without restraint.

Nor were there any signs of excess in how Mamá dressed or decorated the house. She took seriously the Biblical directive "Let your modesty be known to all men." She wore simple tailored wool skirts and soft crepe blouses to work. On those occasions when she dressed formally, she would make herself a long gown which exposed only her beautiful back. Scoop-necked dresses were always modest, and she never showed both front and back at once.

One of my more flamboyant cousins, who wore false eyelashes, lots of makeup, and big wigs and whose living room resembled a turn-of-the-century bordello, used to tease that my mother's living room with its serene cream-colored walls and carpet, tasteful furnishings, and subdued pastoral landscape paintings reminded her of a Christian Science reading room. There were two sets of sheets for each bed, and a modest larder of dried and canned foods. Yet there was always adequate food, beautifully prepared from fresh ingredients, and clothing which she had usually made herself, often using remnants of good-quality fabrics that she had found in the garment district. Rather than buy a new doll every year, she would make my favorite one new clothes. It was the only way she could live within her means. There was very little waste in Mamá's home. And, because we lived simply, we were able to live well, given the modest income she earned as a seamstress. Her secret was temperance, and Mamá's keen use of moderation created miracles.

Self-restraint is a difficult concept for many children. As children, our emotional nature is usually underdeveloped. As a child, I wanted to do what I wanted to do. I hadn't learned that the extra bowl of ice cream could make me sick, or that temper tantrums could cause hurt to myself or to a loved one. Mamá would say, "You have to learn to control your temper," whenever I lost mine.

Mamá would often point out examples of excess when the men in the family drank, too. Drunkenness disgusted everyone, even the young children. In small towns and communities where everyone knew everyone, it was not uncommon to point out examples of both exemplary and undesirable behavior to young children. Families can become their own moral guides by pointing out both appropriate and inappropriate ways of behaving. Temperance or moderation is almost always the key.

"That is not acceptable behavior" was one of my favorite phrases when I wanted one of my children to stop acting a certain way. Conversely, I compliment or reinforce good behavior, or simply lean over and give them a kiss. Mamá taught me early that "a child is like a tree." It needs to be straightened out or pruned so it will grow upright and healthy. We need moderation to create balance, harmony, and excellence in our lives. Temperance is the virtue which helps us develop the skills we need to achieve this balance in the way we live.

In this ancient hymn from Peru, the singer asks for help to behave in the desired way. Mamá always said we have to hold the ideal model of behavior up so that we can imitate it. She also taught me to affirm that which we wish to become so that we bring our action and our words into conformity with that model.

Ancient Quichua Hymn

Aylillay, aylillay
uh huayli
aylillay, aylillay
uh huayli.
Gentlemen dignitaries
gentlemen people
beautiful word
beautiful quiet please
forgive me

make me understand
speak my father
drive away wrath
drive away sloth
aylillay, aylillay
uh huayli.

Those of us who have had the pleasure of knowing Congressman Roybal personally appreciate the dignity with which he conducts himself and the quiet strength he brings to any confrontation. His respectful manner, personal strength, and self-control in the face of outrage have enabled him to challenge injustices on many fronts and defend the rights of Latinos, minorities, women, and the elderly, in the halls of the U.S. Congress.

Edward R. Roybal
Member of Congress, 1963–1993

When I learned not to take a back seat to anyone, I learned to fight for rights due, but without losing control. I learned this from my dad. He would say, "Never lose your temper because if you lose your temper, you lose the fight." I always acted without losing my temper—and I have a temper—I've always controlled it.

Whenever I have stood up to injustice, or discrimination, or other wrongs, I have done it without anger. You can't think if you're angry. That's what my dad used to say. His message goes back many years, but I've remembered it whenever I've encountered challenges and injustice.

Thomas Merton called César Vallejo "the greatest universal poet since Dante." Here Vallejo speaks to the private and soulful conscience of the reader, reminding us of the destructive force of anger, the opposite of temperance.

César Vallejo (Peru/France)
(1892–1938)

Anger

Anger which breaks a man into children,
Which breaks the child into two equal birds,
And after that the bird into a pair of little eggs:
The poor man's anger
Has one oil against two vinegars.

Anger which breaks a tree into leaves
And the leaf into unequal buds
And the bud into telescopic grooves;
The poor man's anger
Has two rivers against many seas.

Anger which breaks good into doubts
And doubt into three similar arcs
And then the arc into unexpected tombs;
The poor man's anger
Has one steel against two daggers.

Anger which breaks the soul into bodies
And the body into dissimilar organs
And the organ into octave thought;

The poor man's anger
Has one central fire against two craters.

Translated by Thomas Merton.

---

*Many children wonder why their parents insist on their learning a par-
ticular task "the right way," or to perfection. It seems so silly to spend
so much time learning to do something which does not seem to have
much importance. But as Marta Monahan, self-mastery teacher and
author of the book* Strength of Character and Grace *tells us, living
with consistent effort and moderation is what leads to mastery and
success.*

Marta Monahan
Author, Speaker

Moderation is order. It's having control over your actions. It's
managing your life with elegance. It's a rhythm. It's the grace of
mastery.

The first time I mastered something I was so proud. I was in
boarding school in El Salvador and had worked very hard to figure out
how to mop the floors without leaving streaks. Mind you, we were all
girls from families that had maids to do all the housework. But the
Mother Superior expected us to learn to do this task with grace—to do
it to perfection. I cannot tell you the feeling of having mastered something to perfection and being recognized for it. It stayed in my head
that mastery was possible.

I told my father the whole story and he said, "You have arrived
at the grace of mastery and that is what makes life easy and beautiful."
And he said, "If you reach that place you will realize you are in a bal-

let in slow motion. I am going to show it to you." He took me to the ocean, and he showed it to me in the waves. There you see the moderation—unless there is a storm, which is not moderation—but there is a beauty and a rhythm to the ocean. The waves build, and crest, and come into shore. He told me, "Tonight is a full moon and we are going to stay and have dinner here." We were at a club at the beach. And he said, "I want to show you the ballet of the fishermen."

At about eight o'clock no one was out on the beach, because everybody was inside with the entertainment, or on the patio with the moon—it was very pretty. So we went to the beach and watched eight or ten of the fishermen run in a rhythm, with moderation, with almost no splashing—because they developed that grace—so that they wouldn't scare the fish. And they didn't go in too deep. And then they moved back. They were muscular and strong young men. They tossed a net that was a thirty-foot-wide circle across the water, and then, with the same grace, they pulled the net so that it didn't hurt the fish. Then they put the fish in a bucket, rolled the net again, and started the dance of jumping in the water. And you saw all of them moving in the same manner. They were not synchronized, but using the same movement, like dancers dancing the same dance at different times. And my father said, "This is the ballet of mastery that you acquired with the mopping."

One day, my father said, "Come here." It was six o'clock in the morning and he had already been up, showered, shaved, put on a suit and tie, and had walked for an hour. He told me to come outside because he wanted to show me another ballet. It was the trashmen collecting the trash. He said, "Watch." And I did. They ran, they ran with a rhythm, picked up the can, swung, and threw it up into the truck, and did it again with the repetition and grace which creates moderation. It's the rhythm. Without moderation there is no rhythm in life, there is just a cacophony, a noise, an abruptness.

It's All in the Frijoles

Ricardo Montalban
Actor

In my religion, we call the difference between virtue and sin *use* and *abuse*. You use something, but you don't abuse it. You can use your job, but you don't abuse your job. Moderation to me falls under use and abuse. For instance, I have one drink every night, but I have never been drunk in my life.

Maybe that is because, when I was very young, there was always wine from Spain on the table and my father would have a glass of wine. And then, when I got to a certain age, he would give me a little wine with water. And so, to me, wine was merely a complement to my food. In this country, they say, "No, you can't drink until you're eighteen." So the young person thinks, "Wait a minute, November seventeenth, I'll be eighteen, then I can drink." Then they go out and get drunk. I think it is wise to teach children that a glass of wine is not something to abuse, but to use for further enjoyment of food.

Trained in the ideas of the Enlightenment from an early age, Simón Bolívar's heart was molded for liberty, justice, greatness, and beauty.

Simón Bolívar (Venezuela)
(1783–1830)
Statesman and Leader of the Revolution Against Spain

Virtue and moderation were the motto of Venezuela. Fraternity, union, and generosity should be yours, so that these great principles combined may accomplish the great work of raising America to the political dignity which so rightly belongs to her.

This essay comes from the book A Pocket Mirror for Heroes, *by Baltazar Gracián, translated by Christopher Maurer. Given its wisdom, it's no wonder the book has become a favorite among those who seek excellence in their lives, three centuries after it was written.*

Baltazar Gracián (Spain)
(1601–1658)

Virtue

Man was made from the rest of creation. His perfections came to him as tribute, but on loan. Heaven gave him his soul, earth his body, fire his warmth, water his humors, air his breath, the stars his eyes, the sun his radiant face, fortune his possessions, fame his honors, time his ages, and the world his home. Friends gave him company; parents, character; and teachers, wisdom. And when he saw that all of these goods were movable, he is said to have asked:

"What, exactly, belongs to me? If all this is borrowed, what do I get to keep?"

"Virtue. It is yours alone, and no one can revoke it. All is nothing without her, and she is complete in herself. Other goods are in jest; she alone is in earnest. She is the soul of the soul, life of life, radiance of all gifts, crown of perfection, perfection of all being. She is the center of happiness, throne of honor, joy of life, satisfaction of the conscience, breath of the mind, source of contentment, font of happiness, and feast for the intellect, the will, and the memory. She is rare because she is difficult, and wherever she is, she is beautiful and well esteemed.

It's All in the Frijoles

All people want to resemble her, and few possess her in truth. The vices hide under her cloak and imitate her action, and even the worst people want to be taken as good. All would like her for others, few for themselves. All want to be treated faithfully and not gossiped about, deceived, or insulted, but few bestow that treatment on others. She is lovely, noble, and gentle, and all the world conspires against her. True virtue has hidden herself away. When we think we've found her, we've seen only her shadow, which is hypocrisy. A kind person, a just one, a virtuous one, is as rare as the Phoenix, and no less immortal."

Pulque, an alcoholic beverage made from the fermented sap of the maguey plant, played a major role in Aztec ceremonial life as both a ritual drink and a sacrificial offering. This beverage was often drunk at banquets and festivals, though public intoxication was strongly condemned, particularly for those of noble birth. According to legend, celestial demons of darkness, the horrific tzitzimime, threatened to destroy the world. Often depicted as female, these night demons are the stars that do battle against the sun at every dusk and dawn.

The Origin of Pulque
An Aztec Myth

While food had been provided to humans, there was little in their lives to inspire pleasure or joy. So, the god Quetzalcoatl concluded that something was needed to make people sing and dance, an intoxicating drink to bring pleasure to people's lives. He woke Mayahuel, the sleeping young goddess of maguey, who lived in the sky with her fearsome *tzitzimitl* grandmother, and the two descended to earth. There, they join themselves into a great forked tree, with Quetzalcoatl as one branch and Mayahuel the other.

Mayahuel's grandmother woke to find the girl missing. Enraged, she called upon her fellow *tzitzimime* star demons to find her errant granddaughter. The furious celestial demons dove headlong from the sky to the tree where Quetzalcoatl and Mayahuel were hidden. Just as they arrived, the tree split in half and the two branches crashed to the ground. Recognizing the girl, the grandmother savagely tore the branch apart and passed parts of her granddaughter to all the other *tzitzimime* to devour. Quetzalcoatl, however, was left untouched and unharmed and, once the demons returned to the sky, Quetzalcoatl turned back into his actual form. Sadly gathering the gnawed bones of Mayahuel, Quetzalcoatl buried them in the earth and, from this simple grave, grew the first maguey plant, the wondrous source of pulque.

Dichos

Todas las virtudes están de acuerdo, los vicios se pelean.
All virtues are in agreement, all vices fight each other.

Cuerpo de tentación, cara de arrepentimiento.
Body of temptation, face of regret.

El que evita la tentación evita el pecado.
Whoever avoids temptation avoids the sin.

Resisto todo menos la tentación.
I can resist everything except temptation.

El que malas mañas tiene, tarde o nunca las perderá.
Whoever has bad habits will lose them later or never.

It's All in the Frijoles

Lo mejor de los dados es no jugarlos.
The best thing about dice is not to play them.

El vicio es sabotaje contra uno mismo.
Vice is self-inflicted sabotage.

La sangre se hereda y el vicio se pega.
Blood is inherited and vice is contagious.

Todo lo excesivo es vicioso.
Everything excessive is licentious.

No hay peor vicio que el exceso.
There is no worst vice than excess.

10

Prudence
Prudencia

Al que madruga, Dios lo ayuda.
God helps the one who wakes up early.

A fuerza, ni los zapatos entran.
Nothing is gained by force.

. . . el que lee mucho y anda mucho,
vee mucho y sabe mucho.
. . . he who reads and travels much,
sees and knows much.

—Cervantes, *Don Quixote*

En dondequiera se cuecen frijoles
If you try hard enough you can accomplish almost anything.

Lo que se aprende en la cuna siempre dura.
What is learned in the cradle lasts forever.

Mamá was a master of practicality, forethought, and common sense. As a child, I lacked these gifts, preferring instead to daydream, to seek adventure, and to follow my impulses. I was forever wandering off unaccompanied into Elysian Park, which backed up to the property where we lived near Echo Park. "Ten cuidado, mija, be careful, my little one," she would warn me when I left her. "Don't go looking for trouble." These were phrases she spoke whenever we parted, even when I was a grownup with my own children. "Be careful! Keep your eyes and ears open," are phrases I repeat often to my son and daughter. I also have passed on the sage advice, "Con pendejos no bañarse porque pierden el jabón" (Never bathe with fools because they will lose the soap) and "Donde fuego hace, humo sale" (Where there's smoke, there's fire).

To take care, to be careful, is to be prudent. It is to think before you act, to prepare for the future, to prepare for unanticipated eventualities so that you are not caught off guard. "Las aparencias engañan" (Appearances betray). "No todo lo que brilla es oro" (Not everything that shines is gold). Prudence involves practical wisdom, good judgment, forethought, and care in living our lives. Prudence also involves care in providing for the future, and the saying "Waste not, want not" is a reminder to be economical and frugal about money and resources so that we will have enough in the future. A prayer answered in the form of a winning Mexican lottery ticket enabled my parents to make a down payment on the home where I grew up, which was located in a nice neighborhood in the Silverlake district of Los Angeles. After my parents divorced, my mother was able to continue making payments on our home by exercising financial restraint and prudence. She always told me, "Put your money away, don't spend more than you earn, and don't use credit cards." She only used credit when she had to buy a major appliance like a refrigerator or washing machine, because she couldn't pay the several hundred dollars it would cost at one time. Then, she would look for a good price. When she used credit, she would pay it off as quickly as she could.

In our home, we never lacked for anything. But it was Mamá's prudence that enabled her to stretch her small check. She would buy beans and rice in bulk and shop downtown where prices were cheaper and the produce was fresh. She made everything from scratch, and all her cooking was delicious. When I needed a coat, she would ask one of the cutters at the shop where she worked to cut a remnant to my size. She would do all the sewing and finishing work at home. As a result, I had beautiful clothes for pennies.

Mamá wanted to be sure I understood the importance of the virtue of prudence. As a result, I grew up listening to folktales like the "The Three Counsels" and "Little Red Riding Hood" to learn how to avoid strangers who could do me harm. There were a string of dichos which she frequently used, such as Los perritos abren sus ojos a los quince días, los pendejos jamás (Puppies open their eyes in fifteen days, fools never do); Entra por aquí y sale por allá (In one ear and out the other); No hay peor sordo que el que no quiere oír (The deafest person is the one who doesn't want to hear). I heard this latter one a lot since I had a tendency not to listen. Then there were the days when I violated all the rules. That's when she told me, "Razones convencen a sabios y a necios los palos" (The wise are convinced by reason, fools by a paddle). If necessary, she would grab a belt or switch and say, "You just don't listen to reason."

Indeed, folk wisdom from Spain, as well as the teachings of the indigenous people of the Americas, emphasizes the importance of developing wisdom. Spanish philosophers such as Baltazar Gracián em-

phasized the importance of prudence in their writings. Latin American historians teach us the philosophy of the Aztec peoples, who also emphasized the importance of developing men of wisdom, men with heart. The Calcamec schools of the Aztec ruling class believed in strict discipline, the separation of the sexes until marriage, and intellectual development based on a knowledge of religion, mathematics, science, and literature in order to create good leaders capable of building a strong nation.

Ricardo Montalban
Actor

Prudence is similar to temperance, or use and abuse. To be prudent you must think before you act. And when you act, you do the best you can. In my mind, these virtues are all closely related.

My father was conservative. He taught me, as did my confessor Father Murray, that freedom is the right to do what you ought to do, not the right to do what you must do, which is suppression; nor the right to do what you please, for that leads to chaos.

Father Murray used to say, "Look, there is a bench in a park with a sign that says: wet paint. You are free to not sit down. If you sit down, you're going to ruin your suit. All right, let's say at a very busy intersection there is a signal, the red light, the green light. The red light comes on, you are free to stop. You have the freedom to stop. And when the light turns green, you are free to go. On this busy street, this intersection, take the signal away and see what happens. There is no freedom there."

I experienced this in France. It was amazing. I was driving a car on my way home from the studio during rush hour. I was approaching *Les Champs Elysées* when, suddenly, we came to a complete stop because there had been a power failure in all of Paris. A collision had occurred in the intersection, blocking the traffic.

And there we were, sitting, the French honking their horns, looking madder than they usually look, even when they're happily driving. Nobody moved. I thought to myself, "This is an intersection without freedom. Freedom is discipline. Without discipline, there is no freedom." It took about forty-five minutes before the lights came back on and a policeman was able to clear the intersection. When he moved the car that was blocking traffic, he whistled and made a signal to proceed. The signal in our street was red so we waited for the cross traffic to go. The light turned green for us and we were free to go, and the cross traffic stopped. Freedom without discipline just does not exist. I think what is happening in the United States is that we are not a disciplined people anymore. We don't obey the law. We have replaced freedom with license.

I believe children are our best teachers. They often challenge us in ways that are maddening so that we learn important lessons. Children also absorb the attitudes around them and often serve to remind us of the important things we must do.

Sandra Guzman
Editorial Director, Soloella.com

One day I was helping my son with his geometry homework and I started to cry. I was upset that my mother was ill and in the hospital. So, my little boy told me this story: "There was an island with all these monkeys, but there was one little monkey, and all the monkeys would exercise every day except the one little lazy monkey. They'd say,

'Come on, let's go run, we've got to get in shape.' So all the other monkeys would run, but the little monkey would say, 'No, go on, I'll go tomorrow.' So every morning all the monkeys would go run and exercise and the little monkey would always say, 'Tomorrow, I'll do it tomorrow.' Well, one day, the monkey catchers came, and guess who was caught? The lazy monkey." I wasn't really following him. He asked me, "Do you get the moral of the story?" I said, "No." "Well, the moral is don't leave for tomorrow what you should do today. I know that we cannot move to New Jersey to be near Grandma, and I know we can't visit her every day, but we don't spend enough time with her. We should visit her more often. Maybe we can go in the middle of the week, and on the weekend." I started to cry some more. He's so wise.

. . . My mother always wanted to build herself a little house in Puerto Rico. A few years ago she said she was ready to do it! She had saved $60,000, working as a seamstress. Imagine. Last December she finished it. How did she do it? She would not buy a Coke; she would drink water. She took lunch to work instead of spending money on food. She lived within her means. Any gift she got she put away. She put money away for twenty years, and she did it! We're going to inaugurate the house at Christmas.

———————

Sandra's memories stirred similar ones for me. I recall my mother talking about growing up during the Depression; they had to make their own soap, make their own clothes, make everything stretch, and last and last and last. They couldn't go out to buy things; they were living on a shoestring. It was a lesson in prudence. How different my life would have been if Mamá had lacked prudence!.

Children need parents to be wise. They need parents who know how to respond to their difficult questions and hurts with intelligence; parents who are able to see the larger picture. This story by television producer Nely Galán is a powerful example of a parent's wise counsel that is now being used as part of the national advertising campaign by a major Spanish language television network.

Nely Galán

President, Galán Entertainment

When I was growing up, my mother always told me little stories and sayings. One day when I was in the first grade, I came home from school crying, "Mami, *estos americanos,* they called me a spick because I am Latina."

She sat me down and she said, *"Tú le dices a esos americanitos que tienes lo mejor de los dos mundos porque tú eres latina y hablas español y tienes una cultura preciosa y puedes contar todos sus cuentos"* (You tell those little American kids that you have the best of both worlds because you are Latina and speak Spanish, and you have a precious culture and you know your history). *"Y tú eres completamente americana y hablas inglés y tienes todo tu futuro en América."* (You are completely American, you speak English, and you have a future here). *"Tú tienes lo mejor de los dos mundos"* (You have the best of both worlds). From then on, it never bothered me again.

I've kept that story with me all these years. Last year, we were trying to figure out the ad campaign for Telemundo. From my experience of launching channels in Latin America I know that in our medium, you touch people when you touch their pain. The pain of Latin Americans is that they have a love/hate relationship with the United States. They want to be like Americans, but they have a resentment toward them.

Here in the U.S., I realize that the pain of Latinos is that we are considered a minority, that we're thought of as not as "good" as our Anglo counterparts. This is our pain.

When the people at Telemundo asked me, "How come you don't feel disempowered as a Latina?" I told them it's because when I was in the first grade, my mother told me I have "the best of both worlds." I always thought that it was added value to be Latina and that speaking another language was a plus, not a negative. And they said, "Nely, that's it." So that's how the campaign *Lo mejor de los dos mundos*—the best of both worlds—came about.

Maria Elena Salinas
Anchor, Noticiero UNIVISIÓN

Icome from an extremely religious family. We were very poor, but I never heard my parents complain. They sent us to Catholic school during the week and took us to church on Sundays. My parents were very wise and believed it was important to provide us with a moral education, that doing the right and good thing builds strong character. They also taught us there is nothing you can't do in life.

At the age of fourteen I started working in the same factory as my mother, clipping threads off clothing, to help out the family. My mother taught me to save one-third of my earnings, spend one-third for my expenses and school, and to give one-third to her to help with the rent. I have always helped my mother financially from that time forward.

She was very prudent when it came to money. There was no choice; there was so little. In addition to teaching me the one-third rule, she also taught me to join a Christmas club where, starting on January 1, I put away money for the next Christmas, just as she did. In this way mother taught me to save for the bigger purchases I would make later in life.

She always figured out ways to entertain us with little money. We would take vacations in the family car. For the holidays my parents would do all the cooking themselves. To celebrate the *Día de los Reyes Magos,* the Day of the Three Kings, my mother, instead of buying the pastry at the bakery, would bake the pastry round herself then place the little toy representing baby Jesus inside the dough. She would give

It's All in the Frijoles

the person who found the little toy a small gift and treat him extra special for a week.

My parents believed in the importance of doing things together as a family. And they would look for entertaining things to do with the children on Sundays. Throughout the year my parents would take us for outings at the beach and picnics in the park, always packing sandwiches and sodas for us to take with us. We were able to do things because my mother would plan celebrations and prepare all the food at home. We enjoyed so many good times together as a family, without spending a lot of money.

Katherine Ortega
Former United States Treasurer

My dad had a *dicho* for every occasion. One favorite was, *"No hay mal que por bien no venga"* (There isn't bad that doesn't bring good). That helps me when things don't quite go my way. I always feel there is something better coming along. He also used to say, *"La esperanza es lo último que se pierde"* (Hope is the last thing that dies).

He used to tell us, *"Dios dijo, ayúdate que yo te ayudaré"* (God helps those that help themselves).

Tanto fue el canario al agua hasta que se ahogó (The canary kept returning to the water until it drowned). He didn't want us to be reckless or take foolish chances.

We also heard "Get that chip off your shoulder." Dad didn't want us to make excuses. He always told us, "You can do anything you set your mind to do. So don't make excuses because you're short, or because you're Hispanic, or anything else like that." When things didn't turn out well he used to say, "Don't cry over spilt milk." He taught us not to dwell on our mistakes or failures, but to channel our energy towards the future. Sometimes my parents had different attitudes about things. My mother would have a little piece of leftover fabric, and she did not want my sister to cut it because she might ruin it. But my father would say, *"Echando a perder se aprende"* (We learn from our mistakes).

His other favorites were *El que adelante no mira, atrás se queda.* Kind of like look before you leap! *Al que madruga, Dios le ayuda* (God helps the one who rises early) or, the early bird gets the worm. *Dime con quien andas y te diré quien eres* (Tell me who your friends are and I'll tell you who you are). *Nadie sabe que trae uno en el costal más que el que lo carga* (Only the one who carries his problems knows what they are and how big they might be). *Una mano lava la otra, y las dos lavan la cara* (One hand washes the other, and two wash the face).

Herman Gallegos
Philanthropist, Community Organizer

I remember listening to my grandmother's voice coming from the kitchen. We lived in small homes where the bedroom was always near the kitchen. You could smell the food being cooked, and you could hear my grandmother and my mother talking. My mother always seemed very happy when my grandmother was around. They would always talk about meaningful things and I learned from those conversations, which I can recall when I smell certain foods. I recall the dicho about *barriga llena, corazón contento,* full stomach, content heart. The smells from the kitchen—*frijoles, tortillas, chile*—were enough to make you think you'd died and gone to heaven, so I really understood the meaning of that *dicho.*

I don't consider myself famous, but people know me. That reminds me of a *dicho* that my dad liked to use. *Candil de la calle, os-*

curidad de tu casa, which is to say, you might light up the streets, but you also have to take care of your responsibilities at home.

Dad also used to say, *le da uno la mano y se toman el pie.* If you help somebody, you give them a hand, and they take your foot. I understood this *dicho* as I grew older and gained more experience.

When I began organizing workers, one of the iron rules I learned is to never do for people what they can do for themselves. You can't just give people what they need. You must teach them the skills they need to change things, to have more control over their lives, in order for them to become really empowered.

Back in the old CSO (Community Service Organization) days, we used to help people who would promise to come back and become members, yet we often never saw them again. One time, César Chavez had an office here in east L.A. We had worked together on a worker's compensation case for a gentleman for months and months and months. He promised when he got his money he would buy a membership.

One day he came into the office, waved an envelope at César and said, "Look, I got my check." He was happy. César asked, "What about your membership?" "Oh, yeah, no problem." We never saw him again, and we were livid. You give them a hand and they take your foot. The lesson is that not everyone is going to be grateful. There is truth to that old *dicho* my father used to tell me.

Polly Baca
Former State Legislator, Colorado

My mother gave each of her three daughters prudent advice. She wanted us to defer marriage until we had graduated from college and worked for a year. Her vision of success was for each of us to get a teaching degree, so we could stay home in the summertime with our children and work the rest of the year. She figured once we had a career, if something happened to the marriage, we'd still be okay.

She really wanted us to be independent and not have to depend on a man. It's funny, because, when two of us were in our late twenties and still unmarried, my father complained to my mother that he didn't think he was ever going to have grandchildren, that the message had been too effective. It appeared we just weren't going to get married at all. Despite this, they gave up some friends who insulted them by questioning why they wanted their daughters to go to college if they were just going to get married anyway.

My mother gave us good advice. All three of us graduated from college. My older sister is associate vice chancellor at the University of Colorado at Denver, and right now, I'm the regional administrator for the U.S. General Services Administration. My younger sister is a director of a division at the Small Business Administration in Washington, D.C. We're all making very good money and are successful. We've even given them the grandchildren they wanted!

Jesus Treviño
Director, Chicago Hope

There is a saying I often remember: *No por mucho madrugar amanece más temprano.* This means the sun is going to come out on its own good time, so no matter what you do you can't really hurry it along, even if you stay up all night. This is the other side of working hard, being skilled and being disciplined; no matter how hard you try to do something, you can't influence the end result. You can be the most hard-working person, but you can drive yourself nuts if you try to take on things that are out of your control.

Life is about patience and about learning to chill out when things are beyond your control. I have learned this in my own work. There are times when you are directing on the set and the makeup is going to take another half hour, or you've designed the shot and are under pressure to finish at a certain time because time is money. Or, you have a big crew, and the producer is on your back, saying "Hey, we want to be out of here at seven o'clock," and you know it's going to take another half an hour to get the scene lit properly. At a certain point you have to detach yourself and say, "You know what? Nothing I can do is going will make it go any faster." Once you learn that, it's kind of liberating, because you know it won't get done any faster if you sweat about it. This, I think, is a good lesson to have learned.

Another *dicho* that was instructive was, *El que con lobos anda, a aullar se enseña* (If you run around with wolves you're going to learn how to howl). That can be both negative and positive. It could mean that you are known by the company you keep, in this case, bad company (wolves). But another meaning is that if you are with good people, you are going to learn good things.

———————

"Hold your tongue" were words my mother often hurled at me when I was about to start a childish tirade, or say something hateful or rude. I have long since learned the wisdom of being prudent, and know it is important to take care in our use of words. After all, once they are unleashed, cruel, thoughtless words can never be retrieved, nor can the damage they cause be undone. There is much prudence in having "A Wise Mouth."

Baltazar Gracián (Spain)
(1601–1658)

A Wise Mouth

How provident Nature was when she made the mouth not only for speech but also for taste! We can examine our words before we pronounce them, and sometimes chew on them, and see if they have substance, and if we notice they will embitter others, sweeten them up a bit. We can find out how a "no" tastes, and how someone will digest it, and coat it with sugar. Let the tongue be used to eat, and for much else besides, so that we can sometimes keep silent. . . .

Antonia Novello, M.D.
Visiting Professor
Johns Hopkins University School of Hygiene & Public Health
Former United States Surgeon General

One thing I learned from my mother is that if you are angry and want to say something in words that might offend, first write it down. "Anger will hold for one day," she would say, "but there are ways that you can say something without offending. So write it down, reread it the next morning, then if it still expresses what you want to say, send it." She would always tell me, "Ink gets the message farther than a lemon pie." The other part of her message was "You must also learn to forgive."

The computer has been a big help in doing this. I can write whatever I want and wait until the next day. That way I can edit it and send

It's All in the Frijoles

it, or throw it away. At the very least this strategy gives me an opportunity to vent my anger constructively.

When I was inducted into the Women's Hall of Fame, I didn't think I should be on that wall. Before giving me the medal they said, "It's not so much how she ascended, but how she descended from her position that was noteworthy." One of the reporters from the *Washington Post* thought I should have gone out in a blaze. I told the reporter "I don't want you to confuse dignity with weakness." Lots of people will tell you how to go up, but very few people will tell you how to step down with dignity. There is a time to step down. When it was time to leave my post as United States Surgeon General, I was very aware that I should do it in such a way as to not hurt any opportunities for the women and Latinas coming up after me. When government officials have been involved in scandals that have come under investigation, I have been saddened beyond belief by its impact on all the people who looked up to them. For that reason, I was committed to not destroy all that I had done in those years in office.

It was hard to bite my tongue and come down with dignity, but it has allowed me to do everything I have done in the past few years. If I had spoken out, I would have been just one more angry woman who *metió la pata en la boca,* put her foot in her mouth, on her way down. It took great maturity in that moment to not do that in that moment. Many good things have happened to me because I stepped down but did not come down as a human being. I think part of that comes from what my Mami told me about God. She taught me "God is everywhere. He sees everything you do and knows everything we think." I am always aware of that. The most important things are those things Mami taught me. She was a strong role model. I'm not a humble bee. Not at all. You have to be aggressive. But I think it's important to combine the feminist with the feminine. You have to know when to use each. You have to be equal to men, but not the same as men. You have to know when to step down in such a way that those who come behind you benefit. That's the wisdom I learned from my mother.

Mamá loved to pass on stories that had a message about how to live with more intelligence. When you think about it, a lot of the trouble and misery we find ourselves in is due to poor choices that fly in the face of what we know to be better ones. Thinking back on her conse-jos, advice, I remember her saying you can win someone over more easily with honey than with vinegar. That dicho has always stayed with me, even through two social movements that stretched one's sense of justice, patience, and grace to the limit. The story that follows, Los tres consejos, The Three Counsels, is a story Mamá enjoyed tell-ing me.

The Three Counsels

There were once three men who lived in a small village too poor to sustain them and their families. Two of them had large families. The third had a wife and one son, who was studying to be a priest. Af-ter complaining about their plight in feeding their families, they de-cided to do something about it. They decided to leave their depleted farms and look for work in the city. So, they gathered up some provi-sions and set off to seek work.

They had traveled several miles when they met an old man who asked them where they were going. They explained their situation and told him they were looking for work and a better life.

"Well," said the old man, "suppose I make you an offer. Would you prefer to take a bagful of money, or three wise pieces of advice that would serve you in life?"

"We'll take the money, of course!" responded two of the men without hesitation.

The man with the one son thought awhile and finally said, "I be-lieve I will take the words of wisdom."

The old man gave the sacks full of money to the first two men, then he turned to the third and said: "Don't leave the well-traveled road for the path. Don't ask about what does not concern you. And don't jump to conclusions about what you hear, and act too hastily."

He then said goodbye to the three men and disappeared. The two who had chosen the money turned to the third man and exclaimed, "Oh, what a foolish thing you've done! What good is that advice going to do you?"

The man smiled. He knew the advice of the old ones was not to be taken lightly. "It may be that the three rules will serve me better than the gold will serve you. I will gladly part with my wealth, so I am going to give you the first piece of advice free: As you return home, don't leave the well-traveled toad for the path."

"That's silly! What do you know?" they answered and went off laughing. And do you know, to get home sooner they decided to take a path through the forest instead of the road. On the trail they were assaulted by thieves who killed them and took their gold.

The man who had been given the advice continued his journey until he came upon a very large ranch house where he asked for lodging for the night. The gentleman of the house invited him in and gave him supper. After he ate, the master of the house took the man to meet his wife. She was very frail and thin, just a skeleton, really. The man felt like asking why she was so thin, but he remembered the second proverb for guiding his life, and he remained quiet. The man then asked for work and was given a job.

Now, it so happened that his host was a rich man who owned a great deal of land and had many servants. In all his years, he had never met a man who minded his own business. When anyone saw his wife, they invariably asked why she was so thin. Then he would become angry and run them off. If his rage was aroused enough he would have them killed. He had purposefully instructed his servants to feed her only leftover food, bones, and pieces of dry tortillas. With such a scanty diet, of course she was thin! He had made a solemn vow not to better her condition until he met a person who would not ask why he kept his wife in such a state. On the other hand, if he met such a person, that person would acquire all of his wealth.

Now, the master thought, this last man I hired has not stuck his nose in my business; I will ask him why.

"Señor," he said to the worker, "why haven't you asked me why I keep my wife as I do?"

"Sir," the man replied, "a husband and wife's business is their own, and I do not ask about what does not concern me."

"Well spoken," the master answered. "At last I have found a man who doesn't meddle in the lives of others. From this day forward you shall be the owner of everything I have, and I will ask my wife's forgiveness and treat her well."

The rich man gave the worker everything he had, then he and his wife left for another city. The man, now that he was the new owner of a vast ranch, decided to return home to fetch his family. He made preparations, packed his pistol, and hurried back to his village.

Now, he had been gone a long time, so when he arrived he decided to surprise his wife. He went to the window, peeked in, and saw something that made his blood boil! A young priest had just embraced his wife! His first impulse was to reach for his pistol and kill his wife, but he remembered the third piece of advice and calmed himself. He listened closely and heard his wife speak to the young priest. Then he recognized this man as his son. The third maxim had served him well. He entered the house and greeted his family and they all wept with joy. The fortune which the rich man had left them was more than enough for the husband and wife to live well the rest of their lives.

Dichos

Razones convencen a sabios y a necios los palos.
The wise are convinced by reason, fools by a paddle.

Ignorar es más que errar.
Ignorance is worse than erring.

Cual el amo, tal el criado.
As master, as servant.
(Set good examples.)

Guarda los centavos que los pesos llegarán.
Save your pennies and the dollars will come.

Despacio pero seguro.
Slowly but surely.

No hay peor ciego que él que no quiere ver.
There is no blinder person than the one who does not want to see.

Antes de que acabes no te alabes.
You shouldn't begin to shout until the end is all worked out.
(Don't count your chickens before they hatch.)

Más vale un hecho que cien palabras.
A deed is worth more than a hundred words.

Al mal paso, dale prisa.
If it's disagreeable, do it fast.

No te sueltes de una rama sin tener otra agarrada.
Don't let go of one branch without grabbing another.

Lo que es de todos no es de nadie.
What is everybody's is nobody's.

Todo en la vida se puede recuperar, pero el tiempo nunca se recupera.
You can recover everything in life, but time.

En la tierra de los ciegos el tuerto es rey.
In a country of blind men the one-eyed man is king.

La mierda, entre más la escarban, más hiede.
The more you sift the shit the worse it smells.
(The more you look into a shady deal, the stinkier it gets.)

Más vale pan con amor que gallina con dolor.
Better bread with love than chicken with grief.

El que mucho abarca poco aprieta.
If you want everything you'll get nothing.

El que adelante no mira, atrás se queda.
Who doesn't look ahead remains behind.

Nadie sabe lo que tiene hasta lo ve perdido.
One doesn't appreciate what one has until it is lost.

No hay tiempo como el presente.
There is no time like the present.

It's All in the Frijoles

11

Justice
Justicia

El derecho nace del hecho.
Right is born from the act.

El tiempo es justiciero y vengador.
Time is just and avenging.

*Quien no oye más que una campana, no oye más que un
sonido.*
Who hears but one bell hears but one sound.
(There are two sides to any argument.)

*La justicia es el equilibrio entre la Moral y el Derecho y
tiene un Valor superior al de la ley.*
Justice is the balance between morality and right and has a
Valor superior to that of the law.

—a Mexican patriot

At times it appears we live in an unjust world. "Might makes right" seems to be the prevalent way of thinking. As a child I had difficulty understanding why bad things happened to good people. I remember Mamá explaining in one of our kitchen seminars on life that there is a higher justice at work. She told me that evil will meet its just reward, even if it does not happen in exactly the way or at the time we would like. El pecado trae consigo la penitencia, *the sin carries with it its own penance.* Haz mal, espera otro tal (*Do wrong, expect wrong in return*).

I remember her talking about the difference between the old Hammurabic code of an eye for an eye, a tooth for a tooth, and the New Testament teachings of Christ to turn the other cheek. "Revenge is not justice," she would say, "because it comes from hatred. Justice comes from God and God is love. Justice, like respect, produces harmony."

She also taught me that if there are things wrong in the world, it is not God's doing or punishment, but a result of man's bad choices. "If you see something that is wrong, or unjust, you must stand against it. Remember, mijita, God helps those who help themselves."

I learned from her that good will prevail, and that it is our responsibility to change ourselves into better, more loving individuals so we can help make the world a better and more just place. She taught me that transformation and the strength to stand against wrong comes

It's All in the Frijoles

from within. She always gave examples from the Bible, like the story in which Jesus challenges the money changers. She also liked to refer to Gandhi, the great spiritual leader of India, who was able to free India from English rule through his nonviolent struggle. She always said that the man who takes up arms against another becomes as much of a beast as his oppressor. "Violence only breeds further unjustice," she said.

Mamá would say that justice, like freedom, is a universal truth and gift which come from God. When we align our thinking and our actions with that truth, we bring justice to light. If the scales of justice are balanced, it will be because the people who make and enforce the laws are just and truthful, that is, virtuous. It's not that justice is blind. It is that we are.

Burt Corona
Activist, Founder, Hermandad Mexicana

I can pinpoint my interest in social justice and in human justice to my grandparents. My grandmother became a Protestant convert when she was about nine years old. Our family owned one of the richest mines in the world, La Mina Prieta in Parral, Chihuahua. They were supporters of the Mexican Revolution—followers of the Partido Liberal Mexicana, led by Flores Magón and his brothers. They recruited a revolutionary committee consisting of the pastors of the Congregationalist, Methodist, and Presbyterian churches in that area, along with the local intellectuals and middle-class people.

So involved were they with the politics of the time that, when the Revolution was initiated on November 20, 1910, my father and some of his friends were on the train that left Chihuahua to assault the first few towns up in the Sierras. He was wounded and had to come back to recuperate. That's how my mother first met my father. She and my grandmother were strong supporters of the Revolution. My grand-mother had graduated from the first school in Chihuahua, Mexico, that trained women as doctors. She was one of five U.S. doctors who helped those wounded during the incident when my father, who was a colonel in Pancho Villa's army, and his troops attempted to capture the last train out in Chihuahua in 1911. That was the train carrying all the foreigners, the middle class, and the rich to the United States.

My mother and my father met through that incident. He went off to fight in many other battles during the Revolution, and was wounded several times. Each time my grandmother would go get him, bring him back to the border, treat him, and put him back in good shape. My parents were married in 1916. Pancho Villa was the best man.

When the Villa forces were defeated in 1917, my parents moved to El Paso. My father then went back to fight with the Villa forces in Mexico. As Villa retreated and gave up arms, my father joined the new Mexican Army. By trade he was an engineer, with expertise in lumber-ing. He established lumber and sawmills in Southern Mexico. He was killed there in an ambush by soldiers who were Carranzistas and did not like Pancho Villa. They were afraid my father and others from Chihuahua were plotting to take up arms again. I grew up hearing these stories as a youngster in El Paso, surrounded by other families who shared those ideals and Revolutionary experiences. Many were veterans of the Revolution. Many were middle-class doctors, engi-neers, and lawyers. What held all of the families together was that they wanted social justice. They opposed the exploitation of the Indians and the poor. They were not Marxists. They were not Communists. They were people who stood up for social justice, people who felt that the poor, the Indians, were not getting a fair shake.

With this background, it is not surprising that, while I was at USC in the mid-1930s, I got involved in a movement in the Protestant churches called the Mexican-American Youth Conference. They were trying to organize Protestant churches in East Los Angeles to tackle so-cial problems, such as improving slum housing. Then, as a student, I

It's All in the Frijoles

got very involved in the Longshoremen's Union during the 100-day strike up and down the Pacific Coast. The union shut down the ports all the way from San Diego to Alaska. I was elected president of the local in 1939 and 1940. I stayed with the union until I volunteered to go into the service in 1941, right after Pearl Harbor.

All of this activism, of course, had its roots in the kind of life we had among our community of friends who were involved in social justice. From them, I learned that you could accomplish those goals with commitment and organization. It's been that way ever since.

Edward R. Roybal
Former Member of the U.S. Congress

I had been recently elected to the Los Angeles City Council while still working as a social worker, when I heard that a real-estate office in East Los Angeles was not selling homes to Mexicans. It was in 1949, right after the war. The GI's, who were of Mexican descent or who were black, were mad about the fact that they were not able to get housing after serving in the military.

The Monday after I took office, I went to the real-estate office. It was located right on the corner of Beverly and Atlantic in east Los Angeles, a beautiful, white building with a very big sign that said, "GI Homes For Sale." Well, I went and picked out the house I wanted. And I wrote a check for $250 before I got there. I didn't even have it in the bank, but I couldn't buy the house anyway, or live in it, because it was out of my district. I just wanted to test them. I gave them my discharge papers and all the paperwork. The realtor looked at them and said, "Everything's in order, but I'm very sorry. My orders are not to sell to Mexicans." I didn't say anything. I took my business card out of my wallet and gave it to him. I walked out of the office with my papers and sat in my car right in front of his building—a city car, incidentally. He showed up on the driver's side before I started up the engine. I rolled the window down.

He said, "I can sell it to you because you're different." I thanked him very much and left. Then I went to the city council and I told them what happened. Newspaper headlines went out all over the country: "GI Refused Housing." Three days later, we put a picket line around the realtor's office on a twenty-four-hour basis.

The realtor called and wanted to talk to me. I agreed to go back to his office. With me was Fred Ross, who was the director of the CSO (Community Service Organization). Accompanying Fred Ross was a young man, very bright, who was training with us. His name was César Chavez. We came out of that meeting able to say that the realtor would sell a home to anyone who had an honorable discharge. That's what the sign said, and that's all we were asking for.

Where did I learn the skills to pull this off? My mother. She taught us fortitude, justice, courage, and faith through her example. I learned at home to do what I think is right.

Antonia Hernandez

President and General Counsel, Mexican-American Legal Defense and Education Fund (MALDEF)

My dad was born in Texas in 1926, but his family was deported to Mexico in the 1930s. He grew up there, where he met and married my mother. When he decided to bring us to the states, we came in through El Paso, Texas, in 1956. This was a time when there were signs stating "no dogs or Mexicans allowed." My father was a very bright man, always discussing history and labor issues. He had been a labor organizer in Mexico, organizing *campesinos,* farmworkers. He read the Spanish daily papers, voted, and always discussed issues and

It's All in the Frijoles

politics. Papi explained prejudice to us. He said he wanted more opportunities for us, but because the leaders of Mexico were corrupt, there were more opportunities here in the U.S.

He told us we could make a difference, notwithstanding the fact that there was a lot of discrimination. He said, "I want you to always be proud of who you are. It's not other people who determine who you are. Who you are is determined by how you live your life. So be proud of being a Mexican. Be proud of your actions."

We were taught to deal with whatever was before us. We knew we had to stand up for what was right, *tus derechos humanos,* your human rights. "You kneel to no one, you bow to no one. You are respectful, always, but you stand up for your rights," my father told us.

My father never lost his concern for the underdog. Back in the turbulent sixties, it was my father who drove me to demonstrations. When *Los Angeles Times* reporter Ruben Salazar was killed during the Chicano moratorium, there was a demonstration at St. Alfonso's Church on Atlantic Boulevard. My father drove me there.

When I moved out of the projects and lived downtown, I picketed the Safeway market to support César Chavez and the United Farmworkers grape boycott. My dad and mom always approved of my political participation and our fight for justice.

Growing up, I never knew a lawyer, but I knew that the law was the vehicle both for change and for improving the quality of life. I decided to go to law school to be a public-interest lawyer to help Latinos. I was very clear that I was going to change the laws. My father didn't think much of the lawyers in Mexico so he asked me, *"Mija, ¿quiere ser como esos ladrones?"* (Do you want to be one of those thieves?) "Oh, no, Papi. In this country there are good lawyers!"

His sage counsel, "Nobody has control of your destiny but you," has also served me well. "They can influence you, *ojo chícharo, mija,* they can always put something in the way, but you can overcome it."

Jesus Treviño

Director, Documentarian

My sense of justice came from both my parents and my experiences as a young man. Certainly, you learned from the teachings of Jesus to love thy fellow man in the Catholic Church. When I was growing up, however, I was also very aware of the Civil Rights movement. I read constantly. One of the reasons I did not get into gangs was because I could read. I spent all my time in the library. At first I read fantasy and science fiction, which I still read today. Then I became interested in politics, then in civil rights. During my high school years, I was absorbed in the Civil Rights movement and became a part of it. When the Chicano movement was initiated, I kind of kicked myself and thought, "Hey, you've been wanting to help the black people. Why don't you help your own people?" That was really an awakening for me.

When the *Movimiento* came, I saw unjustice up close. I witnessed two or three instances of severe police brutality as a documentarian. I covered the Salazar inquest [after the death of *Los Angeles Times* reporter Ruben Salazar] and saw what a whitewash that was. I was at the Chicano moratorium in east Los Angeles on August 29, 1970. I interviewed Reyes Tijerina, founder of La Raza Unida party. As a college student, my first meeting with César Chavez, the founder of the United Farm Workers, had a profound impact on me because I saw what was going on in Delano. When I met him, I thought, "Here's someone to follow. Here's someone I can pattern my life after."

All these elements converged, the sense of justice and the sense of having experienced injustice personally. When people talked about the oppression of Chicanos, I knew what they meant. My problem was that I grew up assuming that injustice was the normal course of events. When I was in elementary school and the white kids always got the opportunity that I, as a Mexicano, never did, I thought that was the order of the universe.

Once, when I was in the fifth or sixth grade, the teacher selected five or six Anglo kids in Lincoln Heights to be members of the Science Club. I wanted to join. I was fascinated by science, but she never picked me. One day they were doing an experiment and she called me. I thought "This is great, I am finally going to get my chance to join with the others in the Science Club."

Instead, she asked me to thread a needle. I guess she figured I had good eyes. After I threaded the needle, she said, "You can go back to your chair now." It was devastating for me, because I saw what I wanted right in front of me, yet I was being sent back to my seat.

Later, when I was in high school, I was awarded a four year scholarship to Occidental College. Before that my high school guidance counselor had told me I should think about attending a community college because I couldn't survive in a four year college. There was a tracking system then, and he was recommending I attend L.A. Trade Technical College, a vocational training school.

It's all our stories—my story is only one of millions—that have shaped my sense of justice. I've talked to many other Latinos who experienced similar things. We were really poor when I was a kid. We would eat bean *burritos* every day. I remember waiting until Friday, when my dad got his paycheck, so that we could have some meat. That was a big deal. We could also have a 7-Up, and that, too, was a big deal. That was my childhood. So, when people talked about justice and about the poverty of the *campesino,* I knew what it was like. I grew up with it.

When I witnessed injustice as a documentarian, I reflected back on my childhood, and reflected on the life I lived as a child, I knew people shouldn't have to live that way. That's why injustice has that visceral quality for me, and why I have sought to point it out and correct it.

Dionicio Morales

Life in Two Cultures

In Steinbeck's books, I began to discover the historical roots of our own Mexican America life. They took place in our same locale, only in an earlier period of California history. I was transported by his descriptions of our people. He inspired me to seek the broader picture.

No public school class had ever taught me that California had been a state under a Mexican governor—a state with a rich spiritual and temporal culture as well as a prosperous agricultural economy. All of this, of course, was before the coming of the "Pioneers" and gold-seekers from the East.

I read other authors and became enthralled by the political courage and foresight of the Mexican *Californio* leadership. I imagined myself sitting as a spectator in Colton Hall in Monterey, witnessing the proceedings of the Constitutional Convention of 1849. I envisioned a delegation of eight distinguished *Californios,* who had been prominent under the Mexican regime, as they created history These brave men stood their ground and spoke their minds, both in English and Spanish, hoping to give our state a good start in its new life. We have only to look around us to see the names of these Mexican American constitutional fathers. They live in the names of the boulevards and cities of modern California.

There was José Antonio Carrillo, who had signed Mexico's first constitution, which abolished slavery four decades before Abraham Lincoln signed the Emancipation Proclamation. There were General Mariana Vallejo, Pablo de la Guerra, and José Covarrubias of Santa Barbara; Miguel de Pedrorena, whom Commodore Stockton had appointed Customs Collector at San Diego; Antonio Pico, the popular mayor of San Jose; Jacinto Rodríguez, a militiaman from Monterey and San Francisco; wealthy landowner and rancher Manuel Domínguez of Los Angeles (described both as a dark-complexioned mestizo and as the "Indian member" of the Convention). What a preview of things to come! They fought for the rights of all California inhabitants to become citizens, regardless of race, a concept not accepted in the rest of the United States.

The presence of Domínguez among the drafters of the state constitution had a considerable impact on the convention, particularly when it came time to debate an Anglo delegate's proposition that "voting in California should be limited to white males only." Had I been a voting member of that delegation, as dark-complexioned as I am, I would probably have felt like an outcast. Santa Barbara's delegate, Pablo de la Guerra, led the argument against the "white males only" policy. He pointed out that the Treaty of Guadalupe Hidalgo, which ended the war with Mexico [in 1848], had guaranteed the former Mexican citizens American citizenship and the right to vote under the new regime without any color discrimination. The "white only" proposition, of course, opposed the dark-complexioned delegate Dominguez's right to sign the very constitution he was helping to draft.

What a lesson for us in the twentieth century! The racists of our own day should know that while bias in California has existed from the very beginning, it was also vigorously opposed from the beginning by Mexican leaders!

Octavio Paz, Mexico's great man of letters and Nobel Laureate, recalls childhood stories in his poem "Interruptions from the West." The son of a lawyer whose ancestors were partly Indian, and a woman whose parents had emigrated from Spain, Paz's paternal grandfather was a journalist and novelist who fought with the patriot Benito Juárez against the French occupation of Mexico in the 1860s. His father was a veteran of the Mexican Revolution of 1910 who went into exile to represent the peasant guerrilla leader Emiliano Zapata in the United States.

Sitting around the dining table, young Octavio listened to his elders talk about the war against the French and the revolution, a scene he captures here.

Octavio Paz (Mexico)

(1914–1998)

Philosopher, Poet, Diplomat

Interruptions from the West

My grandfather, taking his
coffee,
would talk to me about Juárez
and Porfirio,
the Zouaves and the Silver
Band.
And the tablecloth smelled of
gunpowder.

My father, taking his drink,
would talk to me about Zapata
and Villa,
Soto y Gama and the brothers
Flores Magón.
And the tablecloth smelled of gunpowder.

I kept quiet:
who was there for me to talk about?

Translated by Charles Tomlinson.

Pablo Neruda is one of the most influential poets of Latin America and perhaps the best-known. He began writing poetry while in elementary school, although his father forbade him to do so. He had a career as a diplomat, serving in Spain, Mexico, and France. Neruda

It's All in the Frijoles

won the Nobel Prize in Literature in 1971 while he was living in Paris and serving as the Chilean ambassador to France.

Pablo Neruda (Chile)
(1904–1973)

America, I Do Not Call Your Name Without Hope

America, I do not call your name without hope,
When I hold the sword against the heart,
when I live with the faulty roof in the soul,
when one of your new days
pierces me coming through the windows,
I am and I stand in the light that produces me,
I live in the darkness which makes me what I am,
I sleep and awake in your fundamental sunrise:
as mild as the grapes, and as terrible,
carrier of sugar and the whip,
soaked in the sperm of your species,
nursed on the blood of your inheritance.

Translated by Robert Bly.

Uncle Rabbit and Uncle Tiger
A Folktale from Nicaragua

Tiger was making his way through the forest one windy day when, crack! A large branch broke loose from a tree and pinned him to the ground. He was there for quite a while, his body bruised and aching, until Uncle Bull came along.

"Tío Bull, please help me!" he shouted. "I am trapped here, and in pain."

"No, Tío Tiger, you will eat me, I know you will."

Tiger became very agitated and began to cry. "Tío, I am in pain. I will die here if you don't help me. Please get this branch off me! I promise I will not eat you."

Tío Bull was a gentle soul with a good heart. He could not bear to hear Tío Tiger crying. "All right, Tío," he said. "Lie still while I get rid of this branch." Delicately he hooked his horns beneath the branch and tossed it away.

Well, as soon as Tiger was free he promptly forgot his promise. All he knew was that Tío Bull was very plump and looked delicious. He immediately pounced on Tío Bull and sank his teeth into his side. Of course, Tío Bull was very upset by this.

"Tío Tiger, you promised you would not eat me if I rescued you. I saved your life."

"But I am very hungry," replied Tío Tiger. He thought for a moment. "Okay, there is one condition under which I will not eat you."

"And what is that?"

"We will ask whomever we come across for their opinion on this matter. We will see whose opinion makes the most sense."

Tío Bull, knowing he had no choice, agreed.

Tío Tiger and Tío Bull walked through the forest, looking for someone to talk to. Soon Tío Ox came by. He was limping and could barely see.

"Tío Ox," asked Tío Tiger, "How does one repay a good deed?"

"With a bad deed, Tío Tiger. Look at me. I worked for twenty years for my master, never complaining. When I grew old and lame, he threw me out to die."

"See?" said Tiger to Bull. "That's one who agrees with me."

As they walked further into the forest, they came upon an old horse, swaybacked and limping.

"Tío Horse," asked Tiger, "How does one repay a good deed?"

It's All in the Frijoles

"With a bad deed, Tío Tiger," responded the horse, head down.

"How can you say this is true?" asked Tío Bull anxiously.

"Look at me!" said Horse. "I served my master well. I plowed his fields. I carried his children. And every night I waited outside a bar while he drank until he fell out the door. Every night I carried him home, and every morning I worked his fields. The years passed, and I grew too feeble to work. He let me loose to die."

"That's two for me," said Tiger. Bull thought, one more and I am Tiger's dinner.

Just then, Uncle Rabbit leaped into the path.

"Tío Rabbit," called Tío Tiger. "How does one repay a good deed?"

"It depends on the kind of good deed one is repaying," responded Rabbit.

"What do you mean?" asked Tiger

"What kind of good deed we are talking about?" said Rabbit.

"Well," said Bull, "I found Tío Tiger trapped under a branch in the woods. He was in pain, and could not move. I felt sorry for him. When he asked me for help, I moved the branch with my horns. As soon as he was free, he tried to eat me. We are asking for opinions to see if a bad deed repays a good deed. Please, tell us how Tiger should repay me."

"I don't understand," said Rabbit. Tiger repeated the story again.

"I still don't understand," said Rabbit. "Could you show me exactly what the situation was so I can decide?"

So Tiger, Bull, and Rabbit journeyed to the place where Tiger had been trapped. Rabbit looked at the branch.

"I still don't see how it could have happened," said he. "Could you please show me how you were under the branch?"

Obligingly, Bull lifted the branch while Tiger slid under it.

"Drop the branch!" shouted Rabbit. Bull dropped the branch, and once again Tiger was trapped.

"Leave him there," said Rabbit to Bull. "And be careful who you help from now on."

Rabbit and Bull went their separate ways. And Tiger remained, trapped as before, roaring with anger and frustration.

César Chávez
(1927–1993)
Founder, United Farm Workers

You must understand—I must make you understand—that our membership and the hopes and inspirations of the hundreds of thousands of the poor and dispossessed that have been raised on our account are above all, human beings, no better, no worse, than any other cross section of human society; we are not saints because we are poor but by the same measure neither are we immoral. We are men and women who have suffered and endured much and not only because of our abject poverty but because we have been kept poor. The colors of our skins, the languages of our cultural and native origins, the lack of formal education, the exclusion from the democratic process, the numbers of our slain in recent war—all these burdens generation after generation have sought to demoralize us, to break our human spirit. But God knows that we are men.

—from a letter to E. L. Barr, Jr., president of the California Grape and Tree Fruit League

Joan Baez
Musician, Activist

I have been true to the principles of nonviolence, developing a stronger and stronger aversion to the ideologies of both the far right and the far left and a deeper sense of rage and sorrow over the suffering they continue to produce all over the world.

Cruz Reynoso
Former Justice of the California Supreme Court
Vice-Chair, U.S. Commission on Civil Rights

My parents taught me that all of us are children of God, that we all belong to the same family, and so I grew up with a strong notion of fairness. My father was a farmworker in Orange County. During the summers the family used to travel north to the Central Valley of California to pick crops. Once, when I was a little boy, Dad had trouble getting the money due him after the family worked in the Fresno area. I recall hearing my parents comment on that unfairness. There were tremendous abuses of farmworkers in the fields. Those abuses were contrary to our religious teachings, which told us that all human beings should be treated equally, and my family's belief that society should be fair.

I felt compelled to do something about the injustices around me. It did not seem right that Mexican-American workers so often were not paid a fair wage for their hard work; that poor neighborhoods lacked sidewalks, curbs, and parks where children could play; that our rural communities were not served by the U.S. Postal Service.

As a young man, I learned the value of confrontational justice, of standing up against situations and people that thwarted the democratic ideals I learned at home and in school. I also learned the benefit of joining forces with others to accomplish common goals.

≈>|<≈

Soledad O'Brien
NBC Weekend News *Anchor, and* MSNBC Morning Blend *Anchor*

My mother has a tremendous sense of justice and she has never looked down on anyone. She worked as a Spanish teacher in my high school in Smithtown, Long Island, New York. One day when I was in college, I went to pick her up after work. My high school was primarily white. Not only was she one of the few Hispanics in the school, she was also one of a few black people in the school. We were walking through the hallways and came across a young black boy who had been caught running through the hallways.

This boy was surrounded by the principal and the two assistant principals. He'd broken a rule, but he was clearly being given an additional message: that he did not belong. He was terrified, utterly terrified. My mother and I were on our way out but she just stopped. The principal said, "Oh, Mrs. O'Brien, everything's under control. Don't you worry. You can go home now." And she said, "That's okay. I'm just gonna stand here for a little bit."

Well, at the sight of another person of color, this kid looked thrilled. He just couldn't believe his luck because, for a moment, he felt that he wasn't quite so alone in the world. I remember him looking at my mother and my mother looking back at him in an unspoken agreement: "I'm going to stick it out with you until we know what's going on. I'm not going to let you be bullied by these people who are definitely trying to intimidate you."

Eventually the administrators got embarrassed because it was

It's All in the Frijoles

becoming a bigger deal than they had planned, just by my mother saying nothing. She was simply a presence, a five-foot-two-inch presence amid these tall men. Eventually, they let go of the back of the boy's shirt collar and told him, "All right, don't run in the hallways," or something like that, and let him go.

I remember being so proud of my mother. She was great. She always stood up for underdogs. She doesn't necessarily make a scene, but she will stand there and give tacit support to people, sometimes even at her own peril. To do that when those people were her bosses would not make them tremendous fans of hers, but she didn't care.

It was never about personal advancement. It was always about justice, a sense of fair play, and a sense of being there for people who really didn't have a voice. One of the reasons I became a journalist and a writer was because, when I worked in California, I primarily worked in minority communities, and I wanted to give a voice to people who are consistently not heard. This was something I learned from my mother.

Dichos

Voz del pueblo, sube al cielo.
Clamor del pueblo sube al cielo.
The outcry of a people rises to heaven.

Voz del pueblo, voz del cielo.
Voice of the people, voice of heaven.

No debes juzgar sin antes verte juzgado.
Judge yourself before you judge others.

Por un borrego no se juzga la manada.
Don't judge the whole flock by a single sheep.

De juez de poca conciencia no esperes justa sentencia.
From a judge with little conscience, don't expect a just sentence.

Ni absuelvas ni condenes, si cabal noticia no tienes.
Neither absolve nor reprimand, unless you have the facts in hand.

Justicia sin dignidad no es justicia sino crueldad.
Justice that is not benign is not justice but cruelty.

El que hizo la ley, hizo la trampa.
Whoever made the law made the trap.

It's All in the Frijoles

12

Fortitude
Fortaleza

Donde hay voluntad, hay modo.
Where there is a will there is a way.

There is no substitute for persistence. It overrides
everything.
                                    —ANDY GARCÍA, actor

Roma no se construyó en un día.
Rome wasn't built in a day.
                                    —CERVANTES, *Don Quixote*

La constancia hace milagros.
Consistency creates miracles.

Action is the antidote to despair.
—JOAN BAEZ

Si, se puede.
Yes, you can.

—CÉSAR CHAVEZ, President, UFW

D ios, dame paciencia con esta niña" *(God, give me patience with this girl). How often I heard Mamá repeat this call for help! I can remember her uttering these words whenever I would ask too many challenging questions, or begin to provoke her with irksome behavior, as only children can do. Her prayers must have been heard because my mother was a paragon of moral strength and endurance—fortitude. She literally exuded patience, calmness, and stability. She was my rock and anchor.*

Everything about her, including her persistent courage in trying circumstances and her calmness, came from this virtue. She taught me never to put off until tomorrow what you could do today, lo que se ha de hacer tarde que se haga temprano. Even the way she made her frijoles *demonstrated patience, although, until now, I never looked at it in this way. Yes, while making her* frijoles de la olla, *spreading out the beans on a tray and washing them while carefully picking out the grit and shriveled, imperfect beans with such care, Mamá was exercising* fortaleza, fortitude. Strength and tenacity were her middle name. And, through all the travails of her often painful and difficult life, she exibited a courage and strength of character in the midst of pain, affliction, and hardship. It is a characteristic we often see manifested in the best of our women, la fortaleza.

As I think about the many lessons of life she gave to me in her sunlit kitchen, I realize that the exercise of patience, of taking care in the accomplishment of a task, is part of learning how to be a good cook. It is the proper paring of the apples or pumpkins for empanadas, the seemingly endless beating of the egg whites to peaked perfection for meringue or chiles rellenos, the scraping of the chiles to make the sauce for enchiladas or tamales—all these acts of preparation are a metaphor for living successfully. Her words "Con paciencia se gana lo imposible" (With patience you can win the impossible), when I impatiently looked into the pot, or into the oven, still ring in my ears.

Good food, like a good life, doesn't just happen. It takes planning (Do I have a good recipe?), preparation (the right ingredients?), and mindfulness (Am I in a loving mood, so that the meal is delicious?).

Of course, we can improvise at times with great success, but first we must know the basic rules, the recipes of the kitchen and for living. How often do we try to replicate a wonderful recipe and forget a key ingredient, or burn the meal? A bad bean can spoil the pot, Mamá always said. How true this is in life.

Mamá also looked to God for nourishment and, indeed, he was the source of her strength. Her fortitude came from her faith. I can remember her teaching me the Twenty-Third Psalm to remember whenever the going was rough, or when I was afraid. These words are among the first that come to my mind today whenever I face a difficult challenge.

Mamá's determination was also an important part of the equation. As the Spanish mystic Saint Teresa de Avila said, "I decided . . . it is tremendously important to begin with great determination . . . The soul that begins with determination has already traveled a great part of the way. . . ."

Perfection is not easy to achieve, but we must seek to do and be our best. Even in the simplest of tasks, in the most ordinary daily activities we can develop ourselves, our inner strength and our potential. We have a model for doing things well, for doing our best, for rooting out all the "little negative traits and habits," as my mother used to say, in the making of the frijoles.

One of the common themes among the many remarkable people whom I interviewed was how the fortitude of a parent, grandparent, or great-grandparent influenced their lives. It was often the mother or grandmother who was the source of stability and love for the entire family. In that stoicism and strength amidst adversity, turmoil, and even violence, we learn a powerful lesson: No matter what befalls us, we can overcome and perhaps transcend the situation. Without this sense of the ability to overcome, we are like flotsam in the waves, or a ship without a captain. La fortaleza gives us power.

Ten paciencia, mijita, ten paciencia. *Have patience, my little daughter, have patience.* A aquél que esperar puede, todo a su tiempo y voluntad le viene. *Everything willingly comes to one who waits. This was Mamá's message to me. It is a life lesson I am still trying to master. Patience. Patience and determination. I can still hear Mamá saying these words:* El hombre propone, Dios dispone. *Man proposes, God disposes. Knowing this gives us strength for the journey.*

Jesus Treviño
Director, Activist

I think fortitude is part of our culture. It's been called a *macho* code, but I don't think it's just about males. I think it's about people. Fortitude emerges when something happens and the person has the attitude *me encabran,* I'm going to do it anyway, damn it. It's resilience in the face of adversity. I know I got this trait from my mother.

My mother came from Juárez, Mexico, when she was fifteen to work in the Woolworth's in El Paso, knowing barely any English. When she was asked if she knew the language, she lied and said, "Yes, I do." Then she proceeded to memorize the English words for items in the store, getting help from the Mexican-American girls who worked there. They taught her how to speak enough English so she could be a sales clerk.

She helped to support her family across the border and worked all her life as did my father. They loved their kids and provided for us.

Fortitide is just saying, "We have to do this." It's reinforced by our culture, but sometimes it's also reinforced by the fact you have no other options; when you are down, dirty, and poor, and the bill collectors are coming, and you've got to figure out what to do to survive.

When I was growing up, I had this tremendous sense of poverty and making do and always being the outsider, especially when I got into junior high and high school. I was the kid who would go on some school outing and only have a shirt, never had a jacket or sweater. I was always the needy kid. It gets to you after a while. As a result, I was determined to go to college, and break the cycle.

My parents may have been poor and may not have had opportunities for economic and historical reasons, but I vowed that would not happen to me. I decided to do whatever it took to escape poverty, even if I had to put forth two or three times more effort than the Anglo kid next to me. I think my determination came from seeing this fortitude in my mother, seeing how she struggled all of her life, and seeing how she made it.

———————

Fortitude comes from faith. I know this was the case for Mamá. In talking to those I interviewed this belief was reinforced.

Gloria Santiago
Author

Our parents always made us think that we were not poor, that the reason we didn't have all those material things was because we

It's All in the Frijoles

didn't need them. We were told if we would work hard, we would get them, but we did not rely on material goods for our happiness. Happiness came from relying on ourselves, knowing who we were, and loving one another. Whenever I think about my family, I think about how strong they were. When I'm in trouble, I go back to those thoughts—they keep me going.

One can only hope for the kind of determination exhibited by this most famous, yet humble, of all nuns. Born into a wealthy family, exhibiting great beauty and charm, Saint Teresa de Avila made the choice early to make God her life. She joined the Carmelite Order of nuns, one of the most demanding orders, and became an exemplary human being, not only in her ministry, but through her tremendous acts of love, caridad. *Her story is one of tremendous inspiration, whatever path we choose to take.*

Saint Teresa de Avila (Spain)
(1515–1582)

All is nothing. The world is vanity, life is short. I decided to force myself to enter the convent. . . . [*Determinación, decisión,* was a word she used frequently.] I decided . . . it is tremendously important to begin with great determination. . . . The soul that begins with determination has already traveled a great part of the way. . . .

During the 1911 agrarian revolution in Mexico, Emiliano Zapata and his contemporaries wrote the Plan of Ayala, which asked for small farmers to get the "justice they deserve as to lands" and requested that that justice be codified in a national agrarian law. Zapata was single-

*minded in his approach, "I am resolved to struggle against everything
and everybody," he wrote to a friend. Today, Article 27 of Mexico's
revolutionary constitution of 1917 is the foundation, or more accurately, the unfulfilled idea, for agrarian reform. This key article directly resulted from peasant movements such as the one organized by
Emiliano Zapata.*

Emiliano Zapata (Mexico)
(1879–1919)
Leader of the Mexican Revolution

Revolutions will come and revolutions will go, but I will continue
with mine.

Alma Martinez
Actor

Both of my parents were very tenacious people. My mother was
never a woman to sit still. She never gave up. She went to beauty
school after she was married, and finished at the top of her class. The
owner of the school offered my mom her first job, but it was not an
easy time. She had little support from my dad, she spoke no English,
and she had to take the bus to and from class while still carrying out
her responsibilities at home. Then she got pregnant, and dropped out
to have my brother Bobby. She returned to school after three or four
months. Because she spoke no English, she was harassed by a couple
of other students. One of the men in the class came on to her sexually

It's All in the Frijoles

and, as she did not understand what he was saying, she would smile benignly. One of the women who befriended her heard the fellow one day. She grabbed him, shook him, and told him to leave my mom alone. She figured mom was a hard-working woman with enough challenges to overcome without some jerk hassling her.

Years later, I realized just how difficult attending beauty school was for my mom. When I looked at her textbook, I found that she had translated the entire cosmetology textbook. She wrote the Spanish words in tiny script in the margins of the pages. In this way, she created her own roadmap.

Later, when she wanted to own her own shop, she noticed lots of older women started coming to the shop where she worked. She asked them where they used to go. When she found out that the owner of the Powder Puff Salon (where these new clients were from) was too old to keep working, she visited the woman and ended up taking over her business. She also cared for the former owner. My father did not like her working away from home, so he built her a salon in the back of the house so she could work at home. Eventually, he opposed that as well. Mom's ambition sometimes caused conflicts between my parents. Dad was not always supportive of what my mother wanted to do. Despite his disapproval, she kept going. She did whatever she needed to do. She never let it get her down. She had a great disposition and always kept a positive attitude. She was careful not to get us involved in their conflicts.

From my mother I've learned to be a mediator, to be resourceful, and to resolve everything in a calm manner. When things get difficult, I think about my mother, and how she was able to weather any storm. Now, I can keep going in any crisis and do whatever needs to be done, no matter what is going on.

My dad, too, was very resourceful. And he was meticulous about any work or project he undertook. He worked on the assembly line at General Motors for thirty years. When he decided to remodel and enlarge our home, he had to learn the construction, plumbing, and electrical skills needed to complete the project.

Since he had only a slight knowledge of construction and spoke only Spanish, he would take us to the library, describe the type of book he needed on plumbing or electricity, and ask us to find it for him. He always wanted books with lots of pictures to help him learn to do specific things, like installing electrical wiring.

He used the pictures to guide him and help him figure out how to do the next step. He always remained in the car outside the library. We would go in and out, bringing him books for his approval. When he finally selected a book, we would read it in English, translate it, and give him the information in Spanish. That's how he learned to do everything. He would also ask neighbors and friends to teach him certain things. In turn, he would help neighbors with their home-improvement projects. He believed in reciprocity. He would never take anything without giving back.

Dad needed a vehicle to haul all the lumber and other materials he needed for the remodeling project he wanted to complete on our home. He spent nearly a year rebuilding an old '52 Chevy truck before he started. Imagine, working on a truck for all that time in order to accomplish another bigger project down the line.

He worked on our house for five to seven years, turning it from a two-bedroom, one-bath house into a three-bedroom, two-bath home. He added a new kitchen, den, patio, and lighted outdoor trellis. He tore down walls. He did the electrical and plumbing work himself. When he was finished, he was very proud, because he had created a very nice home for his family with his own hands, despite his limited financial means.

From him, I learned that we can learn and do anything we set our minds to, if we make the effort. As a result, I know to tackle the task at hand and keep working at it until it is completed. I've done this with my acting career, moving out from the Teatro Campesino to regional theater, to the Mark Taper Forum with *Zoot Suit,* and on to feature films, television, and commercials.

I've used the same formula with my master's degree, which I received from the University of Southern California. It took ten years. I'm doing it again now that I am at Stanford University, working on my Ph.D. in theater and drama. It's a dream come true. I am making it

It's All in the Frijoles

possible by doing what my parents did to realize their dreams, by taking one step at a time.

Suzanna Guzmán
Mezzo-Soprano

I remember when my mother and my aunt would sit around and talk after family functions. Sometimes they'd get a certain look and I could tell that they were remembering a time when their apartment building in east Los Angeles caught on fire.

The family lived on the top floor. When the building caught fire, they all ran out and were watching it burn. My mother was probably eleven years old. And she said, "My mother's wallet." She just, without even thinking, went back into the burning building, got her mother's wallet, and came back out. She knew if the family lost the wallet that it was over, that they would have nothing. She didn't think about it. She just said to herself, "I've got to do it," and she went up and got it.

When my mother went to work in her early sixties, after she and my father separated, she hadn't had a job aside from "Mom" for years. But she found a job she was *perfect* for: greeting people from behind a counter. It was a very safe situation for her. As a receptionist, her natural gifts, her warmth, charm, supportive demeanor, love of people just blossomed. After two years of not leaving the house—she went through a tough period after her marriage ended—it was a remarkable rebirth. She started calling people she hadn't seen in years to set lunch dates and to reestablish old friendships. She took joy again in the little, precious things in life.

She also starting *learning* again, never afraid to try anything new. When I made my debut at Carnegie Hall, she flew out from Los Angeles four days before the concert to be with me. I always got really nervous when she was in the audience and this concert was incredibly important. While I was happy to have her be with me, the last thing I wanted to do was play "tourist" when I needed to focus so intently. And it was her first visit to New York City! When she arrived, we did all the typical tourist things and I secretly hoped that she would be too tired to do much of anything else. Was I wrong! She was like the Energizer Bunny. The miracle was that before I could freak out about it, she announced that she didn't want to wear *me* out, and that she was going to go exploring on her own. I was so grateful that I didn't even question letting her go out into the big city all by herself. This was the first time she'd ever been on the East Coast, much less the biggest, busiest city on earth. I figured she'd be gone a couple of hours and back for lunch. She left at 10:30 A.M. and was *still* gone by 5:00 P.M. Just as I was about to call the police, she strolled in smiling from ear to ear, bursting with her adventures. She had met a German woman in Central Park who not only treated her to a carriage ride around the park, but took her to brunch at Tavern on the Green, and strolled home with her down Columbus Avenue! She exchanged letters with that lady for years! And, while I know she was proud of my success at the concert, I know that secretly the highlight of that trip was that special day on her own.

One need only read the universal classic Don Quixote *by the great sixteenth-century Spanish writer Miguel de Cervantes to understand the virtue fortitude. His masterpiece has been translated into more languages than any other work, with the exception of the Bible. This wonderful, inspiring tale has also been made into the play* Man of La Mancha *for the entire family to enjoy.*

It's All in the Frijoles

Miguel de Cervantes (Spain)
(1547–1616)

Don Quixote

The God of love behold in me,
mighty on land and in the air,
and on the broad and tossing sea;
great is my power everywhere,
e'en though in Hell's dread pit it be.

Fear is a thing I never knew,
all that I wish must needs come true,
howe'er impossible it seem;
for my will and word are still supreme,
I command, enjoin, forbid, subdue.

People who devote themselves to the arts are an elite group, who must daily draw from their own internal resources and creativity to create a work. Artists, writers, and composers are people who have learned the meaning of perseverance, of fortitude. They pursue their goals no matter what, often at great personal sacrifice. This exerpt from a lecture given by composer Daniel Catán about how he has shaped his career as a composer speaks about fortitude and its relationship to the creative process. We discover that, as individuals, we are rarely a finished product. We grow and change as we move through barriers. By moving past our challenges as we develop our God-given gifts, we continue to grow. This reflection from composer Daniel Catán is an excerpt from his lecture "Composing Opera: A Backstage Visit to the Composer's Workshop," presented in the Andrés Bello Auditorium of the

Inter-American Development Bank on August 14, 1997 as part of the IDB Cultural Center's Lectures Program.

$\sqrt[3]{l}\sqrt[3]{l}$

Daniel Catán

Composer, Florencia en el Amazones

Writing opera is a work of perseverance. We persevered and eventually found our characters; we found our story too. In the early 1900s, the great opera star Florencia Grimaldi reprises the river journey she made twenty years before with her one true love, the naturalist Cristóbal Ribeiro da Silva. Searching for the rarest of butterflies, he mysteriously disappeared into the Amazonian jungle. Her stated mission is to sing at the fabled opera house in remote Manaus, but her secret desire is to find her lover once more.

Florencia Grimaldi, a native of South America who has triumphed all over the world, undertakes the journey that will bring her back to her origins. It is, I believe, the story of the return journey that we all undertake at a certain point in our lives: *nel mezzo del cammin di nostra vita,* the moment when we look back at what we once dreamed of becoming, and then confront what we have now become.

The story of Florencia's return journey resonated very loudly within me. So I suspect I should now tell you a little about my childhood and about my musical training. How did I decide to become a composer?

When I was fourteen years old, I left Mexico to go and study in England. I was a reasonable pianist in those days, and taking advantage of the fact that a distant relative lived in London, I decided to go there hoping to become a professional pianist. I completed my school years successfully, though not without a small crisis that felt at the time like the end of the world: the realization that I did not want to become a professional pianist after all struck me like a slap in the face. I was aghast and did not know how to react, but the message was loud and clear: I was not to go down that path. It was difficult, as you can imagine, to justify a journey that had taken me so far and that seemed to be heading towards a tragic miscarriage.

England, however, was generous to me. It opened my eyes to the infinitely varied world of music, well beyond the confines of the piano . . . I decided then, not without some trepidation, that I would become a composer. This put an end to one small crisis but set in motion a whole new one.

How do you become a composer? If you want to become, say, an architect or a doctor, there are indications for you to follow, carefully mapped out, at the end of which you become what you have set out to be. Becoming a composer seemed enigmatic by comparison. And reading about the great composers did not help a bit. They all seemed to have been born knowing how to do it. I was obviously not in the same situation. I panicked. I talked to friends. I studied scores of scores. And slowly I came to understand something that has been with me ever since: composing is neither something you are born with, nor learn at some point in your life in order to apply it later; it is a continuous process of discovery and a continuous attempt to express, in musical terms, that most curious activity we engage in so passionately that we call our lives.

In this sense it is not unlike mastering a language. We don't learn how to speak and then proceed to speak the rest of our lives; we start at some point, no matter where, and slowly get better as we do it. And just as our words are the result of our interaction with what surrounds us, our music is the reflection of all those experiences we call our lives. Looking at it in this way, there is some truth in saying that one does not learn how to compose, one only gets better at it.

. . . And when I feel extremely courageous and ask whether I have become what I once dreamed of becoming, I try to be kind with myself. I confess that, with all my heart, I'm still trying.

Parents teach children the virtues by modeling them for us. Like Mamá, actor Edward James Olmos's parents taught him fortitude as well as the importance of education by making the sacrifices necessary to work and attend school while raising a family.

Edward James Olmos
Actor

Fortitude means that you have a sense of self-worth sufficient to sustain you and move you forward against insurmountable odds. The fortitude to cope. The fortitude to manage. The fortitude to accept. The fortitude to share. The fortitude to be able to understand others. I wouldn't have gotten where I am today if I hadn't had the example of fortitude set by my parents.

My father went to school through the sixth grade, my mother through the eighth grade, but the fortitude that my mother and father showed in pursuing an education was unbelievable. I remember so well going to see my father get his high-school diploma when I was a young man. I was eleven, twelve, thirteen when he was going through high school, and he was in his late thirties. He studied English, mathematics, psychology and literature, in school. I saw him do it; I used to go to night school with him. The experience made me realize that education must be really important because there were a lot of older people sitting in those uncomfortable chairs that were made for little children my size, and they were filled with adults who would sit there for three hours after working all day, twelve hours a day.

When my father graduated from high school, I graduated from junior high, and I never thought about not graduating from high school. I went on and graduated. My mother started high school when I did and when I graduated, so did she. I went on to college. My mother has been in college for about ten or eleven years now. She's not aiming at graduation, she just enjoys taking the classes and learning.

Even my youngest sister, who had three children, ten months apart, starting at the age of fifteen, got her education after each baby was born. She now has six children, but she made it through high school and college and became a registered nurse. So consistent was the lesson of triumph over all adversity taught to us by our parents that my little sister could handle it. She didn't lose it. She didn't quit school, even with six children. She didn't become a welfare mom. She finished high school, finished college and went on to become a nurse and support herself.

Bill Melendez
Cartoonist, Producer

My grandmother was always telling us stories about the ranch. One time, one of her contemporaries was saying how terrible things were back then because of the Mexican Revolution. "Oh, that was nothing," she told us. "When your mother was very little, the Apaches would raid the ranches in the middle of the night. We would have to get up in our bedclothes and hide on the roof. They would take what they wanted. Finally, the shooting would alert the *vaqueros* on the next ranch and they would come and chase them off. Now *that* was something." And she said that they shot at the Apaches from up on the roof. "You shot them?" "Yes," she told me. "Did you hurt any of them?" "I sure hope so!"

Losing a child is the most difficult of all losses. Abraham Quintanilla's daughter Selena was killed in 1996 by the woman who was the treasurer of her fan club. Here he talks about fortitude and faith.

Abraham Quintanilla

President, Q-Productions

Nobody can understand the pain of losing a child unless they go through it. It's been devastating for me and my family, but we get involved and continue with the work that Selena was doing. We keep our minds occupied.

What keeps me going is my belief in the Resurrection, the idea that one day I'll be able to see Selena. A lot of people ask me about Yolanda [the woman who killed Selena] and, I can tell you, in all honesty—I've said this from day one—I've tried to dislike her and I can't. I don't think that I could live with that hatred inside me. Even if I did hate her, nothing's going bring my daughter back. I don't think about the negative things. I think about the wonderful time that we had with Selena, the positive things that we've done, how she was a positive role model for young people, and how she affected so many kids. We will continue the positive work that made people love Selena.

Ramón Vargas

Tenor

Fortitude comes from faith, love, friendship, and from the family who supports you in your work and your personal life. Life would be overwhelming if you didn't have faith and fortitude. In moments of tragedy, there are two ways to respond. You can have a negative reaction, or you can have faith and be at peace with the situation.

My first son, Eduardo, was born with brain damage. He is five years old now and he doesn't speak, he doesn't walk, and he has a lot of problems. One needs a strong faith at times like this. I have learned that my faith, and the love of my family and friends, has helped me live with my son's condition. My faith has deepened as a result of my son's birth. At first I reacted against the situation. Now I understand, now I believe. *Soy creente,* a believer. *Fortaleza* is something that is nourished by faith. It is very important to learn how to be strong in life and to teach this to our children.

Dichos

La perseverancia toda cosa alcanza.
Perseverance attains all.

Donde hay gana hay maña.
Where there is desire, there is skill.

Más hace él que quiere que él que puede.
The one with heart beats the one who's smart.

Dicen que del agua fría nacen los tepocates.
They say tadpoles are born from cold water.
(Said upon setting out on an impossible task.)

El que persevera triunfa.
Whoever perseveres, triumphs.

13

Chastity

Castidad

Chastity of the mind is the well-ordered movement of the mind that does not prefer the lesser to the greater things.

—SAINT AUGUSTINE, *De Mendacio xx*

"*Why buy the cow when the milk is free?*" *It was an odd thing for Mamá to say as we were making* tortillas de harina. *Her lessons were often told in colorful phrases and sayings designed to make a point. I was finishing a glass of milk one morning, so that day's lesson naturally evolved from milk to chastity. It was to be one of her more direct lessons, as I would discover. "What do you mean, Mamá?" I asked. "As you grow into a woman you will have men who will want you to have sex with them. But you mustn't do this unless the man is in love with you and is prepared to marry you first. If you have sex first, it's like giving the milk away for nothing. There's no need to buy the cow. And there is nothing worse for a woman than to be used and tossed aside." "But I'm not a cow, Mamá, I don't understand." "You will someday,* mijita, *someday you will."*

Chastity means being chaste, that is, to avoid having sex before or outside of marriage. Chastity is often equated with virtue, particularly when speaking of a woman. In the Latin culture, as in most cultures, chastity is a very desirable quality in a woman. This vision of woman is exemplified by the Virgen de Guadalupe *to whom young brides give flowers during the traditional wedding ceremony. In earlier times, a man could end his marriage if it was discovered on the wedding night that the wife was not pure or chaste.*

Es una mujer decente is to say the woman is undefiled, unsoiled. Couples are expected to be chaste at the time of marriage, and to re-

main faithful to each other in marriage. This is still a vital goal. Indeed, being chaste within a marriage, known as fidelity, is one of the pillars which forms the foundation of a good marriage. Today, divorce rates are soaring, even within Latino families, where divorce has been considered a religious taboo, because one of the spouses has been unfaithful. Sadly, today there is sexual promiscuity almost everywhere, even in the more conservative small towns of Mexico and other Latin countries. The increase in sexual activity outside marriage is creating an epidemic of out-of-wedlock pregnancies (one in eight Latina teenagers in Los Angeles) in large cities here in the U.S. Interestingly enough, these numbers reflect the behavior of U.S.-born Latino teens rather than recent immigrants. Sociologists believe this is because the traditional religious and cultural mores are still in place among the immigrant population.

It may seem unfair in this era of women's rights, but it is clearly up to the woman to maintain this virtue. It is an ancient role which women should not take lightly. It is the woman in her role as mother who is responsible for transmitting cultural mores and values from generation to generation. To aid in this role, the dichos are specifically concerned with the regulation of social relationships between the sexes. Cuiden sus gallinas que mi gallo anda suelto (Watch your hens so that my rooster can go about loose), is a dicho often addressed to young girls to justify restraints placed on her social activities.

The proverb is usually a warning directed by the parents of young men to the parents of young girls as a reminder that, in the view of the community, responsibility for proper conduct lies principally with the girl and her family.

Males are also admonished in proverbial terms to be aware of their own responsibilities and to avoid casual relationships, as in Agua que no has de beber, déjala correr. Water that you should not drink, let it run. Or, Si no compras, no magulles. If you aren't going to buy (it), don't bruise (it). However, most proverbial concern is directed towards females. The reason is obvious. It is the woman who gets pregnant, who is left alone with the child, and whose family must bear the burden of her indiscretion.

Tanto va el cántaro al agua hasta que se rompe. *The jug goes to the water many (times) until it breaks.* Age-old wisdom acknowledged that passion, if unleashed, might compete with virtue and bring negative consequences, however they were defined. The above saying is appropriate to a wide variety of contexts. However, it is often used to warn a daughter that if a girl runs around with a lot of boys she's likely to end up pregnant. Likewise, young women are often directed by mothers to refuse an expensive gift from a boyfriend on the grounds that El que da bien vende y el que lo recibe bien lo entiende, *which is to say, acceptance of the gift would amount to recognition of an obligation to reciprocate in some way. Mature women would do well to ponder this* dicho *as well.*

Latino cultural teachings not only teach girls and women to conduct themselves with care, but also to learn to discern between the quality of male suitors. I can remember my mother encouraging me to date a man who would be "a man of good character, from a good family, who will be a good father, a loving and kind husband."

Too often today, these teachings are forgotten, considered old-fashioned, or ignored in the search for superficial attractions and short-lived physical pleasure. My mother would also tell me to look closely at my suitor's parents, especially the father, because "chances are your husband will probably behave just like his father."

I recall chafing against the strict restrictions placed on my dating behavior by my mother. I would comment that their severity indicated an unjustified lack of trust on her part, only to hear, Bajo la desconfianza vive la seguridad *(Beneath the lack of confidence lives security). This is an excellent example of the wonderful way proverbs take away any personal sting, but are reinforcements for traditional wisdom. I've shared these with my daughter, along with the painful, practical reasons why young girls should avoid casual sex. Common sense and traditional wisdom play an important role in teaching children how to behave.*

My discussions with my daughter have gone beyond "Just say no" and "safe sex." I have talked with her about the emotional, psychic, and spiritual aspects of sex, as well as her value as a woman. I

It's All in the Frijoles

have told her that sexual relations involve more than body parts, that sexual relations engage our very being, our soul. Do we really want to treat this deeper part of who we are casually?

Technology can reduce or prevent obvious risks, but it cannot relieve the feelings involved in this delicate and important area of our lives. We need to teach our children about the nonphysical side of sexuality. This form of teaching goes beyond pronouncement of slogans such as "Just say no," which only induce fear. Guiding young people through dichos *and other wise teachings and discussion helps them build self-understanding, self-respect, self-worth, and a commitment to what is for their greatest and highest good.*

The hard won freedoms of women of recent decades should not be confused with license. Women are the gatekeepers of virtue and the transmitters of their culture. It is an ancient role which should not be taken lightly.

Serving as "gatekeeper" is not an easy role. Nor is abiding by this virtue any less demanding than being honest, prudent, or courageous. Some may argue a bit more vehemently against chastity, because through medical technology we have been able to reduce certain risks. However, we are still left with the impact of casual sex on the emotions, the psyche, and the spirit or soul. I believe the standards of conduct set forth in the dichos *of an earlier age and the teachings of our elders were also an attempt to help young people avoid the pitfalls of licentious sexual behavior. Every culture has attempted to rein in the passions in order to protect and preserve cherished cultural beliefs and values. Isn't it likely that they were also intuitively aware of the nonphysical aspects of sex in a way we seem to have lost touch with in our mechanistic, modern-day world?*

Many people today are also exploring the spiritual side of sexuality. Books on the subject are easily found in bookstores. There is a popular interest in Tantric sex, and men and women are discussing their frustrations with casual sexual relations and a desire for sexual relations that are more intimate, connective, and loving.

This virtue is no less relevant as we approach the new millennium than it was in past centuries. Avoiding sexual activity outside of marriage, like abstaining from lying, gluttony, cowardice, slothfulness, and so forth, is a goal for those on the path of virtue. Like the other virtues, chastity is the standard we aim for as we seek to develop and strengthen our mind and soul.

Liz Torres
Actor, Comedian

I grew up in Puerto Rico in a very traditional family. My mother had a very strong message about chastity. "Don't ever bring a baby home." That shocked me. I didn't understand at all what she was saying to me. I never thought that my mother thought that I would do something like that.

There was a very rigid code of behavior. Sex was not discussed. I never knew anything about it. The girls were carefully chaperoned. We were never left alone with boys. If we went out to a party we always were accompanied, even if we were with one of our cousins. Adults believed it was an invitation for disaster to leave a teenage boy and girl alone together.

I remember the night of my junior high-school prom. I was not allowed to date, although I begged my mother to let me go. "Absolutely not," she said. "I'll go with you." "No, Mom, you can't do that." I was desperate. I wanted to fit in and join my friends. I told her a group was going to the prom together, but it didn't matter. She was adamant about accompanying me.

I went to the prom but, as I was going into the YMCA where the dance was held, I saw my mom with a group of other mothers. My mom had talked these other mothers into chaperoning the young people in our group! Nobody else in the group would talk to me. I was all bummed out because my mother was outside. We thought we would take a walk in the park, and she said "No."

It's All in the Frijoles

She thinks the American custom of dating, of allowing your fifteen-year-old daughter with boiling hormones to go out alone with a boy with raging hormones, is an invitation for disaster. And she's right. But I didn't see it that way back then. I was trying so hard to be an American. I would rebel at anything that didn't allow me to conform to what my American friends were doing. I never rebelled about being Hispanic, just at some of our customs, which were very restrictive compared to American society.

Sor Juana Inés de la Cruz, the brilliant nun, poet, philosopher and writer from Mexico, dealt with the topic of chastity with tremendous wit and humor in this poem that Mamá herself would have enjoyed writing.

Sor Juana Inés de la Cruz
(1648–1695)
Mexican Philosopher and Poet

You Men

Stupid men, quick to condemn
Women wrongly for their flaws,
Never seeing you're the cause
Of all that you blame in them!

If you flatter them along,
Earn their scorn, their love incite,
Why expect them to do right
When you urge them to do wrong?

You combat their opposition,
And then gravely when you're done,
Say the whole thing was in fun
And you did not seek submission.

You expect from action shady
That some magic will be done
To turn courted courtesan
Quickly into virtuous lady.

Can you think of wit more drear
Than for one with lack of brain
To smear a mirror, then complain
Since it is not crystal clear?

Tempt us not to acquiesce,
Then with justice can you censure
Any girl who dares to venture
Near you, seeking your caress.

Women need be strong, I find,
To stay safe and keep unharmed
Since the arrogant male comes armed
With Devil, flesh, and world combined.

Translated by Willis Knapp Jones.

———————

In this era, in which we often confuse freedom and license, chastity has too often fallen by the wayside. This excerpt from Mexican philosopher, diplomat, and poet Octavio Paz's book The Double Flame *provides us with an erudite overview of the subject, and explains the purpose of chastity.*

Octavio Paz (Mexico)
(1914–1998)

The Double Flame

The rules and institutions meant to tame sex are numerous, ever-changing, and contradictory. It is pointless to list them; they range from the incest taboo to the marriage contract, from obligatory chastity to legislation regulating brothels. Their changes defy any attempt at classification that is anything more than a mere catalog: a new practice appears every day, and every day an old practice disappears. But all are comprised of two terms: abstinence and license, neither of which is an absolute. This is explainable: *the psychic health of society and the stability of its institutions depend in large part on the contradictory dialogue between the two.*

Since earliest times societies have gone through periods of chastity or continence followed by periods of licentiousness. An example from close at hand are Lent and Carnival. Antiquity and the Orient were also acquainted with this double rhythm: the bacchanal, the orgy, the public penitence of the Aztecs, the Christian processions of amends, the Ramadan of the Muslims. In a secular society such as ours, the periods of chastity and license, almost all of them associated with the religious calendar, are disappearing as collective practices hallowed by tradition. This is of no import: the dual nature of eroticism is preserved intact. No longer a religious and cyclical commandment, it turns into a rule to be followed on an individual level. This rule almost always has an ethical foundation, although it sometimes appeals to the authority of science and hygiene. The fear of disease is no less powerful than the fear of divinity or the respect for moral law. The double face of eroticism—fascination with both life and death—appears once again, divested now of its religious aura. The meaning of the erotic metaphor is ambiguous—or, rather, it is plural. It says many things, all different, but in all of them two words figure: pleasure and death.

. . . . The cult of chastity, in the West, is an inheritance from Platonism and other philosophies of antiquity that held the immortal soul to be the prisoner of the mortal body. . . . In the Orient the cult of chastity began as a method for attaining longevity. . . . Despite the difference, chastity fulfills the same function in the East as in the West: it is a test, an exercise that strengthens us spiritually and allows us to make the great leap from the human to the superhuman.

————————

Considered the greatest Spanish poet of the second half of the nineteenth century, Gaspar Nuñez de Arce was considered an honorable gentleman of high ideals who lived ill at ease in a venal and corrupt society.

Gaspar Nuñez de Arce (Spain)
(1831–1903)

On License

Liberty, liberty! Alas! Thou art not she,
That Virgin chaste, in robe of shining white,
Whom in my dreams I thought to see.
In naught resembleth thee that goddess bright.
Who, like the Morning Star in purity,
Shed on earth's gloomy haunts her radiant light.

Thou art no fountain of perennial fame,
Stirring the heart with hopes sublime and grand,
And giving life true dignity and aim,

Nor heavenly spirit with avenging hand,
Sent down from heaven the tyrant's neck to brand
For evermore with crimson mark of shame.

Thou'rt not that vision, that long-coveted prize,
I vainly follow with my soul athirst;
But what wild words are these? Away disguise,
Dishevelled license, of all fiends the worst,
Sedition's paramour, with staring eyes
I mark thee well. Be thou for aye accurst.

Translated by Ida Farnell.

Mario Obledo

*Attorney, Founder, Mexican American Legal Defense
and Education Fund (MALDEF)*

My sisters were not allowed to date until they were of legal age.
They were escorted everywhere, as women were in the old days.
We all were taught to have control over our bodies, to preserve them
and to take care of them. We were taught to be only with the one we
married. And, to this day, eleven out of the twelve brothers and sisters
have been married thirty and forty years. This commitment is tied to
self-respect, to a strong faith system—we prayed every night—and to
a strong mother who waited up for each of us and made sure we each
arrived home safely every night.

———————————

*This charming memory deals with honesty as much as chastity. But it
points out the severe consequences a breach in chastity held for actor
Luis Avalos.*

Luis Avalos

Actor, Writer, Director

We were in Florida, and I was about twelve years old. And my friend Bernie—Bernie was sort of the neighborhood trouble-maker—had gotten hold of some cigarettes. At that age, we were experimenting and trying everything. So, we got this pack of cigarettes, and we went underneath the house to smoke. In Florida, there are grates decorated with flamingoes and palm trees that cover the entrance to the crawl spaces underneath the houses, attached to the house by two pins on either side. We removed the grate and climbed under.

We were there with a girl who was a couple of years older than we were, a neighbor. We figured we'd smoke a cigarette and, you know, give her a kiss, sort of like playing adults.

All of a sudden, I heard a car in the driveway. In a panic we ran out of there and, in the process, broke that grate. That evening my mother said, "I know what you've done, and you're going to pay for it." I thought to myself, "Oh, my God, I'm going to have to marry this girl." And Mom said, "You know what you've done." "No, Mom, I didn't do anything." I denied it adamantly. Finally she said, "Yes, you did. You broke that grate, and I'm going to take it out of your allowance." I think she made me sleep the night in the bathroom so I would never be dishonest again. If she had only known!

It's All in the Frijoles

Carmen Zapata

Actor, Founder of Bilingual Foundation for the Arts

I grew up in the roughest barrio in New York, Spanish Harlem. My dad was from Mexico, and my mother from Argentina. We were very, very poor, but I was raised with very strict rules and values. Years after I became an actress and was able to afford to buy my mother a house, a new car, and a mink coat, my mother told me that material things were not important. What was important, she told me, was that I was able to survive in an industry which was so often destructive to young women . . . that I was able to remain pure and clean and to know the difference between right and wrong.

. . . . When I said I wanted to be an actress, my mother opposed my career choice because the industry was known to be hard on women. I knew acting was my calling and that I had no other career choice. I told her that while I would pursue my chosen career, I would do nothing wrong . . . that she would have to trust me.

I didn't smoke, drink, or engage in sex. I just worked at a career I loved. I went on the road, I played on Broadway. When I returned from being on the road, she looked at me and said, "You're as pure as when you left, but that's what you've learned and what we've taught you to do."

Vicki Carr

Singer

I come from a very, very strict family. I wasn't allowed to go out much. I remember being told, "Once you do that, once you make that mistake, no man will want you." I didn't know what mistake they were talking about. What did they mean by *mistake*? One of the things we were taught about relationships was that you didn't live with a man unless you were married. As the oldest child, I was expected to set the example for my brothers and sisters. I realized that I did have a responsibility. Years later I told my dad, "In a way, you forced me to marry when I really didn't feel I was ready," but I understand why he did it.

I respected my parents and grandparents and realized that my family wasn't quite ready for the modern-day lifestyle, nor would they accept any arrangement but marriage. I got married twice because of that. This time I told my dad, "It's my decision this time, okay?" I'm sure they were doing it out of caring. I was setting that example and taking responsibility. It's kind of nice but, sometimes, there's a little bit of a pressure to being the oldest. It's really difficult.

Although we chafed against those rules, there was a reason for them. Today we live in scary, scary times. The consequences for casual sex are dire, so the important thing is to instill in your kids those virtues of respecting yourself and respecting other people, expecting you will be respected. That's really what chastity is about.

***

Nely Galán
President, Galán Entertainment

My parents were continually telling me what was really important in human beings. They were strict. I couldn't even spend the night at a friend's house. When I would ask why, my mother would tell me, *"Porque yo no sé los valores o las morales de esa familia. Y para mí, lo más importante es que tengas valores y una moral estricta"* (Because I don't know the values or morals of this family. And for me, it is most important that you have strict morals and values). It's so funny.

One of the things my American girlfriends never understood is why Latinas enforce virginity so much.

I remember growing up and thinking, "What is this virginity thing? It's so stupid." Now that I'm older, I really get it. I *really* get it. I think how wonderful it was for me to have parents who said, "You are worth everything and you should never give that away to anyone so easily." It's not like they were being extreme in order to teach the lesson, but it's that they were right.

My mother would also say things like, "Why buy the milk when the cow is free." It was really this thing that *Lo que tú tienes que vale no se regales a nadie* (Don't give away this thing that is so valuable to anybody). It's all tied in to your sense of worth and your sense of what is worth giving a part of your worth to. What are the things that are a part of you? What are the things that you must never give away, like your sense of worth, your virginity? These are a physical reflection of who you really are. It's like they are part of your soul, and it is true.

$$\frac{1}{2}$$

Polly Baca
Former Member, Colorado State Legislature

My mother expected her three daughters to postpone marriage until after we graduated from college and worked for one year. We were also expected to be good girls, not to play around, to save ourselves for marriage. Mom's two messages were: One, a man would never marry you if he got to play around first, and two, you would recognize the man you loved when you were in the arms of somebody else.

She encouraged us to date more than just one person, to experience dating different men, but to be very cautious about ever getting too involved with them. It was okay to kiss them, but you didn't let them touch where they weren't supposed to. It was based more on not getting pregnant. It was not as religious as I would have assumed. My mother also talked a lot about fidelity. She told us never to put up with a man playing around. She said if we started dating somebody and he was not faithful to just let him go. She taught us to respect ourselves and to stand up for our rights as women.

Dichos

Cuerpo de tentación, cara de arrepentimiento.
Body of temptation, face of regret.

El que evita la tentación evita el pecado.
Whoever avoids temptation, avoids the sin.

El vicio es sabotaje contra uno mismo.
Vice is self-inflicted sabotage.

Contra el vicio de pedir, hay la virtud de no dar.
Against the vice of asking is the virtue of not giving.

It's All in the Frijoles

14

Charity
Caridad

Oh, child of the Sun, loving and kind to the poor.
—INCA GREETING

Una buena acción es la mejor oración.
A good deed is the best prayer.

. . . by love serve one another. For all the law is fulfilled in
one word, *even* in this; Thou shalt love thy neighbor as
thyself.

—GALATIANS 5:13–14

If I speak in the tongues of men and of angels, but have not love, I am a noisy gong or a clanging cymbal. And if I have prophetic powers, and understand all mysteries and all knowledge, and if I have all faith, so as to remove mountains, but have not love, I am nothing. If I give away all I have, and if I deliver my body to be burned, but have not love, I gain nothing" (I Corinthians 13:1-3).

Cariño y caridad are often used interchangeably in this frequently recited passage by Saint Paul. Indeed, is is said that God's greatest gift to humankind is his love for us, and our greatest gift in return is to love our fellow human beings. The true meaning of charity comes from this awareness.

Mamá instinctively knew that faith without works is empty. She knew that when we see a need and meet it, it is not out of guilt, but because we must—because it is the right thing to do. She taught me that it is important to give out of love, as one child of God to another. "Love thy neighbor as thyself" was a commandment which she practiced as part of her daily living. Like Saint Teresa de Avila, Mamá believed it was important to help one another, to be compassionate, "not only to show goodwill but tenderness with it . . . to look after the sick, to serve in the lowliest tasks is a form of prayer." It was Saint Teresa who also admonished the nuns in her charge to "Get beyond your little practices of piety, abrillas . . . . Your love must not be the product of your imagination but be proved by acts."

Mamá was always doing for others, bringing friends and family members into her home when various crises struck; giving advice when asked, even to strangers she met on the street; gathering up clothes for poor families in Tijuana. She also had a special way of celebrating every event through some act of sharing or giving. There was always a small gift, often homemade, for me for every occasion: a small box of chocolates for Saint Valentine's Day, a pretty initialed handkerchief for Saint Patrick's Day, an extravagant handmade costume for All Saints' Eve, and tamales for Christmas Eve. Mamá took care of me, took care of everyone in her life with graciousness and love. Of course, I took so much of this for granted. It wasn't until she passed away and my favorite cousin Rudy Castro delivered a eulogy at her memorial service that defined the core of my mother's essence as love that I understood that love is giving. It was a powerful reminder of Christ's words telling us to "Love thy neighbor as thyself."

Charity is the love of one's fellow human beings. We manifest love by taking care of loved ones and neighbors just as we would take care of ourselves. Caridad is service, and service is one of the defining qualities of Latin people.

Antonio Caso, the great Mexican philosopher and poet, tells us that "Faith is impossible without charity, just as light is impossible without the sun, just as a corollary is impossible without the axiom. Good works are faith itself upon reflection in the conscience of him who performs them . . . to believe is to act, to see, to live. Without the good act there is no faith nor hope." It is a rare thing not to witness strangers as well as family members reaching out to help someone in need, like the Mexican woman who tried to give money to Gary Soto so he could have a bus ride home.

Gary Soto

Poet

Charity comes from wanting to help and, if I locate its source inside me, I think of when I was a third grader at St. John's Catholic School in Fresno. My father had died a couple of years before, and being left alone was terrifying. Also worrisome for me was the poverty that was real. I remember walking home from school, holy in my little Catholic soul, and seeing a kid approaching from the opposite direction down a leaf-strewn street. I know it was October from the way the light slanted through the nearly bare trees. I sensed a change in the climate and sensed that I could be looking at myself when I saw that he wore socks with heels completely ripped. In fact, I knew I was looking at myself—me with my own torn socks and cardboard in the soles of my shoes. I was sneaky, because I figured out a way of hiding my plight by tugging my socks down into my shoes so that the holes were invisible except to me and my own little ego. But the kid coming toward me, well, he wasn't nearly as bright. His poverty was so evident. The holes rode way up high on the backs of his heels. Although small and not earth shattering, he was a miserable sight; I was looking at myself, except that kid was going one way and I the other. We call that empathy, and empathy is what kickstarts charity.

Charity is not just an emotional response but action. It's responding to the least of our brothers and sisters, as the Bible says. I was also on charity's needy end; I ran away from an ugly home situation when I was seventeen and lived on the streets for a while before renting a room in a house that was similar to the one from which I had escaped. I was working at a tire factory in Burbank. The work was difficult, nearly impossible even for a young man like me, hard in muscle and with a lot of youthful energy in my legs. I used to walk six miles home each day, and while I tried to hitchhike, no one would give me a ride because I was completely covered with black soot from the tires.

It's All in the Frijoles

From a distance I probably resembled a coal miner, black around the eyes with my long hair spiked up from the dust, which was like eraser rubbings from a pencil. I was a sight to behold. I wasn't looking for charity but, my God, a ride part way home wasn't asking much. In my eight weeks, no one ever offered help except one woman, a Mexicana, of course, who stopped her car though she was going in the opposite direction. She ran across the street to give me a dollar for bus fare. I raised my hand to fend off the money, but not her act of charity. She begged me to take it. But I didn't which, as I look back, was the wrong response. I should have taken that dollar in order for her to complete her act of charity.

I still marvel over her selfless gesture. That was many years ago and since then I think I have demonstrated what some may see as charity. My wife and I tithe ten percent of what we earn towards the Chicano arts and some educational programs. Charity is an unselfish act; yes, it's a conscious act, but when you give, in money, time, or even wisdom, your charity goes out to others, and even though you may never see your gifts again, they circle around for everyone's good.

———

Charity goes beyond giving help or alms to the needy. Charity means brotherly love in action. Engaging in acts of goodwill, giving back, is part of this important virtue.

Rafael Catalá
Author, Mysticism Now

Service, to me, is something very personal. It has nothing to do with your ego. It has to do with doing in each moment that which in each moment is necessary. I've always had the philosophy that if you become aware of anything that is required of you or of an injustice, the act of becoming aware makes it your privileged responsibility. Then you do the best you know how to serve that community or that person. I think the first time I ever experienced that was in 1959, when I was still working for the Cuban Revolution. I must have been about fifteen. A few friends and I were given an area to canvass in order to count all the children who would be receiving toys on the Epiphany. But the toys never arrived. I called all my friends and said, "Look, the toys never arrived, but we are responsible. We gave our word." So we all got our money—we broke into our piggy banks, borrowed money, and asked for money from our parents. We bought the toys and distributed them, not in our names, but in the name of the Cuban Revolution.

Bill Melendez
Animator, Producer

My grandfather on my mother's side had a ranch near Hermosillo in Mexico where I was born. He collected horses, but he also had an interesting cause. When anybody in the district died a pauper, he would go get the body and see to it that the person got a good Christian burial. It seemed crazy to me, but that is what he did . . . made sure everybody got a good Christian burial. And the irony of his life is that when he died, we could never find his body. We think he was ambushed by some *bandoleros*. It was during the Revolution, and there were a lot of things going on back then. He had an argument with some men in a *cantina* one evening while he was looking for a stray horse. Of course, given his reputation, everybody went looking for him, but we never found him.

I was raised by my maternal grandmother. She was just like the old lady in the film *Like Water for Chocolate*. The ranch looked the same, too. We were taught that it was our duty to take care of the downtrodden and those who needed our help.

There is a story my grandmother told me about the time she went to visit my father on a military base. He was a soldier in the Federal army, who traveled from one campaign and military base to another. He lived a very strange, nomadic life. On one occasion, she had gone to see him at a base and heard someone screaming her name. She turned and recognizing some of her workers said, *"Mis peones, mis peones,"* my peons, my peons. They had worked for her back home and my father had pressed them into the army. She was furious, but there they were. Back then, you could buy out a soldier's enlistment. The poor devils had been enlisted for who knows how many years, so my mother paid to buy out their time of service, and then she gave the workers money, and told them to go back home. She knew that they shouldn't be there. It wasn't right. It wasn't the way to care for those entrusted to your care. They had been pressed into service like indentured servants, and to make it worse, my father had done it.

———————

Mexico has always been sought out as a place to escape the political turmoil of other countries. It was a popular immigration point for Jews escaping Nazi persecution in Europe. The genuine charitableness of the people not only welcomed newcomers, but the virtues taught there became an integral part of those who were raised there.

Raquel Bessudo
President, Medisend

I am a Mexican-born Jewish girl of European parents who arrived in Mexico just before the Second World War. I feel I have internalized many Mexican traditions and values, because you are, in a way, formed by your social and cultural environment. My parents escaped the persecution of Jews in Poland at a time when Jews were not approved of by their neighbors and considered unwelcome foreigners. When I asked my mom what she feels for Mexico, she always refers to the great country that opened her arms to the needy. In a way, I suppose this is one of the great qualities of Mexican people—their open friendship toward their fallen neighbor, even if their own situation is not the greatest. Here the poor are even more open-hearted than others. They will always have a piece of *tortilla* and some *frijoles* and, of course, the *mole* will never be missing if the reason is to greet you and make a feast for you as the most important person in the world. When you have the chance and the luck to approach an authentic Mexican, the tradition will always be out in front—the good manners, the care for their people, the ethics in their way of life.

I have been involved with my countrymen in different ways: in the Centro de Estudios Mayas, learning about the ancient inhabitants of this sector of the Mesoamerican world, their traditions and manuscripts that tell us of their millennial culture; and, in a different way, with my social work, helping to get medical equipment that is no longer being used in the States from American hospitals to clinics and institutions that deliver health support in Mexico. This giving back to my country for all it has provided our family is an important part of the cycle of life.

Fernando Chavez
Attorney

My grandmother, my father's mother, who helped raise me, was very religious. She was a devout Catholic, very compassionate, never self-righteous, always caring, and wise. She was, I imagine, probably like a lot of grandmothers, but she was very influential in my upbringing because those are the qualities that were always important to her—more important than wealth and material things.

It's All in the Frijoles

She said that acts of *caridad* were how one should be judged, because those kinds of acts could be carried out by either rich or poor people.

She used to say, "You need to do this because these are the important things in life. If you have, then you share whatever you have." I remember always having people who had less to the house for dinner and making food to take to people. And my dad [César Chavez] would tell me stories about when they were growing up and were traveling migrants. They always lived in tents.

It was not uncommon to take in an additional family or two who, for some reason or another, had no shelter, not even a tent. My dad was always picking up stray people, bringing them home. I would say, "Who is this?" He would answer, "Oh, some guy who doesn't have a home. We're going put him up for a few days."

I remember a story my father told me about my grandmother taking in a family to share their tent in Ventura or Santa Paula where they were picking lemons or oranges. The husband was injured. Because he was living in a labor camp, they ran him out when he couldn't work, even though he had a wife and five or six children. They were supposed to stay with my grandparents and dad for a week and ended up spending four months, everybody living under the same tent.

When I was a little boy, my dad would often take me with him when he was organizing. We'd go to someone's house to eat and my dad would ask, "Can I bring such and such a person?" I was amazed, because the person might have been hitchhiking, or the person might have been somebody who told my dad he was down and out, or might be a guy with his wife and three kids. But people would always say, "Sure, come on in. Bring your friends, come on in."

These memories have impacted me deeply. I find that I do the same thing. I don't bring people to the house, but I find myself caring for people like my dad and grandma. I recently had a case representing a man and his family who had been involved in an accident involving an electric stove and were seriously hurt. They were living in Coalinga in someone's garage. It had no heating, and they were running an electric cord from the house into this garage which was the size of a room. They used a little electric stove to make food and to heat their room. It's amazing that people still live under these conditions.

The man told me that, depending on how cold it was, they'd sometimes sleep in the car. I knew I wasn't going be able to do anything for these people. The case wasn't going in our favor. I don't know why that particular incident affected me more than others, because I see it a lot. I could see they had nothing, absolutely nothing. So I gave them a thousand dollars. I knew it wasn't going to cure their ills, but I just could not see myself leaving them in the same situation that I found them in without doing a little something. I do this a lot because it's something my grandma would expect.

Last Christmas, my sons received a gift of a hundred dollars. We were in the car driving to visit some friends, and we pulled up to a traffic light near some homeless people. My boys asked, "What are they doing there?" And I said, "Well, they're homeless. They have nowhere to go." My boys gave them twenty dollars. That gesture touched me deeply.

How do we teach caridad? *By being loving. By engaging in all the little acts of kindness and love we express to our children and to those around us, on a daily basis. After all, love is reflected in love. This children's song is a favorite of mothers and teachers because it comforts, nourishes, and makes children feel safe and loved.*

Children's Song and Rhyme

Duérmete, mi niña,	Go to sleep, my little girl,
duérmete, mi sol,	go to sleep, my sun,
duérmete pedazo	go to sleep, piece
de mi corazón.	of my heart.

Un elefante se balanceaba
sobre la tela de una araña.
Como veía que resistía
fue a llamar a otro elefante.

One elephant balanced
atop a cobweb.
When he noticed it supported him,
he called another elephant.

Miguel Martinez
Artist

One of the fondest memories I have of my boyhood is my mother's ritual of making homemade bread every Saturday. She was employed outside our home to make a living for us, but she found the time and energy to make delicious bread and homemade jelly, which were shared with all our playmates when they visited us. The Saturday baking was supposed to last all week, but it was so popular that the loaves disappeared by mid-week.

As I think about this, I realize my mother's easy generosity taught me that part of the joy of life is in giving and sharing. Even to this day, after all these years, many of my boyhood friends continue to remind her of their enjoyment in having homemade bread and jelly at our house.

Probably my mother was a role model for more than just her own children. I would hope to leave a legacy such as that.

In the first part of the eighteenth century, a Spaniard of noble blood took leave of his only relatives, a nephew and his nephew's little daughter, and left for the New World. After crossing the ocean, he came to what had been the splendid capital of Moctezuma, where he settled in an elegant mansion with many servants.

The Spaniard, Don Mendo Quiroga y Suárez, Marquis of Valle Salado, came with a great amount of money and recommendations to

Charity/Caridad

be presented to the viceroy. Thus, it was easy for him to find friends among the high government officials and the rich people of the capital. But because he was humble, generous, and compassionate, Don Mendo preferred to spend his days helping the poor and the sick instead of attending the parties of the rich.

Somersault Street

One day, Don Mendo, somewhat worried, went to visit his best friend, the Viceroy of New Spain.

"I have come to ask your advice, Don Rodrigo," said the Marquis.

"Speak freely, my friend. You know that you can trust me."

"Yes, I know, and I thank you for it. Well, I have just received news from Spain of the death of my nephew. May he rest in peace! Now, his young daughter, Paz, who is fifteen years old, is an orphan. Fortunately, her nanny, old Eulalia, takes good care of her. But what should I do?"

"I advise you to invite them to live in your home. What happiness the young lady will bring to your solemn mansion! There will be cheerful laughter, romantic serenades, parties, and dances."

"I agree. This very day I shall send her the invitation and the money for the trip and other expenses."

The niece accepted the invitation with pleasure. But she and her nanny did not arrive at their new home until the Christmas season, which everyone celebrated with *piñatas* and *posadas*.

Don Mendo gave a great ball to present his niece to the capital's high society. Everyone, including Don Mendo, was charmed by the beautiful young woman. She was tall and slender. Her eyes and hair were as black as the wings of a blackbird, her skin was very white, and she had aristocratic hands and feet. Truly, she was as gracious and beautiful as a spring day.

It's All in the Frijoles

But in the following months, everyone noticed that in contrast with her physical beauty, Paz had an unpleasant personality. She was ungrateful, ill-mannered, and even proud.

"My dear niece," Don Mendo advised her, "you ought to be more courteous. Otherwise, you will have very few friends."

"I don't care. The people here are ignorant. I don't want their friendship," answered Paz.

The uncle was right. At the end of a year, Paz only had two friends left: her uncle and her nanny. In spite of her unpleasant personality, the two loved her greatly.

One day, a tragedy occurred in the great mansion. Don Mendo suddenly became very ill and died before sunset. Upon receiving the news, the whole city was saddened. All the people cried over the loss of their good friend.

In Don Mendo's mansion, the niece shed many fake tears with one of her beautiful eyes, while she had the other eye fixed on an old chest locked with a key. Paz knew very well that her uncle's will was kept there.

The day arrived when the notary was to come to the mansion. He opened the large chest with a key and took out Don Mendo's will. He read it very solemnly in the presence of Paz, the Viceroy, and other friends.

I, Don Mendo Quiroga y Suárez, Marquis of Valle Salado, leave all my property to my niece, Paz Quiroga, but . . .

"Yes, of course. I deserve everything," Paz interrupted rudely.

The notary smiled while he was preparing to read the other part of the will.

. . . but on the condition that she pay for all the torments that she made me suffer while I was alive; otherwise, all my assets will go to the Orders of Saint Francis and Mercedes, equally. The payment that I demand from my niece is this: dressed in a ball gown, she will go in an open carriage

through the main streets of this capital; then, in the pavil-
ion built in the center of the Main Square, she will lower
her head and turn three somersaults in the presence of all
the spectators who are assembled there. Otherwise, the in-
heritance will go to the religious orders. (Signed) The Mar-
quis of Valle Salado

If a bomb had exploded at the feet of the proud young woman, it would not have had a greater effect than the reading of the last part of the will.

"Oh, no! What am I going to do?" shouted Paz, weeping sincerely this time. "I cannot do that."

"The decision is yours and . . ." but the notary did not finish the sentence because the young woman ran out of the living room.

Remembering that money means power and influence, Paz made her decision. So, on a sunny morning when it seemed that there were millions of people in the Main Square, the niece got down from her elegant carriage and went over to the pavilion.

For a while, she looked at the people. She saw many of her uncle's friends. She saw the young men and women who had tried to be her friends. How serious they all seemed!

"Without a doubt, they have come to laugh at me," thought Paz. "But it does not matter. I will not see them again. After receiving my inheritance, I will leave for Spain."

Then, with trembling hands, the young woman picked up her long gowns, got down on her knees with her head on the floor of the pavilion and turned the first somersault.

She expected to hear laughter, but she did not hear any.

The young woman quickly turned her second somersault and then the third. Then she got up and ran toward her carriage. "Take me home right away," Paz ordered the coachman.

As she left, she could hear the shouts of the people. But what were they saying? The young woman listened with surprise.

"Long life the niece! Long live our brave little friend!"

Paz heard those voices many times. She then wept inconsolably.

It's All in the Frijoles

The following week, when the notary came to speak with the niece, she told him, "I wish to be worthy of my uncle, who was a saint. Therefore, please give the greater part of my inheritance to the Orders of Saint Francis and Mercedes. Furthermore, instead of going to Spain, I will remain here. I am going to help the nuns in the orphanage."

"Very well, I will obey your wishes," answered the notary with a happy smile. "Now I know that you are worthy of your uncle, who loved you so much."

In memory of this legend, the street in front of Don Mendo's mansion bore the name of Somersault Street for a very long time.

Celebrities have a powerful impact on people all over the world. Their words, songs, music, movies, and art have uplifted people in ways we cannot imagine. I am moved by the generosity of jazz musician Poncho Sanchez as he was greeted by a group of young boys when he recently visited Peru for the first time. His gesture was a tremendous act of caridad, something he learned at home from his parents. "I get the warmth, the caring, and the giving part from my mother. The hard work, stubbornness, and fortitude come from my father."

Poncho Sanchez
Latin Jazz Musician, Composer, Performer

My mother is nothing but heart. Everybody that has ever known her says, "Your mother is beautiful, she's just a beautiful woman." She cares about everybody. I used to think she was too friendly, because if anyone came to the door, she would invite them in to eat. She was always warm and open and treated everyone like family. Because she cooked a lot and made fresh homemade *tortillas* every day, my friends used to like to visit our home. We often joked that if a man came to rob her she would probably first invite him to sit and eat before he did anything. That's the kind of person she is.

On my recent tour to Peru, I was greeted at the airport at six in the morning by about eight little boys. They looked like they were between fourteen and eighteen years old. They were calling out, "Don Poncho! Poncho! Don Poncho!" I had never been there before, but there they were with pictures of me and album covers. It was six in the morning! I was signing the stuff for them and I asked, "Are you coming to the concert tonight?" And all of them looked at me and said, "No, it costs too much money to go to the concert." I said, "What are your names?" I told them, "You meet me in the back and I'll get you guys in." Sure enough, that night they were at the concert. The guard told me they had been waiting there about two hours before I arrived. I told him, "They are with me."

The next morning the boys were at the airport again. I told them they ought to visit California one day. And this kid looked at me and said, "Poncho, I've been trying for a long time, me and my mother, to get visas to go to the United States, but I can't get one. I may never get one." He added in Spanish, "Poncho, I'm gonna tell you one thing. I leave Lima, Peru, every night when I listen to your music."

Here is a kid that is living in a Third World country. Lima is like Tijuana, or worse. And music helps take him away from there and give him hope. Hearing him I got chills that went through my body. I never knew that I had touched anybody in the world like that.

This story about caridad *by the former Governor of New Mexico, Toney Anaya, is similar to Mamá's deathbed message about the frijoles. Sometimes the most profound wisdom is so simple that the deeper meaning evades us.*

It's All in the Frijoles

Toney Anaya
Attorney, Former Governor of New Mexico

Both my mother and grandmother were *mayordomas* at the local church when I was growing up. They took on the responsibility of making sure the church was always cleaned and taken care of. They were deeply religious, which had a tremendous influence on me. Before going to bed, we always said the rosary. Each time we visited the church we always said the stations of the cross. We prayed at the table before meals and before we went to school.

Many years later, just before I was elected governor, my mom passed away. She had had cancer a couple of times. She'd been in and out of the hospital, and the second time she went in, it was obvious she wasn't going to come back home. The family was scattered around the country. My older brother was in the military, stationed on the East Coast. My family was also there. Mom sent for us all and waited until we all got there. Then she lined up all of the children at the foot of her bed, the oldest first, down to the youngest, and called each one of us individually up to her, starting with the oldest. She spoke something into each of their ears, dismissed them, and then went on down the line.

I was third youngest so I had to stand there patiently, wondering what she was saying. I knew she was a very godly woman and I wondered what message she was conveying to each one. When it finally came to my turn, she pulled me down to her, one hand on each side of my face. By now, her breath was almost gone and she struggled to whisper. *"Tone,"* is how she pronounced my name, *"Tone, cuida a tu familia."* Take care of your family.

As I walked away, I couldn't help but think to myself, "Mom, I waited all this time. And the only thing you had to say to me was *Tone, cuida a tu familia."* Frankly, I was kind of looking for more. I was disappointed. She spoke to my younger sister, then my younger brother. Then she closed her eyes and passed away.

It was many years later, after I was elected governor and had gone through the turmoil of working to accomplish the good we were trying to do that I finally started understanding what she meant that night. It would have helped me in my personal relationship with my family as well as in what I was trying to do as an elected official had I grasped the deeper meaning of her message sooner.

I realized then that she certainly meant *cuida a tu familia* in terms of my wife and my three kids. When she died I had already served as attorney general and I had run for the United States Senate. She no doubt sensed that things were not as focused in my family life as they should have been because of all these other distractions. But I think she also sensed I was going to be governor. I think she also meant *cuida a tu familia* in a broader sense, as in a community, as in the larger family of human beings.

It was towards the end of my career as governor when this message finally dawned on me. It caused me to look at my public service in that light, as *caridad,* caring for the larger family of people I had been elected to serve.

Dichos

Dan más donde conocen menos.
They give more where they know less.

Ni todo dar, ni todo negar.
Do not give all, nor deny all.

Ofrecer y no dar es deber y no pagar.
To offer and not give is to owe and not pay.

It's All in the Frijoles

Dar por recibir no es dar sino pedir.
To give in order to receive is not to give but to ask for.

Hay más dicha en dar que en recibir.
It is more blessed to give than to receive.

Qué lindo es vivir para amar; qué grande es tener para dar.
How beautiful it is to live and love; how great it is to have and give.

Caridad de la buena en casa y luego en la ajena.
The best charity begins at home, and then moves on to the neighbors.

Haz bien y no mires a quien.
Do good and never notice to whom.

Al potro y al niño con cariño.
Treat animals and children kindly.

Amor primero, amor postrero.
Love, first and last.

For Further Reading

Jerome R. Adams. *Latin American Heroes: Liberators and Patriots from 1500 to the Present*. New York: Ballantine Books, 1991.

Rudolfo Anaya. *Bless Me Ultima*. New York: Warner Books, 1972.

The Arizona Historical Society. *Frontier Tucson: Hispanic Contributions*, 1987.

Peg Augustine. *A Child's Garden of Virtues: Stories About Virtues*. Nashville: Dimensions for Living, 1996.

St. Thomas Aquinas. *Treatise on the Virtues*. Translated by John A. Oesterle. Notre Dame, Indiana: University of Notre Dame Press, 1966.

Genevieve Barlow. *Stories from Latin America*. Lincolnwood, Illinois: Passport Books, 1997.

William J. Bennett. *The Book of Virtues: A Treasury of Great Moral Stories*. New York: Simon & Schuster, 1993.

William J. Bennett. *A Children's Book of Virtues*. New York: Simon & Schuster, 1995.

Juan de Betanzos. *Narrative of the Incas*. Edited by Roland Hamilton and Dana Buchanan from the Palma de Mallorca manuscript. Austin: University of Texas Press, 1996.

Jose Antonio Burciaga. *In Few Words/ En pocas palabras: A Compendium of Latino Folk Wit and Wisdom, A Bilingual Collection.* San Francisco: Mercury House, 1997.

Miguel de Cervantes. *Don Quijote de la Mancha.* Translated by Charles Jarvis, with an introduction by Milan Kundera. New York: Oxford University Press, 1999.

Father Bernabe Cobo. *Inca Religion and Customs.* Translated and edited by Roland Hamilton. Austin: University of Texas Press, 1990.

Robert Coles. *The Moral Intelligence of Children.* New York: Random House, 1997.

Lulu Delacre. *Golden Tales: Myths, Legends, and Folktales from Latin America.* New York: Scholastic Press, 1996.

Linda and Richard Eyre. *Teaching Your Children Values.* New York: Fireside, 1993.

Corky Gonzalez, "I Am Joaquin." *The Latino Reader, An American Literary Tradition from 1542 to the Present.* Edited by Harold Augenbraum and Margarite Fernandez Olmos. A Marc Jaffe Book. New York: Houghton Mifflin, 1997, p. 266.

Roberto Gonzalez Echevarria. *Oxford Book of Latin American Short Stories.* Oxford: Oxford University Press, 1967.

Ralfka Gonzalez and Ana Ruiz. *My First Book of Proverbs: Mi Primer Libro de Dichos.* Emeryville, California: Children's Book Press, 1995.

Rosie Gonzalez. *The Fire in Our Souls: Quotations of Wisdom and Inspiration by Latino Americans.* New York: Plume, 1996.

Jose Griego y Maestas and Rudolfo A. Anaya. *Cuentos: Tales from the Hispanic Southwest: Bilingual Stories in Spanish and English.* Santa Fe: The Museum of New Mexico Press, 1980.

Margot C. Griego, Betsy L. Bucks, Sharon S. Gilbert, and Laurel H. Kimball. *Tortillitas Para Mama and Other Nursery Rhymes, Spanish and English.* New York: Holt, Rinehart and Winston, 1981.

Oscar Hijuelos. *Our House in the Last World*. New York: Persea Books, 1983.

T. J. Knab, Ph.D., and Thelma D. Sullivan. *A Scattering of Jades: Stories, Poems, and Prayers of the Aztecs*. New York: Touchstone, 1994.

Tiffany Ana Lopez. *Growing up Chicana/o: An Anthology*. New York: William Morrow & Company, 1993.

Olga Loya. *Momentos Mágicos/Magic Moments: Tales from Latin America Told in English and Spanish*. Little Rock: August House Publishers Inc., 1997.

Roberta H. Markman and Peter T. Markman. *The Flayed God: The Mythology of Mesoamerica*. New York: HarperSanFrancisco, 1992.

Robert Ryal Miller. *Mexico: A History*. Norman, Oklahoma: University of Oklahoma Press, 1985.

Pablo Neruda. *Extravagaria, A Bilingual edition*. Translated by Alastair Reid. Austin, Texas: University of Texas Press, 1969.

Jose-Luis Orozco. *De Colores and Other Latin-American Folk Songs for Children*. New York: Dutton Children's Books, 1994.

Anton C. Pegis. "Introduction" to *Saint Thomas Aquinas*. New York: Modern Library, 1943

Miguel Leon-Portilla. *Aztec Thought and Culture*. Translated by Jack Emory Davis. Norman, Oklahoma: University of Oklahoma Press, 1963.

Laura E. Richards and Fairmont Synder. *The Little Book of Values, Moral Fables and Rhymes for Kindly Children*. New York: Glorya Hale Books, 1996.

Luis J. Rodriguez. *Always Running, La Vida Loca: Gang Days in L.A.* New York: Touchstone, 1993.

Mercedes Díaz Roig and María Teresa Miaja. *Naranja Dulce, Limón Partido: Antología de la Lírica Infantil Mexicana, Selección, Prólogo y Notas*. México, D.F.: El Colegio de México, 1996.

J. Barrie Shepherd. *Aspects of Love: An Exploration of I Corinthians 13*. Nashville, Tennessee: Upper Room Books, 1995.

Gary Soto. *Junior College: Poems*. San Francisco: Chronicle Books, 1997.

Dr. Benjamin M. Spock. *A Better World for Our Children: Rebuilding American Family Values*. Chicago, Illinois: Contemporary Books, 1994.

Karl Taube. *Aztec and Maya Myths*. Austin, Texas: University of Texas Press, British Museum Press, 1993.

Barbara C. Unell and Jerry L. Wyckoff, Ph.D. *20 Teachable Virtues, Practical Ways to Pass on Lessons of Virtue and Character to Your Children*. New York: Perigee, 1995.

Victor Villaseñor. *Rain of Gold*. New York: Delta, 1991.

Westridge Young Writer's Workshop. *Kids Explore America's Hispanic Heritage*. Santa Fe, New Mexico: John Muir Publications, 1996.

Guy A. Zona. *Eyes That See Do Not Grow Old: The Proverbs of Mexico, Central and South America*. New York: Touchstone, 1996.

For Further Reading

Contributors' Biographies

Pepe Aguilar is one of Mexico's most prominent film stars and recording artists. His recording "Como Mujeres Como Tú" topped the Billboard charts, winning him the Premio Billboard and the Premio Lo Nuestro in four categories in 1999. Under the auspices of his company, Pepe Aguilar Productions, he has made five records with his father, singer-actor Antonio Aguilar.

Isabel Allende was born in Peru and raised in Chile. She is the author of the widely acclaimed international bestseller *The House of the Spirits*, which was soon followed by the novels *Of Love and Shadows; Eva Luna; The Stories of Eva Luna; The Infinite Plan; Paula*, the story of her daughter's death; and *Daughter of Fortune*.

María Conchita Alonso was born in Cuba and raised in Venezuela. She starred in ten different Spanish soap operas and four feature films in Latin America before moving to the United States, where she starred opposite Hollywood's hottest actors. She has garnered critical acclaim for her feature roles in *Moscow on the Hudson, Colors*, and *Caught*, among other films. Ms. Alonso has garnered three Grammy nominations.

Linda Alvarado is president of Alvarado Construction, Inc., a commercial general contracting firm based in Denver, Colorado. In keeping with breaking nontraditional roles, she made history as the first Hispanic owner of a Major League baseball franchise.

Toney Anaya is an internationally recognized Hispanic leader and a nationally sought speaker. A licensed attorney for thirty years, he served as attorney general for New Mexico from 1975 to 1978, where he transformed the previously obscure office into a major force in government. He was elected governor of New Mexico in 1983 and was the highest ranking elected Hispanic at the time.

Anthony Stevens Arroyo is a professor of religion and Director of the Program for Analysis of Religion Among Latinos (PARAL) at Brooklyn College, the City University of New York. He is general editor of a four-volume series on Latino Religion — An Enduring Flame; Old Masks, New Faces; Enigmatic Power; and Discovering Latino Religion. Dr. Stevens is also the author of three other books and numerous research monographs, social science publications, and theological and pastoral publications.

Luis Avalos was born in Havana and became a Latin from Manhattan when his parents moved to New York City when he was one year old. Upon graduating from New York University's School of the Arts, he was hired as a member of the Lincoln Center Repertory Theater. On television, Mr. Avalos was a regular on the Emmy and Grammy award–winning The Electric Company. He also wrote, directed, and produced the award winning special El Regalo de Paquito, for which he received an Emmy nomination as director.

Lee Baca was born in East Los Angeles. Sheriff Baca began his public service career in 1965 when he joined the L.A. County Sheriff's Department as a deputy sheriff trainee. He rose through the ranks and was appointed to captain, commander, and later chief. The first Hispanic sheriff in Los Angeles, he was elected in a hotly contested race in 1999. Believing strongly in education, Sheriff Baca continued his studies, having graduated from the University of Southern California with a Ph.D. in Public Administration.

Polly Baca, a former Colorado state senator, was the first woman elected to chair the Democratic Caucus of the Colorado House of Representatives (1977), the first minority woman elected to the Colorado State Senate (1978–1986), the first Hispanic woman to be nominated by a major political party for the United States Congress (1980 Democratic Party congressional nominee), the first Hispanic woman to cochair a National Democratic Presidential Nominating Convention (1980 and 1984), and the first Hispanic woman to serve in leadership in a State Senate in the United States. (Chair,

Colorado Senate Democratic Caucus, 1985–1986). She is one of the original fourteen members to be inducted into the National Hispanic Hall of Fame.

Joan Baez is a singer known for her contributions as an activist in the peace movement. Born in Staten Island, New York, she first became known for her recordings of folk ballads and protest songs during the mid-1960s. She is the author of two autobiographies, *Daybreak* (1968) and *And a Voice to Sing With* (1987).

Raquel Bessudo is the founder and president of Medisend/Mexico A.C., an institution which serves as an intermediary for medical resources and goods donated by American Hospitals for distribution to Mexican institutions dedicated to helping the needy. In 1966 she was awarded the Silver Star for her outstanding social and altruistic work for the needy by the Journalists Association in Mexico City.

Simón Bolívar, the liberator of Venezuela, Bolivia, and Peru, has inspired every Latin American generation for a century and a half. He was president of Gran Colombia and, after being named dictator of Peru, whose government he organized, became the new country's president for life.

Gloria Bonilla-Santiago, Ph.D., is a leading scholar, researcher, speaker, and cross-cultural training consultant with more than fifteen years of experience in program development, strategic planning, fund-raising, and leadership training. She is a professor at the Department of Urban Studies and Community Planning at Rutgers State University. She is the author of two books, *Breaking Ground and Barriers: Hispanic Women Developing Effective Leadership* and *Organizing Puerto Rican Migrant Farmworkers: The Experience of Puerto Ricans in New Jersey.*

Jorge Luis Borges was one of the leading lights of poetry and letters in Latin America. For many years Borges served as an official of the state library system of Buenos Aires and later as director of the National Archives of Argentina.

Cruz Bustamante was elected lieutenant governor of California in November 1998. He is a first-generation Californian who became the first Latino to serve as speaker of the Assembly and the first Latino elected to statewide office in California in more than 120 years.

Vicki Carr is a Grammy Award–winning artist. In her thirty-nine-year career as a recording artist, she has released fifty-five bestselling records, including seventeen Gold Albums. Born in El Paso, Texas, she currently resides in San Antonio, Texas.

Antonio Caso, one of the great minds of the nineteenth and twentieth centuries, was a professor of philosophy and letters at what is now Universidad Nacional Autónoma de México (UNAM) and served as ambassador extraordinaire to Peru, Chile, Argentina, Uruguay, and Brazil. He was named doctor Honoris Causa by the universities of Havana, Lima, Guatemala, Buenos Aires, and Rio de Janeiro.

Rafael Catalá is an accomplished writer and lecturer and an internationally recognized speaker. He is president of the Ometeca Institute (devoted to the relationship of the humanities and science) and editor of its journal. He is the author of three books, *Sufficient Unto Itself Is the Day, Letters to a Student* and *Mysticism Now*. He resides in New Jersey.

Daniel Catán is a prolific composer of operatic and orchestral works. Born in Mexico City, he studied music in London and obtained his Ph.D. from Princeton University. His operas *Rappacine* and *Florencia en el Amazonas* have been performed and recorded to high acclaim. He has published numerous articles on music and the arts in Mexico's most prominent literary journals and a book, *Partitura inacabada (Unfinished Score)*.

Miguel de Cervantes Saavedra, a novelist, playwright, and poet and author of the classic novel *Don Quijote de la Mancha,* ranks as the outstanding writer in Spanish literature.

César Chavez was the founder and president of the United Farmworkers Union. His adherence to the principles of fasting and nonviolence enabled the UFW to stand victorious against both powerful growers and the Teamsters Union to secure labor contracts that provided the people who pick our food better wages and treatment.

Fernando Chavez is an attorney specializing in personal injury, commercial, and corporate litigation in the Bay Area of California. The son of farmworker leader César Chavez, he has served as a member of the California Rural Legal Assistance Foundation, as president of the Mexican American Political Association (United States) and is a winner of the Benito Juárez Award for Outstanding Work for the Latino Legal Community of Santa Clara County.

Henry Cisneros is president and chief operating officer for Univisión Communications, Inc., the nation's largest Spanish-language television network. The former U.S. Secretary of Housing and Urban Development under President Clinton, Mr. Cisneros was formerly the chairman of Cisneros Asset Management Company, a fixed income money-management firm operating nationally, and the mayor of San Antonio, the nation's tenth largest city.

Paolo Coelho is one of the most popular writers in the world. His books, led by *The Alchemist,* have sold more than 17 million copies in seventy-four countries and have been translated into thirty-four languages. He lives in Rio de Janeiro.

Burt Corona, founder of Hermandad Mexicana, is a community and labor leader in California whose efforts at community and coalition building spans much of the twentieth century. He embodies the persistent struggle by Mexican Americans against injustice and racism. Born to immigrant parents in the border town of El Paso in 1918, he was inspired by his father's participation in the Mexican Revolution.

Alfonso Cortés was a legend in his time. He was the mystical poet of Nicaragua and translated Baudelaire, Verlaine, Mallarmé, and Edgar Allan Poe.

Rubén Darío lived in Chile, Argentina, and Spain before returning to his native land, Nicaragua. He read widely in French and Castilian literature and fused Modernism and European symbolist elements with Latin American themes, creating a Hispano-American version of continental symbolism, and is thus considered the "prince of modernism."

Rodolfo Díaz was born in El Paso, Texas. Illiterate until he was an adult, he learned to read in 1994 when he joined an adult literacy program. His poems have been published by the City of Commerce Public Library Adult Literacy Program.

Hector Elizondo is the Emmy award–winning actor who portrays Dr. Phillip Watters on CBS's *Chicago Hope.* He has successfully moved back and forth between starring roles on Broadway, television, and feature films, including *Runaway Bride, Entropy,* and *Pretty Woman.* A native of New York, Elizondo first gained recognition on the New York stage for his portrayal of God in *Steambath,* which earned him an Obie Award.

Jaime Escalante is a former East Los Angeles math teacher whose black-board heroics were immortalized in the hit movie *Stand and Deliver,* starring Edward James Olmos. Escalante was able to transform a troubled barrio school into an institution that produced more advanced placement calculus students than all but three public high schools in the country.

Moctezuma Esparza is a multitalented award-winning filmmaker, pro-ducer, and entertainment industry executive. He has received more than 100 honors, including an Academy Award nomination, an Emmy, a Clio Award, and a Cine Golden Eagle Award. Mr. Esparza, along with Robert Katz, is a partner in Esparza/Katz Productions. Mr. Esparza's film credits include *Selena, The Roughriders, The Ballad of Gregorio Cortez, The Milagro Beanfield War,* and *Gettysburg.*

Nely Galán was born in Santa Clara, Cuba, and emigrated with her family to Teaneck, New Jersey, at the age of two. At age twenty-two, Galan became the youngest television station manager in the United States and rose to her former position as president of entertainment for Telemundo. She is now pres-ident of GaLAn Entertainment.

Herman Gallegos was born in the small mining town of Aguilar, Colorado, and raised in San Francisco, California. He has broken the color barrier on dozens of boards. A veteran of the civil rights movement, he has experience that ranges from community organizing in the barrios to service as a director and trustee of American corporations and foundations.

Baltazar Gracián was a Jesuit priest and major prose writer educated in Toledo, Spain, and is the author of the classic *El héroe.*

Lalo Guerrero is a master of a matchless repertoire of *canciones típicas* and *canciones rancheras* — Mexican folk songs — whose performing career spans five decades. He has received a National Heritage Fellowship from the Na-tional Endowment for the Arts and the Medal of National Merit for the Arts and Humanities.

Sandra Guzmán is an Emmy award–winning journalist with more than ten years experience in broadcast, newspaper, and magazine journalism. She is the editorial director of the soon to be launched website Soloella.com, which targets U.S. Hispanic women. She is the former editor in chief of *Latina* magazine and is the author of *The Latina Bible: The Hispanic Woman's Guide to Love, Sex, Beauty and "La Vida" for the Modern Hispanic Woman.*

Susana Guzmán is a native Californian, born in the East Los Angeles barrio known as El Sereno. Guzman is an associate artist of the Los Angeles Music Center Opera. She performs as a principal artist with many international companies including the Metropolitan Opera, the Kennedy Center Opera, Le Grand Théâtre de Genève, and the Edinburgh Festival.

Antonia Hernandez is president and general counsel of the Mexican American Legal Defense and Educational Fund (MALDEF). She is a member of the President's Commission on White House Fellowships and also serves on the John F. Kennedy School of Government Senior Advisory Committee.

Laura Hernandez is an internationally renowned artist. A member of the School of Oaxaca, she began painting as a young girl and studied at the Academy of San Carlos. The artist divides her time between Amsterdam, Holland, and Mexico.

Luis Jimenez is a prolific and highly acclaimed and internationally renowned artist and sculptor whose work has been exhibited each year since the mid-1960s. His large-scale fiberglass sculptures have been installed at major institutions in New York; Washington, D.C.; Chicago; and New Mexico.

Saint John of the Cross was drawn into service in the Order of Our Lady of Mount Carmel, founded by Saint Teresa de Avila as the nun was establishing her reformation of the Carmelites, and was the author of *Dark Night of the Soul,* a classic spiritual work.

Sor Juana Inez de la Cruz was the greatest poet of the baroque movement in colonial Latin American literature and one of the greatest intellectuals of her time. Born near Mexico City, she became a nun in 1667 and is the author of *Response to Sor Filotea de la Cruz,* considered a landmark of feminist literature.

Benito Juárez was one of the greatest Mexican political leaders. He began far-reaching economic and political reforms and also directed Mexican liberals in a civil war against conservatives, and later led his country in a war of freedom from French control. A Zapotec Indian, Juárez practiced law and began championing the rights of the underrepresented as a young attorney. He was elected governor of Oaxaca; served as minister of justice, where he enacted the famous Juárez Law; and was elected president of Mexico in 1861, a position he held until his death.

Joe Kapp is the only man in history to quarterback in a Rose Bowl game, a Grey Cup Championship, and a Super Bowl. He is the ninth-rated passer of all-time in the CFL and a first-ballot inductee to the CFL Hall of Fame. Today he is a restaurateur and the owner of Team Dynamics, a corporate development company.

Ginny Mancini enjoyed a flourishing singing career, performing with Mel Torme, the Mel-Tones, and the Tex Beneicke Orchestra before marrying composer-conductor Henry Mancini in 1947. She is a longtime supporter of the Southern California arts community.

Alma Martinez is an actress whose long and prestigious career encompasses work in film, television, and theaters across the country. Notable performances include *Under Fire* and *Barbarosa* in film; *Black Death, Seguín,* and *Adam 12* in television; and *In the Summer House* and *Green Card* on Broadway and Off-Broadway. In addition to being a highly acclaimed actor, she holds an Master's Degree in Fine Arts from the University of Southern California and is completing her Ph.D. in drama at Stanford University.

José Martí is one of the most important figures of Latin America's wars of independence. He articulated the revolution as a journalist, poet, and orator and was a leader in the struggle to free Cuba, the last New World colony that Spain held, at the end of the nineteenth century.

Miguel Martinez began his painting career in the mid-1970s and has become well-known for his colossal images of women. The artist has been honored for his important contribution to the arts and to the status of women through his unusual work. A native and lifelong resident of Taos, New Mexico, he lives with his wife and daughters.

Bill Melendez is one of the world's most experienced and highly regarded animators. He has worked continuously in film production since he was hired by Walt Disney, where he worked on *Fantasia, Pinocchio, Bambi, The Wind in the Willows, Dumbo,* and many Mickey Mouse and Donald Duck cartoons. His first television special, *A Charlie Brown Christmas,* is a classic that has aired on CBS every year since 1965.

Amalia Mesa-Baines is an independent artist and cultural critic whose works are primarily interpretations of traditional Chicano altars. She is currently the Director of the Visual and Public Art Institute California State University at Monterey Bay. She is a recipient of the MacArthur Genius Award.

Gloria Molina was named by *Time* in 1996 as one of the Democratic Party's "10 Rising Stars," and is considered one of the most influential Hispanics in the nation. She is the first Latina in history to be elected to the California State Legislature, the Los Angeles City Council, and to the powerful five-member Los Angeles County Board of Supervisors.

Marta Monahan, the author of *Strength of Character and Grace,* has been teaching character refinement since 1975. She has made more than 3,000 lecture appearances internationally, and is a frequent seminar speaker for Fortune 500 corporations, in which she leads Strength of Character and Grace programs. Born in El Salvador, she resides in Los Angeles.

Ricardo Montalban's extraordinary career spans several decades as the actor moved from stage to live television and film. His name became a household word as Mr. Rourke of ABC's *Fantasy Island.* In 1970 he founded Nosotros, an organization dedicated to improving the image of and expanding opportunities for Spanish-speaking people in the entertainment industry.

Pat Mora, author of *House of Houses* and *Agua Santa: Holy Water,* is a recipient of many awards, including a Kellogg Leadership Fellowship, Southwest Book Award, and a recent National Endowment for the Arts Fellowship. She divides her time between Cincinnati and Santa Fe.

Dionicio Morales, author of *Dionicio Morales: A Life in Two Cultures,* is the founder of the Mexican American Opportunity Foundation, one of the largest community-based service organizations in the United States.

Greg Nava is a director whose film credits include, with his wife, Anna Thomas, *El Norte,* which garnered many international awards and was nominated for an Academy Award for Best Original Screenplay; *My Family/Mi Familia; Selena;* and *Why Do Fools Fall in Love.* Last year Nava signed a first-of-its-kind studio deal with New Line Cinema and his newly founded company, El Norte Productions, to produce and direct Latino theme movies.

Pablo Neruda, the 1971 Nobel Laureate in Literature, is the most popular, best-known, and most influential poet of Latin America. A native of Chile, he is the author of *Elemental Odes,* among other works.

Amado Nervo studied for the priesthood but left the seminary to enter an active public life as a diplomat, journalist, fiction writer, and biographer of Sor Juana Inés de la Cruz. His simple and esteemed poems earned him the name the Monk of Poetry. A contributor to the periodical *Revista Azul* and a co-founder of the influential magazine *Revista Moderna,* Nervo was appointed secretary to the Mexican diplomatic delegation in Madrid in 1905, where he remained until 1918.

Nezahualcóyotl is the well-known poet-king of the Aztec empire.

Antonia Novello, M.D., was sworn in as the fourteenth Surgeon General of the U.S. Public Health Service in 1990. As such, Dr. Novello became the first woman and the first Hispanic ever to hold the position. She later served as United Nations Children's Fund (UNICEF) Special Representative for Health and Nutrition, and currently is Visiting Professor of Health Policy and Management at the Johns Hopkins University School of Hygiene and Public Health.

Gaspar Nuñez de Arce was an important poet and literary figure of the nineteenth century in Spain. He expressed an aggressive patriotism in the book titled *War Cross*, published in 1875.

Soledad O'Brien is the anchor of NBC's *Weekend Today* and MSNBC's *Morning Blend,* a three-hour news talk show on Saturday and Sunday mornings. She is the contributing technology editor for *USA Weekend Magazine;* and a technology columnist for Women's Wire's website, women.com. O'Brien studied at Harvard University and currently resides in Brooklyn, New York, with her husband.

Mario Obledo has had a distinguished career as a civil rights advocate, attorney, government official, educator, and consultant. He has served as secretary of health and welfare for the State of California, on the faculty of the Harvard University School of Law, as president and general counsel of

MALDEF (an organization that he cofounded), and as assistant attorney general for the State of Texas.

Edward James Olmos is an actor, producer, director, and community activist born and raised in East Los Angeles. After years in the theater, he came to national attention when his mesmerizing performance in the musical *Zoot Suit* led to a Tony nomination. He re-created the role on film, and went on to star in such films as *Wolfen, Blade Runner, Triumph of the Spirit, Mi Familia, Selena, American Me, Talent for the Game,* and *Caught.* He received both a Golden Globe and an Emmy Award for his work as Lieutenant Castillo on the popular television series *Miami Vice.*

Katherine Ortega was appointed by President Reagan and confirmed by the Senate as the thirty-eighth Treasurer of the United States, from 1983–1989. Prior to serving as treasurer, she served as a commissioner of the copyright on the royalty tribunal and as a member of the President's Advisory Committee on Small and Minority Business. Before entering government, Ms. Ortega practiced as a certified public accountant with Peat, Marwick, Mitchell & Co. in Los Angeles, served as vice president of the Pan American National Bank of East L.A., and then as president and director of the Santa Ana State Bank.

Manuel T. Pacheco, Ph.D., the first-born son of migrant workers turned small farmers, became president of the four-campus University of Missouri System in 1997. Prior to this post he served as president of the University of Arizona in Tucson, a position in which he won national recognition for programs designed to improve the academic experience for students at the university.

Violeta Parra was a woman of complex talents as a musician, as a poet, and as a sculptor and ceramicist. She is the only Latin American artist to have had a one-person exhibition at the Louvre.

Octavio Paz, Mexico's premier poet and essayist, was one of the towering giants of letters in the second half of this century. A prolific and brilliant writer, Paz produced more than forty volumes of poetry and essays; served as Ambassador to India during the 1950s, and was awarded the 1990 Nobel Prize in Literature. He was perhaps best known for his book *The Labyrinth of Solitude.*

Anthony Quinn, the Academy Award–winning actor best known for his performance in the film *Zorba the Greek,* was born in 1915 in Chihuahua,

Mexico. He paints in New York and sculpts in Italy, while continuing to make motion pictures all over the world. He is the author, with Daniel Paisner, of *One Man Tango,* his autobiography.

Abraham Quintanilla is the owner and president of Q-Productions in Corpus Christi, Texas. He started in the entertainment business in 1957 touring and recording with his group Los Dinos. He was portrayed by Edward James Olmos in the film *Selena.*

Cruz Reynoso is a former justice of the California State Supreme Court and California Court of Appeals. He grew up in a farmworker family in Orange County, California. The holder of several honorary degrees, he currently serves on the faculty of the UCLA School of Law and is vice-chair of the U.S. Commission on Civil Rights.

Gloria Rodriguez, Ph.D., is founder, national president, and CEO of AVANCE, Inc. Founded in 1973, AVANCE has become a nationally recognized model and pioneer for parent education, family support, and fatherhood programs, as well as programs for the prevention of poverty, child abuse and neglect, crime, delinquency, and school dropout. She was inducted into the Texas Hall of Fame and has been featured in *Hispanic Business* magazine as one of the 100 most influential national Hispanic women.

Phil Roman has produced and directed animated series, theatricals, and commercials for four decades and is founder and chairman of Film Roman, Inc. A six-time Emmy-winner (four for Garfield specials, two for Peanuts) his company currently produces the renowned series *The Simpsons* and *King of the Hill* for FOX Television.

Lucille Roybal-Allard is the first Mexican-American woman elected to Congress (1992). She made history again in 1997 when she was elected as chair of the twenty-nine-member California Democratic Congressional Delegation. She serves on the House Committee on the Budget and the House Committee on Banking and Financial Services. Born and raised in Boyle Heights, California, the congresswoman is the eldest daughter of retired Congressman Edward R. Roybal.

Edward R. Roybal served as a Member of Congress for thirty years supporting civil rights, public-health programs, and help for the elderly before retiring in 1993. A native of Albuquerque, New Mexico, Roybal grew up in Los Angeles. He was the first Mexican American in this century elected to the Los

Angeles City Council. He founded the Mexican American Political Action Committee with attorney Henry Lopez, and cofounded the National Association of Latino Elected and Appointed Officials and the congressional Hispanic Caucus. He established the Edward R. Roybal Institute for Applied Gerontology at California State University–Los Angeles, and is president of the Edward R. Roybal Foundation.

Don Miguel Ruíz is a master of the Toltec mystery school tradition. He combines his unique blend of knowledge in workshops, lectures, and guided journeys to Teotihuacán, Mexico. Trained as a surgeon, Don Miguel is also the author of *The Four Agreements: A Practical Guide to Personal Freedom,* and *The Mastery of Love: A Toltec Wisdom Book.*

Jaime Sabines is one of the most important writers of Mexican literature of his generation. Born in Chiapas, Mexico, in 1926, Sabines died in the spring of 1999.

Maria Salinas is coanchor of *Noticiero Univisión,* Univisión's nightly national newscast seen throughout the United States and Latin America.

Loretta Sanchez is a member of Congress, representing the 46th District of California, and holds an M.B.A. in finance from American University in Washington, D.C.

Poncho Sanchez has seventeen recordings to his credit and is considered one of the great Latin jazz and salsa percussionists.

Arturo Sandoval, originally from Cuba, made his new home in Miami, Florida, when he was granted political asylum in July 1990. He is one of the world's most acknowledged players of jazz trumpet and flugelhorn, as well as a renowned classical artist. He was awarded a Grammy Award in 1999.

Gary Soto is one of today's most praised and celebrated Chicano poets. He is also a playwright, essayist, and author of several children's books. He has received the Andrew Carnegie medal and The Nation Discovery Prize, and was a finalist for the National Book Award. He is the author of *Junior College* and *New and Selected Poems.* He divides his time between Berkeley and his hometown of Fresno, California.

Saint Teresa de Avila entered the Carmelite convent at eighteen. In 1562 she founded her first reformed convent of St. Joseph de Avila, and from that year until her death she opened thirty-two new houses. She is author of *The Interior Castle,* one of the veritable textbooks of mystical prayer that ranks as a classic of Spanish literature.

Liz Torres is a native of the Bronx, New York. An accomplished actor, comedienne, and singer, Torres began her career singing and performing stand-up comedy in small New York clubs, where she and Bette Midler shared Barry Manilow as a musical conductor. Subsequently, she opened for headlining performers such as Liza Minnelli, Tony Bennett, and Lionel Hampton.

Jaime Torres Bodet's commitments to poetry, to mass education, and to human rights have infused both of his careers, as writer and as public servant. He worked as a professor of French literature, as director of the Mexican government's Each One, Teach One literacy programs in the 1940s, and as director general of UNESCO in the late 1950s.

Jesus Treviño is a writer/director whose television directing credits include *NYPD Blue, Chicago Hope,* and *Star Trek: Voyager.* His national PBS documentaries about Latinos include *Yo Soy Chicano, Chicano Moratorium,* and *The Salazar Inquest,* and *Chicano! History of the Mexican American Civil Rights Movement,* which he coproduced. Mr. Treviño's collection of short stories, *The Fabulous Sinkhole and Other Stories,* was published in 1995. He is completing a memoir of his experiences as an activist filmmaker during the turbulent 1960s, a book which also addresses the status of United States Latinos in the next millennium.

Luis Valdez is founder and artistic director of the internationally renowned El Teatro Campesino, council member of the National Endowment for the Arts, and founding member of the California Arts Council. His play *Zoot Suit* became the first play by a Chicano to be presented on Broadway. The film version received a Golden Globe Award nomination for Best Musical Picture. He wrote and directed *La Bamba: The Ritchie Valens story,* and adapted his critically acclaimed stage play *Corridos: Tales of Passion and Revolution* for PBS, for which he won the coveted and prestigious George Peabody Award.

César Vallejo was raised in the highlands of Peru and wrote his first book of poetry at the age of twenty-six. He lived in France and Spain, where he worked with Pablo Neruda and others to raise support for the Spanish Republican cause. Vallejo is considered the most eloquently lyrical, personally rich voice in Latin American poetry.

Ramón Vargas is one of the most acclaimed tenors of today and has been praised internationally for his appearances in the world's leading theaters, such as the Metropolitan Opera, Vienna State Opera, Teatro alla Scala, the Bastille in Paris, Teatro Colón in Buenos Aires, and many others.

Danny Villañueva is the cofounding partner of Bastion Capital Corporation in Los Angeles, the country's only Latino-controlled venture capital firm. The ninth of twelve children born in Calexico, California, Villañueva began his professional football career as a kicker, the only Mexican American in the National Football League (NFL). He parlayed his popularity as a football player into a job as sports director and later general manager at KMEX-TV in Los Angeles, later becoming a partner and director of Spanish International Communications Corporation (SICC), which oversaw KMEX.

Victor Villaseñor is the author of the novels *Macho!* and the acclaimed best-seller *Rain of Gold,* and of the nonfiction work *Jury: The People vs. Juan Corona.* He has also written several screenplays, including the award-winning *The Ballad of Gregorio Cortez.* He continues to live on the North County San Diego ranch where he grew up.

Carmen Zapata began her acting career in 1945 on the Broadway stage in the musical *Oklahoma,* followed by such other musicals as *Bells Are Ringing, Guys and Dolls,* and many others. She has appeared in numerous TV series, including nine years as star of PBS's bilingual children's television show *Villa Alegre,* as well as in the feature film *Sister Act.* In 1973 she cofounded the Bilingual Foundation of the Arts.

Emiliano Zapata championed the widespread effort by Mexican Indians to reclaim land taken by Europeans and mestizos. He organized an army to combat Victoriano Huerta and is considered one of the great leaders of the Mexican Revolution.

Index

Credits & Permissions